DESERT ANIMALS
Physiological Problems
of Heat and Water

DESERT ANIMALS
Physiological Problems
of Heat and Water

KNUT SCHMIDT-NIELSEN
Department of Zoology
Duke University

Dover Publications, Inc.
New York

Published in Canada by General Publishing Company, Ltd., 30 Lesmill Road, Don Mills, Toronto, Ontario.
Published in the United Kingdom by Constable and Company, Ltd., 10 Orange Street, London WC2H 7EG.

This Dover edition, first published in 1979, is an unabridged and unaltered republication of the corrected 1965 printing of the work originally published in 1964 by the Oxford University Press. The author has written a new Preface for the Dover edition. This reprint has been authorized by the Oxford University Press, Walton St., Oxford OX2 6DP England.

International Standard Book Number: 0-486-23850-4
Library of Congress Catalog Card Number: 79-52528

Manufactured in the United States of America
Dover Publications, Inc.
180 Varick Street
New York, N.Y. 10014

TO THE MEMORY
OF
MY FATHER

PREFACE TO THE DOVER EDITION

DOVER PUBLICATIONS has suggested that I write a preface to their reprint edition of my book. I will use this opportunity to summarize some significant developments that have taken place since the book was first written. My preface will therefore be terse and technical.

The literature pertaining to problems of heat and water has expanded tremendously, and even a modest review would require much space. I will therefore cite only a few contributions that add new information and increase our understanding of how desert animals function. While these add to our perspective on underlying principles, a large number of worthy publications will remain unmentioned.

An increase in body temperature during heat loads has obvious and well-known advantages. It allows heat to be stored in the body and also reduces the temperature gradients in a hot environment, thus reducing the amount of water used for evaporation. An unexpected but highly significant finding is that the temperature of the brain, which presumably is the most heat-sensitive organ in the body, can be maintained several degrees lower than the temperature of the body core and the arterial blood. How can the brain be cooler than the arterial blood? The answer is simple. The arteries that carry blood to the brain run through the cavernous sinus where they are surrounded by a pool of relatively cool venous blood that has drained from the nasal region where evaporation cools the tissues (1). East African antelopes in which the body core temperature was increased by vigorous exercise had brain temperatures as much as 2.7°C below the central arterial blood temperature (2).

When the heat load becomes excessive, cooling is achieved by evaporation of water. However, the relative merits of sweating and panting as cooling mechanisms remain unclear. It is well known that the muscular work required for panting can be minimized by utilizing the resonant frequency of the respiratory system; this observation has been extended to include birds (3).

The overall heat balance of an animal in a natural environment is extremely difficult to quantify. The relative importance of air temperature, relative humidity, wind and convection, solar radiation, radiation exchange with ground and sky, evaporation, etc., lead to considerations of formidable complexity. Nevertheless, using the approach pioneered by Porter and Gates, the overall heat balance was accurately quantified for two East African ungulates (4) and later for other animals. The same approach has been equally successful when applied to desert lizards (5).

The suggestion that the clear desert sky, because of its low radiation temperature, could serve as a heat sink, has been tested in field studies. For the desert jack rabbit radiation from the large ears to the sky seems to be, at best, of marginal importance (6). It was observed, however, that when the air temperature exceeded the body temperature, heat influx through the large ears was reduced by a drastic reduction in thermal conductance, caused by vasoconstriction (7). Similar reductions in thermal conductance have been reported for birds (8), showing a useful mechanism for reducing heat loads at high ambient air temperatures.

The most important mechanism for reducing water expenditure for rodents and other small mammals is the cooling of the exhaled air to temperatures much below body core temperature, thus reducing the amount of water the exhaled air will hold (9). The mechanism of cooling the air has been the subject of theoretical analysis (10), and observations have been extended to birds (11) and reptiles (12). More recently, it was observed that even mammals of large body size exhale air cooled to below body temperature, thus achieving considerable economies in the use of water (13).

Desert animals seem to live at a low pitch—on the whole they have lower metabolic rates than close relatives in less demanding environments, and dehydration further decreases their metabolic rates (14). The interpretation is presently unclear; a low metabolic rate may be of value in reducing metabolic heat loads, or it may be an adaptation to the scarcity of food resources.

Our view of reptilian water balance has been changed by two major contributions, one relating to the evaporation of water and the other to excretion. The dry and horny integument of reptiles, long considered nearly impermeable to water, permits relatively high rates of evaporation. In fact, the rate of evaporation through the dry skin of lizards, turtles, and snakes exceeds the evaporation from the moist surfaces of their respiratory tracts (15). The reptilian kidney, unable to produce a highly concentrated urine for excretion of salts, is supplemented by a nasal salt-secreting gland, analagous to the salt gland of marine birds (16). In many desert reptiles this gland is concerned primarily with the excretion of excess potassium (17). In reptiles as well as in birds the insoluble fraction of the urine, consisting mostly of precipitated uric acid, may contain substantial amounts of sodium and potassium, thus aiding in the excretion of these major cations without any osmotic commitment of water (18).

The most striking new discovery in desert physiology pertains to amphibians. Loveridge (19) reported two highly un-amphibian characteristics of the South African frog *Chiromantis*. The rate of evaporation from its skin is a minute fraction of that from the moist skin of all ordinary amphibians; it is of the same magnitude as the evaporation from the dry skin of reptiles. An even more revolutionary discovery is that *Chiromantis*, instead of excreting urea (believed to be a universal characteristic of amphibians), excretes uric acid which requires only minimal amounts of water for elimination. Thus, *Chiromantis* displays reptilian characteristics in this regard as well. These astonishing discoveries led to an examination of South American frogs, and similar physiological traits were found in *Phyllomedusa*, a frog only distantly related to *Chiromantis* (20). *Phyllomedusa* excretes uric acid and has a low rate of cutaneous evaporation, although the mechanism for waterproofing the skin may differ from that of *Chiromantis*.

I have chosen these few reports because they broaden our perspective on the adaptations of desert animals to their environment. A recent symposium (21) gives much additional information. I am happy that otherwise I find little reason to change what I wrote 16 years ago about desert animals and how they cope with the demanding but fascinating environment in which they live.

K. S.-N.

Duke University, December 1978

REFERENCES

1. BAKER, M. A., and HAYWARD, J. N. 'The influence of the nasal mucosa and the carotid rete upon hypothalamic temperature in sheep', *J. Physiol.* (Lond.), **198**, 561–79 (1968).
2. TAYLOR, C. R., and LYMAN, C. P. 'Heat storage in running antelopes: independence of brain and body temperatures', *Amer. J. Physiol.* **222**, 114–17 (1972).
3. CRAWFORD, E. C., JR, and KAMPE, G. 'Resonant panting in pigeons', *Comp. Biochem. Physiol.* **40A**, 549–52 (1971).
4. FINCH, V. A. 'Thermoregulation and heat balance of the East African eland and hartebeest', *Amer. J. Physiol.* **222**, 1374–9 (1972).
5. PORTER, W. P., MITCHELL, J. W., BECKMAN, W. A., and DEWITT, C. B. 'Behavioral implications of mechanistic ecology. Thermal and behavioral modeling of desert ectotherms and their microenvironment', *Oecologia* (Berl.), **13**, 1–54 (1973).
6. SCHMIDT-NIELSEN, K., DAWSON, T. J., HAMMEL, H. T., HINDS, D., and JACKSON, D. C. 'The jack rabbit—a study in desert survival', *Hvalrådets Skrifter*, No. 48, 125–42 (1965).
7. DAWSON, T., and SCHMIDT-NIELSEN, K. 'Effect of thermal conductance on water economy in the antelope jack rabbit, *Lepus alleni*', *J. Cell. Physiol.* **67**, 463–72 (1966).
8. HINDS, D. S., and CALDER, W. A. 'Temperature regulation of the pyrrhuloxia and the Arizona cardinal', *Physiol. Zool.* **46**, 55–71 (1973).

9. JACKSON, D. C., and SCHMIDT-NIELSEN, K. 'Countercurrent heat exchange in the respiratory passages', *Proc. Nat. Acad. Sci.* **51**, 1192–7 (1964).

10. COLLINS, J. C., PILKINGTON, T. C., and SCHMIDT-NIELSEN, K. 'A model of respiratory heat transfer in a small mammal', *Biophys. J.* **11**, 886–914 (1971).

11. SCHMIDT-NIELSEN, K., HAINSWORTH, F. R., and MURRISH, D. E. 'Countercurrent heat exchange in the respiratory passages: effect on water and heat balance', *Resp. Physiol.* **9**, 263–76 (1970).

12. MURRISH, D. E., and SCHMIDT-NIELSEN, K. 'Exhaled air temperature and water conservation in lizards', *Resp. Physiol.* **10**, 151–8 (1970).

13. LANGMAN, V. A., MALOIY, G. M. O., SCHMIDT-NIELSEN, K., and SCHROTER, R. C. 'Nasal heat exchange in the giraffe and other large mammals', *Respir. Physiol.* (1979), in the press.

14. SCHMIDT-NIELSEN, K., CRAWFORD, E. C., JR., NEWSOME, A. E., RAWSON, K. S., and HAMMEL, H. T. 'Metabolic rate of camels: effect of body temperature and dehydration', *Am. J. Physiol.* **212**, 341–6 (1967).

15. BENTLEY, P. J., and SCHMIDT-NIELSEN, K. 'Cutaneous water loss in reptiles', *Science*, **151**, 1547–9 (1966).

16. SCHMIDT-NIELSEN, K., BORUT, A., LEE, P., and CRAWFORD, E., JR. 'Nasal salt excretion and the possible function of the cloaca in water conservation', *Science*, **142**, 1300–1 (1963).

17. TEMPLETON, J. R. 'Nasal salt excretion in terrestrial lizards', *Comp. Biochem. Physiol.* **11**, 223–9 (1964).

18. MCNABB, R. A., and MCNABB, F. M. A. 'Urate excretion by the avian kidney', *Comp. Biochem. Physiol.* **51A**, 253–8 (1975).

19. LOVERIDGE, J. P. 'Observations on nitrogenous excretion and water relations of *Chiromantis xerampelina* (Amphibia, Anura)', *Arnoldia*, **5**, 1–6 (1970).

20. SHOEMAKER, V. H., BALDING, D., RUIBAL, R., and MCCLANAHAN, L. L., JR. 'Uricotelism and low evaporative water loss in a South American frog', *Science*, **175**, 1018–20 (1972).

21. MALOIY, G. M. O. (ed.). *Comparative physiology of desert animals.* Symposia of the Zoological Society of London, No. 31, London: Academic Press (1972), 413 pp.

PREFACE TO THE FIRST EDITION

I T is the purpose of this book to examine what we know about desert animals and how they manage to live in an environment of excessive temperatures and water shortage. To establish a basis for comparison the first chapter presents a discussion of man's physiological responses to this harsh environment. The second chapter has as its subject the perhaps most consequential single aspect of an animal's physical endowment, its body size. Camels, for example, are obviously too large for the burrowing habits which permit the small rodent to retreat underground during the hot desert day. But more important, bulk is the principal factor in determining the rate of heat exchange between a body and its environment—in hot surroundings a large body gains heat more slowly than a small one. The discussion which establishes the theoretical advantages of a large body is intended to lend perspective to the sequence of the succeeding chapters, which discuss the physiological principles of life in the desert. Often our knowledge is sparse, and where information about domestic animals helps clarify the principles of life in arid climates, such material has been included. As this book proceeds from one animal to the next, it attempts to fit information and fact into a general picture, to emphasize the simplicity of the underlying principles, and to illustrate the resourcefulness of biological adaptation to a hostile environment.

No doubt, the book contains errors, both of fact and interpretation. While taking sole responsibility for its shortcomings, I wish to thank the many friends, colleagues, and students who have helped me along the way. Some have been collaborators in the laboratory and in the field, others have helped with discussions and advice. Those who have generously permitted me to use information from their unpublished work I have tried to acknowledge in the text, but undoubtedly I may have failed to mention all. Some friends have read parts of my manuscript and a few have read it in its entirety. To the many persons who have contributed in these and other ways I wish to convey my deep feelings of appreciation and gratitude.

K. S.-N.

Duke University, 1962

CONTENTS

LIST OF PLATES

DESERT ANIMALS
Physiological Problems
of Heat and Water

1

MAN

INTRODUCTION

THE deserts of the world are hostile to man but have a richer animal life than we usually imagine. It is estimated that between one-fifth and two-fifths of the earth surface is desert.[1] Over vast areas of these arid lands there is no permanent water, and years may go by between rains. Although man can penetrate and sometimes prosper in deserts, he does so only because of cultural adaptations—he depends on water that he brings with him or obtains by digging or drilling. It is our technological culture, not our physiology, that permits us to live there. Without a water-supply, man can live for a day, or at most two, in a hot desert. Even the most primitive of living men, the Stone Age aborigine of Central Australia, depends on water. He has no agriculture and lives off the arid land as a hunter and gatherer. Occasionally he obtains some water by digging out a water-filled frog from the hardened mud in a dried-out depression but permanent springs and pools control the range of his extensive travels.

Yet in these same deserts, and in all the deserts of the world, we find a variety of animals that seem to get along well under conditions too adverse for man.

The desert heat. This is not the place to review extremes of desert climate. Suffice it to say that air temperatures on a summer day are frequently between 40° and 45° C, and extreme air temperatures between 55° and 60° C have been reported from several locations both in the Old and in the New World deserts (76).

The effect of the high air temperature is intensified by solar radiation. The low atmospheric humidity and the absence of clouds in the desert permit a high proportion of the solar radiation to reach the ground, both in the visible range and in the infra-red. Furthermore, part of the solar

[1] The extent of the world's deserts depends on the definition used. Estimates based on vegetation which is adapted to arid conditions give 35 per cent of the earth's land area, while careful computation of arid and semi-arid climatic areas gives 36 per cent (311). Thus, in an area about one-third of the land surface of the earth, water is a chief limiting factor in plant growth and animal life. In most of this area, low and irregular rainfall, high summer temperatures, and intense solar radiation prevail and make life precarious. The term 'desert' is loosely used to designate the most extreme of arid climates where regular agriculture is impracticable, and for our purpose no further definition is necessary.

radiation is scattered and reflected from the ground. In addition, the
ground, which is warmed rapidly, becomes a radiator of its own. The
ground often attains surface temperatures of 60° or 70° C. In the Sahara
in June the surface of the sand becomes so hot that one can no longer
walk in the dunes in open sandals because the burning sand trickles
down between the toes. Arab friends told me that if their course took
them into the dunes during summer travel or hunting, they protected
their feet with woven woollen shoes. The heat radiation from the ground
alone is appreciable, but the combined heat load from air, sun, and
ground may become so great that it exceeds by a factor of 10 the metabolic heat production of a man.

At night temperatures fall rapidly, and it may be bitterly cold. A
difference of 30° C between day and night is probably not unusual,
while in the humid tropics day and night temperatures usually differ by
no more than a few degrees.

The main reason for the extreme temperature fluctuations in the
desert is the low humidity. Solar radiation during the day is unimpeded,
the ground has a low heat capacity owing to the absence of water from
the surface layers, conduction of heat to deeper layers is slow because
insulating air has replaced the better-conducting water, and no heat is
removed by water evaporating from the surface. At night the reverse
conditions prevail. Radiation to the clear sky is high and heat is rapidly
lost from the soil surface. In spite of the precipitous temperature drop
the dew point is rarely reached, for the atmospheric humidity is very
low, and in summer dew is seldom formed. The many reports that
describe excessive dew formation in the desert are from the winter, the
preferred time for most desert travel.

KEEPING COOL AND ALIVE

Man is an excellent temperature regulator.[1] In a normal climate he
loses heat from the body at the same rate as it is formed, and therefore
the body temperature remains quite constant. From day to day and
from year to year body temperature varies by at most a few degrees,
which means that the heat loss very closely equals the gain—we remain
in heat balance. In very cold surroundings we tend to lose heat faster,
and if we do not stay in our own private indoor climate we either protect
ourselves by clothing or produce more heat by shivering.

On the other hand, in a hot environment, such as the desert on a
summer day, keeping cool becomes a real problem. Our body tends to

[1] Temperature regulation is an active field of physiological investigation and the
subject is frequently reviewed. For recent contributions see, e.g. (118), (143). See
also (152).

become heated, both from the hot surroundings and from its own production of metabolic heat. Unless it is possible to escape, the only way for man to prevent a rise in body temperature is to be cooled by evaporation.

Man's ability to tolerate temperatures higher than that of his body was dramatically demonstrated 200 years ago by Dr. Blagden, then Secretary of the Royal Society (54, 55). With some friends, he went into a room at 260° F, or 126° C, and remained there for ¾ hour. A steak he took with him was thoroughly cooked, but a dog, kept in a basket to protect its feet from being burned, was unaffected. This simple but impressive demonstration showed that both man and dog can keep cool under very hot conditions. It also showed another thing, that the dissipation of heat depends on the evaporation of water. A pot of water which was covered by oil to prevent evaporation was heated to boiling, while water with a free surface remained much cooler, and if the air was made humid by putting water on the hot floor, it became impossible to stay in the room.

Evaporation of water

If a man is in an environment warmer than his body, heat must move from the hot surroundings to the cooler body. On a hot desert day, therefore, he must dissipate by evaporation of water the heat gained from the environment as well as his own metabolic heat. Some water evaporates from the respiratory tract, but the greater part appears as sweat on the body surface.

For the purposes of heat balance, it makes little difference where the water is evaporated. As one gramme of water changes from liquid to vapour, it binds about 580 calories of heat.

The reason that a precise figure for the heat of vaporization for water cannot be given is that this changes with temperature. At 33° C the heat of vaporization of water is 544 calories, while at the boiling-point of water, 100° C, it is only 498 calories. This, however, is not the full story. The water is vaporized at the temperature of the skin surface, and a small correction should be applied for the change of the temperature of the vapour to that of the air. More important is the fact that the vapour expands as it diffuses into the dry air, and any expansion of a gas lowers its temperature. Consequently, in dry air, additional heat is bound by the expansion of the water vapour, and the effective heat of vaporization exceeds the value we can look up in a table.

The precise determination of the heat of vaporization is important for an accurate estimation of heat balance in man under carefully controlled laboratory conditions. Under natural conditions, on the other hand, it is close to impossible to establish to what extent the heat of

expansion benefits the organism, and for practical purposes we will use
the compromise value of 580 calories per gramme water. (The subject of
the heat bound by vaporization of water has been excellently reviewed
by Hardy (142).)

Sweating rates

In the dry desert air, sweat evaporates as rapidly as it is formed, the
skin remains virtually dry, and we are almost unaware that the sweat
glands are active. However, sweating rates in man can be amazingly
high. The ability to sweat increases with repeated exposures to high
temperatures, and the highest sweating rates are reached only in men
acclimatized by prolonged and severe heat stress. During a really hot
day in the desert, as much as 12 litres of sweat may be produced, giving
an average rate of over 1 litre per hour.

Of course, sweating is not always this high. Ladell (188, 189) observed
sweating rates of about 0·5 litre per hour in Arabia, but Adolph and Dill
(2) working in the Nevada desert measured maximum sweating rates in
six persons which varied from 1·3 to 1·7 litres per hour with an average
of 1·5.

This by no means gives the maximum capacity of the sweating mechanism. Moss (231) reported rates as high as 2·6 litres per hour in coal
miners, and 8·5 litres in a 5-hour period. Under experimental conditions these rates have been exceeded for short periods. In men close
to the tolerable limits of high temperature combined with high humidity
Eichna found extremely profuse sweating (114). Most men averaged
2·5 litres per hour with a range of 1·24 to 3·88 litres per hour. These
men carried out work for 1 to 4 hours in a saturated atmosphere at
$35\frac{1}{2}°$ C. The highest rate mentioned above, 3·88 litres per hour, was
sustained for $1\frac{1}{2}$ hours, but the highest rate observed by Eichna reached
4·2 litres per hour. Eichna states that: 'Men have completed 4 hours
work in good condition while sweating at rates of 3·0 liters per hour, a
loss of 12 liters of fluid in the four hours.'

Such very high rates of sweating seem even more impressive when it is
remembered that the hourly rate of 4 litres is of the same magnitude as
the total amount of water present in the blood. Although the water is
taken from the blood as it passes through the capillaries of the sweat
glands, the loss is partly replaced from the body water in general and
is more evenly distributed over all body water. Furthermore, such high
loss of water cannot be sustained for very long without replacement in
the form of drinking water, a problem that we shall discuss below.

The rate of sweating is not altered by moderate dehydration, it is
still adjusted to the need for heat dissipation (114, 282). Neither does
drinking in excess increase the rate (190).

Occasionally persons are found who have no functional sweat glands, and these unfortunate individuals clearly demonstrate how necessary sweating and evaporation of water is in heat regulation in man.

The function of the sweat glands is under nervous control. Excellent studies have been made of the reflex mechanisms involved, showing that many complex factors interact in the control of sweating. This is not the place to review this subject.[1] For our purposes it suffices to state that even under the most extreme desert conditions the rates of sweating suffice for adequate heat dissipation.

The salt problem

Aside from water the most important constituents of sweat are chloride, sodium, and potassium. A number of other substances normally present in blood-plasma are found in the sweat in insignificant amounts. In fact, all the plasma crystalloids may be present but generally in lower concentrations than in the blood. Urea and lactic acid, however, are found in higher concentrations. At high sweating rates, the amounts of urea eliminated in the sweat are sufficient to be important in excretion, and in studies of nitrogen balance serious errors arise if this factor is overlooked. It is, however, not possible to regard the occurrence of lactic acid in sweat as a form of excretion. Although lactic acid is formed during heavy work, it is not particularly useful to have it eliminated, for it is normally used in the body, being resynthesized to glycogen in the liver. It is quite possible that lactic acid, which may be ten to twenty times as high in sweat as in the blood-plasma, does not at all originate from the lactic acid circulating in the blood. It could be formed by breakdown of glycogen in the sweat glands (349).

For our purposes here, it remains rather unimportant where the lactic acid originates. For the energy balance it makes little difference if 1, 2, or even 3 grammes of lactic acid are lost in a litre of sweat, but it is indeed important if it saves a corresponding amount of chloride. This is a subject which has received insufficient attention since Dill suggested the replacement hypothesis. The loss of salt in the sweat is extremely important, secondary in its physiological effects only to the loss of water.

Salt concentration in sweat. Sodium and chloride always seem to be present in lower concentrations in sweat than in the blood-plasma (see Fig. 1). Earlier reports that salt concentrations were higher in sweat were probably due to faulty collection techniques. It is necessary to guard against evaporation during the collection, and the skin must be free from previously accumulated salt. Furthermore, the collection

---

[1] Detailed discussions of the sweat glands and their function can be found in books by Kuno (187) and Rothman (284). See also (350).

technique itself is likely to interfere. For example, covering the hand or arm with an impermeable rubber glove increases skin temperature and, as we shall soon see, this in itself changes the salt concentration in the sweat. Another difficulty in the evaluation of sweat concentrations is that samples from various parts of the body do not have the same composition (224).

Values for sodium and chloride reported for sweat vary a great deal, and range from about 5 to over 100 mEq per litre. Normal plasma concentrations are around 140 mEq per litre for sodium and 105 mEq per

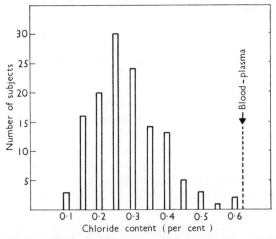

Fig. 1. The chloride content in human sweat is lower than in the blood-plasma. This graph illustrates the distribution of sweat concentrations in normal British subjects in southern Iraq. (Reproduced with permission from Ladell *et al.* (188).)

litre for chloride. There is a tendency for the salt concentration in sweat to decrease with acclimatization to heat (105) and, in addition, the salt concentration tends to increase with increasing sweating rates (168). It was suggested by Robinson (283) that these variations in salt concentration were due to changes in skin temperature, rather than to the rate of sweating. Robinson kept the two hands and forearms of his subjects at different temperatures as sweat was collected in elbow-length rubber gloves. The concentrations of sodium and chloride were significantly lower in the sweat collected from the cooler hand, and the concentration could be changed by raising or lowering the hand temperature. This effect of skin temperature was not dependent upon an increased rate of sweating from the region of higher temperature, and it was found at all stages of acclimatization to heat.

These many possibilities for variations make it evident that it is difficult to estimate salt loss from the skin by collecting representative samples of sweat. However, the rough estimates correspond fairly well with investigations where the sweat has been absorbed in clothing and washed out for analysis, and also with estimates of over-all salt balance in persons kept on known experimental diets with collection of the excreta for long periods, thus giving the possibility for an accurate evaluation of intake and output. Such investigations also indicate that when sweating rates and states of acclimatization are constant, the cutaneous output of salt depends on the dietary intake.

The upshot of all these considerations is that general rules cannot be given for cutaneous salt loss, but we can assume that, at high sweating rates, the total loss may easily run to some 10 to 30 grammes of sodium chloride per day. The highest well-documented rate that I know of was reported by Ladell (191) for men working in a room at 38° C and 80 per cent relative humidity—it was 25·02 grammes chloride, estimated as NaCl, in 162 minutes. This is a heavy drain on the resources, for the body contains an estimated total of only 165 grammes NaCl. During sweating the effects of salt loss are not apparent, but when the water is replenished, the body fluids become diluted and this may lead to serious consequences.

Heat cramps. It has been known for years that workers in very hot occupations tend to be afflicted with heat cramps. Colliers in the deep English coal-mines and stokers on steamships were frequently disabled by painful and exhausting cramps until the work of J. S. Haldane established that these cramps depend on the salt loss connected with heavy sweating rather than on exposure to heat as such (137, 329). This also explains why Norwegian ships had less difficulty with stoker's disease than the British merchant marine. The descendants of the Vikings ate a high proportion of salted meat and fish, while the more plentiful supply of fresh foods on the British ships worked to the disadvantage of the crews in the boiler rooms.

Stoker's disease and miner's cramp became rare after it was realized that the salt loss must be replaced and could be provided with the drinking-water. The addition of 10 grammes of sodium chloride to each gallon (Imperial gal = 4·54 l.) of water for colliers abolished all cramps. There was a general improvement in all workers; both those who had suffered from cramps and others felt more fit and could work longer in the hottest shafts (231). No doubt, the fact that extra salt is necessary is an old experience, but it was neglected until its real value was demonstrated by modern physiology. In the country in Norway I have often heard that salt should be added to the home-brewed beer in the haying season, and one is frequently warned against drinking too freely from a cool mountain brook on a hot summer day. The warning that you may get severe cramps unless you wait without drinking until you sit down and cool off (and eat!) makes sense, for water flowing over the Norwegian granite is about as salt free as distilled water.

My own experience in the desert is that there is no need to take salt with the drinking-water. For normal activities the salt taken with food suffices. A curious thing, however, was that food was unusually bland and tasteless. When we reached for the salt shaker it seemed that the salt was less salty than it should have been. Much greater quantities than usual were necessary to make the food taste 'right', and the tendency was to pour very liberal amounts over all food. This reaction could be a subjective result of our knowing about the need for salt, and it would therefore be interesting to find out whether the taste threshold for salt is actually increased under desert conditions.

Biologically the great need for salt in the desert is a curious phenomenon. Although the urinary output of salt may go down virtually to zero (less than 1 mEq per litre), the occurrence of the salt-depletion syndrome is evidence that the salt output from the skin cannot be similarly reduced, even when the need for conservation is at its greatest. Thus water alone is not sufficient to make a successful desert dweller out of man, and the value of salt is evident from its price in hot countries. It is a main article of trade and taxation, it has caused wars, and at times it has been weighed up against gold.

Restoring the water, drinking

The need for water is manifested as thirst. This ill-defined sensation has been the subject of many investigations and much speculation on the mechanism involved. Theories range from thirst being caused by the dryness in the mouth and throat, to complex central nervous system reflexes. The beautiful investigations of Andersson have clarified that the major stimulus for drinking arises in the hypothalamus, directed by the osmotic concentration of the blood that reaches specific osmoreceptor cells. Direct stimulation of these cells was brought about by injection of minute amounts of concentrated salt solutions in their immediate vicinity, or by stimulating electrodes. Such stimulation made goats drink insatiably, overhydrating themselves up to 40 per cent of their body weight (12).

In the thirsty animal the mechanism is not so simple, for drinking stops before the water has been absorbed from the stomach and has diluted the blood. The distention of the stomach seems to inhibit the drinking, as shown by blowing up balloons inside the stomach (335). The amount of water passing through the oesophagus also has an influence. If dogs are provided with an oesophageal fistula no water reaches the

MAN   9

stomach. A thirsty dog will now drink much larger quantities of water,
but will stop when the amount passing down its throat has reached
about 2½ times the amount it would normally drink. Since the dog is
still physiologically 'thirsty' it will soon drink again, and the amount of
sham-drinking may reach proportions that a beer-drinker would view
with envy.

Thirst in man is a baffling phenomenon. Paradoxically, when man
evaporates water in the desert, he does not drink enough to replenish the

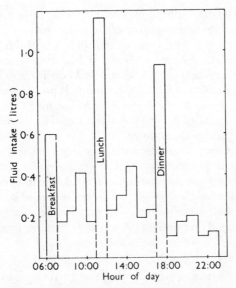

Fig. 2. Man has a tendency to take most of his
fluid during meals. The person recorded here
was moderately active and needed about 6 litres of
water per day—about one-half of this was taken
at mealtimes. (Reproduced with permission from
Adolph *et al.* (5).)

loss, even if a plentiful supply is available. He undergoes a voluntary
dehydration which often reaches 2 to 4 per cent of his body weight, for
his thirst is satisfied before water intake equals loss. The usual pattern
is that he drinks perhaps one-half of what is needed, and when he
sits down for a meal, he fills up the rest (2) (see Fig. 2). This pattern is
not a question of the quality or taste of the water, for Adolph and his
collaborators found that no matter how tasty they made the water, the
drinking pattern remained the same (5). Warm, cool, or iced water made
no difference, and added salt, sugar, or fruit flavour gave the same
result.

Dill suggested a good explanation for the strange drinking pattern (106). When man sweats he also loses salt, and if he drinks to restore all the water lost, the result is an undesirably low blood concentration of salt. Therefore, the bulk of the water, sufficient to restore completely the amount in the body, must wait until food is also taken. This suggestion fits the observation well, but Adolph (286) showed that replacing the salt loss hour by hour only slightly reduced the voluntary dehydration. Thus, we must accept, without adequate explanation, the fact that man is a slow drinker.

Once when I was quite impressed by the amount a donkey could drink, I wanted to test my own capacity for water. I went without water for a few hours until I was extremely thirsty and felt that I could imbibe tremendous volumes of liquid. I had measured out 1 litre of water to begin with and thought that I could easily down it in a minute, for the donkey drank 7 or 8 litres per minute. It proved hard to drink the full litre, and I could barely down it in the assigned time. All desire to continue with another litre was gone, and I could only drink additional mouthfuls by forcing them down.

Ladell found that when the water loss from the skin is rapid, man cannot replace it by drinking even if he tries. When the sweat rate approached 50 ml per minute, efforts to obtain full replacement by drinking usually led to vomiting, whether water or saline was given (190). As we shall see later, drinking patterns in animals such as the camel, donkey, and dog are quite different, with much greater quantities of water being ingested in much shorter periods of time.

LACK OF WATER, DEHYDRATION, DEATH

The paradoxical situation that man's thirst does not suffice to re-plenish his body water means that, even when water is freely available, he undergoes some degree of dehydration. If he has little or no water to drink, dehydration progresses further, and his physical and mental performance deteriorate even at a relatively moderate water depletion. Some of the more obvious changes in the dehydrated man will be mentioned to provide a basis for discussing the physiological effects of water deprivation.

Obviously, experimental dehydration of human subjects has not been carried to the point where the life of the subject is endangered, so most of the information we have has been pieced together by inference from animal experimentation and occasional reports of persons being lost in the desert without water. In the latter cases, if a person has been found before death, the concern has been with recovery rather than obser-vation of the ultimate stages of death from dehydration, and, even so, only rarely is a trained observer present to note the condition and symptoms during recovery.

Effects of moderate dehydration

Kidney function. The major adjustments of the body's water content are made by the kidneys. In a moderate climate, the kidneys usually excrete from 1·0 to 1·5 litres of water each day, but if for some reason water intake is increased, they can eliminate an excess of some 20 litres per day. When water intake is restricted urine volume will be reduced and may be less than ½ litre, but urine formation ceases entirely only in the severest dehydration when physiological processes deteriorate and kidney function fails.

In a desert climate, if sufficient drinking-water is available, urine volumes are usually somewhat less than 1 litre. Adolph and Dill (2) found an average urine volume of 825 ml per day, which was about 25 per cent lower than the average observed in the same subjects during winter. However, exposure to heat and hard work frequently causes water loss not fully compensated by drinking, and the voluntary de-hydration incurred leads to a further reduction in urine volume with values between 0·4 and 0·5 litres (106). The lowest rate observed by Adolph and his collaborators was 230 ml per day (7). As far as we know, similar volumes of urine continue to be formed as dehydration progresses, until kidney function ceases in advanced stages.

When the kidney conserves water it does so by forming a urine where the excretory products are in as high concentrations as possible. When the maximum concentrating ability of the kidney is reached no further amount of water can be withheld, and the urine volume is therefore determined by the amount of excretory products. Of these the two most important are urea and sodium chloride, and the kidney's ability to concentrate them is inherent in its detailed structure which varies from animal to animal. The kidney of man is not particularly powerful; rats and dogs have kidneys about twice as powerful and can therefore eliminate a given amount of excreta with only half as much water. There is no indication that man can be trained to excrete a highly concentrated urine; the maximum concentrating power of the kidney is not subject to any appreciable modification. Also, since the urine output remains about the same under increasing dehydration, no saving in water use is accomplished by permitting man to become increasingly dehydrated.

The minimum urine volume is dictated by the amounts of excretory products and is modified with changes in the diet. The amount of urea depends on the protein intake, but does not decrease to zero even on a protein-free diet. As we have seen, the quantity of sodium chloride to be handled by the kidney may be very low when large losses in sweat demand its conservation, and this is likely to happen during water deprivation in the desert. On the other hand, a man who drinks saline waters, or the castaway at sea who drinks sea water, is in an entirely different situation. Sea water is almost twice as concentrated as the maximum urine concentration in man, and its ingestion therefore leads to progressive and rapid dehydration. Drinking of urine by dehydrated men accomplishes nothing, for the urine, as it was formed, was about as concentrated as the kidney could make it. Its reingestion demands the excretion of the same solutes, which will again require the original amount of water.

Sweating during dehydration. The total water expenditure for sweat formation may easily reach some 10 to 15 litres per day, and a reduction in this tremendous volume would be quantitatively far more important than a reduction in the small amount of water spent for urine formation. If the kidney of man should be, say, twice as efficient as it is, the saving of water would be perhaps 200 ml in a day. Compared to the use of water for sweat, such a saving would be only some 1 or 2 per cent and would be relatively insignificant. On the other hand, a reduction to one-half in the amount of water used for sweat would indeed be important.

The quantity of water used for sweating is dictated by the need for heat regulation. Since the heat load depends primarily on physical factors, such as the difference between air temperature and skin temperature, and radiation load from the sun and the hot ground, one would not expect that any significant saving of water could be accomplished. The notion that man should be able to train himself to the use of less water in the desert, such as he can train himself to improved sport performances, is based on wishful thinking rather than logic.

During the extensive observations of man in the desert carried out by the University of Rochester group headed by Adolph, there was no evidence that man could learn to get along with much less water than dictated by the existing physical conditions (131). In one test, two groups of young men were closely matched in weight and hiked on the same desert trail at the same time. Thus the groups should be comparable, but one drank freely throughout the hike while the other drank nothing. In an 8-hour march at a temperature of 35° C the average water evaporation in the group with water was 5·24 litres, while the group without water had an average evaporation of 4·68 litres. Thus the latter group used for evaporative cooling 11 per cent less water. This shows that the rate of sweating is in the same order of magnitude, whether one drinks or not, but it also indicates that there may be a slight reduction in the water expenditure in the men without water. It is difficult to evaluate whether this was due to a true physiological difference as one of the groups became more dehydrated (7·4 per cent weight loss against 4·3 per cent in those that drank as much as they wished), or to subtle differences such as a more economical way of walking or a reduction in exertion in the group without water.

Decreased blood-volume. As the sweat glands remove water, the immediate source of this water is the blood flowing to the skin. However, since the amount of sweat produced in a few hours can far exceed the total volume of the blood, the water loss must at least to some extent be distributed to the water present outside the vascular system. The exchange of water between the blood capillaries and the tissues is extremely rapid, but is governed by complex laws which are only partly understood.

When the Rochester investigators studied the effects of dehydration in man, they observed that the plasma water contributed more than its proportional share to the water loss. In men dehydrated by 1 to 11 per cent of their body weight, the reduction in plasma volume amounted to about two and one-half times that expected from the total water loss (8). Similar results were obtained by Robinson (282) who found an average reduction of 6·5 per cent in the plasma volume in men who were dehydrated by 3 per cent of the body weight. In these experiments there were no significant changes in the total volumes of circulating cells or plasma proteins, an observation which was made also by the Rochester group. Thus, an important consequence of the loss of plasma water is an increase in red-cell concentration (hematocrit) and in protein concentration. This means an increase in the viscosity of the blood which places an additional load on the heart, for it now takes more work to pump the blood through the blood-vessels. As we shall soon see, the preferential loss of plasma volume and the increased viscosity are indeed very unfortunate.

Pulse-rate and heart function. Almost 200 years ago Blagden observed an increased pulse-rate when men were exposed to great heat (54, 55). Many later investigators have made the same observation, and Adolph and his collaborators have made systematic observations on the heart-rate at various degrees of water deficit (285). In these studies the increment in pulse-rate was closely related to the degree of water deficit and reached about forty beats per minute above the normal when 8 per cent of the body weight had been lost. Physical work, of course, further increases the pulse-rate and adds more strain to the hard-working heart of the dehydrated organism.

If the stroke volume of the heart is measured in a dehydrated person, it is found to decrease as the pulse-rate goes up. The percentage is similar, so that when the pulse-rate increases by 40 per cent over the initial value, stroke volume has fallen about 40 per cent. Thus, the amount of blood pumped out by the heart in each minute (cardiac output) remains approximately unchanged (285).

The embarrassment of normal circulation caused by the increased heart-rate, decreased stroke volume, and increased blood viscosity is a most important factor in the reactions to heat and dehydration. If body temperature is to be controlled, the heat produced in the deeper parts of the body must be transferred to the skin where it is dissipated. This transfer is effected mainly by the circulation of blood to the skin, for the conduction of heat from deeper parts to the surface is slow and accounts for a very minor part of the total heat transfer. Unless all the heat produced in the body is removed and dissipated, the body temperature rises, and the tolerance to this situation is limited. The blood used for transportation of heat to the skin is arterial in character and is, in a way, diverted from its normal function of carrying oxygen to the tissues. Therefore, the tissues in general must now be supplied by a smaller part of the total blood, which already has been reduced in volume by the dehydration. If, at the same time, the viscosity of the blood is increased the demands on the heart may reach a magnitude that cannot be sustained.

Limits of dehydration, death from 'thirst'

In their studies on man in the desert, the Rochester group never carried the experimental dehydration of man beyond 8 to 11 per cent weight loss. In general, they found that people at water deficits of less than 10 per cent of the body weight are in no danger of death, and most signs of discomfort disappear within an hour after water is drunk freely. In the range we know, the symptoms are bad enough. At 2 per cent weight loss, thirst may be violent, but does not seem to increase much in intensity as the water deficit increases. At 4 per cent the mouth and throat feel dry, and functional derangement is manifested in apathy, sleepiness, lagging pace, and impatience. At 6 per cent the symptoms increase in severity and at 8 per cent salivary function has stopped, the tongue feels swollen and sticky, and speech is difficult, a condition which corresponds to what old desert prospectors called cotton-mouth.

What the signs are when the water deficit exceeds 10 per cent of the body weight is known only from reports of men who have been accidentally lost in the desert. A dramatic account of one such case is found in McGee's description of the recovery of a man lost near the Mexican border for 8 days with 1 day's water, a desert record perhaps without equal (208).

Even at moderate dehydration urine volume is reduced to a minimum. Complete failure in urine production never occurred in Adolph's observations, but others have reported the passage of bloody urine or complete anuria in extreme dehydration. It is quite likely that the failure in kidney function is due to the inability to maintain sufficient circulation for adequate renal function.

Formation of sweat did not stop in any of the Rochester subjects, and nothing is known about the degree of dehydration at which sweat production fails. If sweating stopped in a hot environment, a man would soon be killed by the rise in body temperature.

By observing the symptoms in man as they occur with increasing water deficit, and comparing these with observations on animals, it can be assumed that the lethal limit in man is about 18 or 20 per cent weight loss. The exact point will probably depend on air temperature and the speed of dehydration, as well as individual differences. It may be safer to

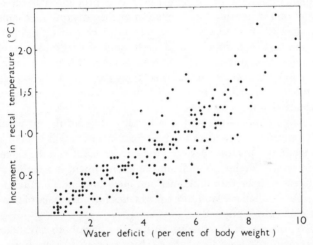

FIG. 3. With increasing dehydration the rectal temperature of man tends to rise. At 10 per cent water deficit the increment in temperature is about 2° C. (Reproduced with permission from Adolph *et al.* (5).)

state that the lethal limit is somewhere between 15 and 25 per cent deficit (9). However, man is physically and mentally unable to take care of himself at 10 per cent weight loss, and at about 12 per cent water deficit he is unable to swallow and can no longer recover without assistance. Adolph claims that a man dehydrated to this point must be given water intravenously, intraperitoneally, by stomach tube, or through the rectum.

Body temperature during dehydration

As dehydration in man progresses, his body temperature tends to rise. The Rochester group accumulated much material, both in the laboratory and in the desert, to support this observation. They found that the rectal temperature increased linearly with progressing water deficit, reaching 2° C increase at 10 per cent water deficit (Fig. 3). If work was performed at the same time, the rise in rectal temperature was faster, reaching 2° C at about 6 or 7 per cent dehydration. It is usually assumed that it is desirable for man to keep his body temperature constant,[1] and the increase in body temperature with progressing dehydration is regarded as a failure in heat dissipation. The reasoning in this interpretation runs as follows. 'Since it is a function of the circulation to transport heat from the tissues in which it is produced to the periphery, a rise in body temperature indicates that the circulation is not transporting heat as rapidly as it is being formed, and therefore represents inadequate peripheral blood flow' (285). It is probably correct that the heat retention is not due to a limitation of the sweating mechanism, for the temperature rise occurs also in persons acclimatized to heat whose ability to sweat is unimpaired. The retention of heat must therefore be due to a decrease in transportation from deeper parts to the surface, and it is a reasonable conclusion that this is related to the increased viscosity of the blood, coupled with the inefficiency of the heart as stroke volume decreases and pulse-rate rises.

The rising temperature may also be viewed in a different way. A rise in body temperature reduces the heat load in a hot environment, for the difference in temperature between the environment and the cooler body is diminished. The heat flow from the environment is roughly proportional to the temperature difference and goes down as the difference gets smaller. As we shall see later, the camel takes full advantage of this simple rule of elementary physics.

Clearly, the rise in body temperature may have both advantages and disadvantages. At least, it might be better to avoid classifying it as a failure of heat regulation.

An accurately regulated increase in body temperature does occur during exercise. The old assumption that one gets 'hot' because more heat is produced and not dissipated has been proven wrong. In a series of experiments Nielsen showed that the increase in rectal temperature was always the same for a given work intensity, and that there was a linear relationship between temperature rise and the work load (Fig. 4) (238). The temperature rise took place irrespective of the conditions for heat dissipation, whether the work was done at room temperature or nearly nude at the freezing-point so that excess heat could be lost easily. This rise then, is not due to an inability to dissipate the heat, but is accurately regulated to the particular level of work.

---

[1] For simplicity, we will disregard the diurnal temperature fluctuations which occur in the absence of heat or cold stress and activity. The baseline we will use is the temperature that could be considered 'normal' for the particular individual at that time of the day. This also eliminates the need to consider variations in individual 'normal temperature'.

Explosive heat rise. As man becomes progressively dehydrated in a hot desert, death is probably not caused by the direct effects of water depletion, but results from what Adolph called explosive heat rise. There is good reason for this assumption, which is based on observations of other species.

In Adolph's experiments a dog exposed to air of about 50° C promptly started to pant (9). Through evaporation it lost 1 to 1·5 per

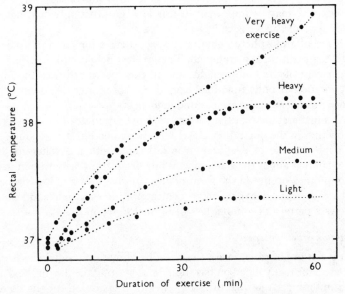

FIG. 4. During exercise the rectal temperature increases, but it levels off after about ½ hour. The level at which it stabilizes depends on the severity of the exercise. In this experiment no plateau was reached at the highest work load. (Reproduced with permission from Nielsen (238).)

cent of its body weight per hour, showing the same progressive symptoms as man: weakness and increases in pulse-rate, rectal temperature, and plasma concentration. All these effects of dehydration were expected, but when the dehydration reached 14 per cent of the body weight, the animal's rectal temperature began to rise explosively. At this stage the animal survived only if immediately removed from the hot atmosphere or given water to drink. With water, dogs proved excellent heat regulators and survived indefinitely in air at 55° C.

What was the cause of death? The dog continued to pant and the mouth stayed cool while the rectal temperature climbed. Evidently the deeper temperature rose explosively because insufficient amounts of heat were moved to the cooling surfaces. Presumably, the increased viscosity of the blood and the strain on the heart, in combination with the reduced blood-volume, had reached a point where blood was not carried fast enough to the cooling surfaces. However, the failure of circulation is not necessarily due to the blood viscosity; all the symptoms of explosive heat rise have a striking similarity to circulatory shock. The two major factors in shock, decreased blood-volume and extreme vasodilation, are prominent under conditions that cause explosive heat rise. What we need to know is the arterial blood-pressure during its onset—if it is high the viscosity may be important, if it is low the situation would have all the criteria of shock.

In a cool atmosphere dehydrated dogs survive longer, and a normal rectal temperature is maintained. The greatest dehydration reached was 17 per cent of the body weight, and in this case death was due to the deterioration of body functions caused by those water-depletion effects whose mechanism is even less understood.

We must assume that the pattern of dehydration death in man would follow that in the dog rather closely. Both are good heat regulators, and although the site of evaporation is different, both use water for heat dissipation at about the same rate. While death from dehydration in hot surroundings occurs in the form of an explosive heat rise it is probable that death from dehydration in cool atmospheres is not sudden, but follows a pattern of gradual loss of normal function.

Can man store water?

It is not out of place to ask the question about a physiological storage of water, for many a person has thought of starting the day in the desert with imbibing large quantities of water in preparation for the coming needs. The popular notion is that the camel does exactly this, filling his stomach with water in preparation for a long waterless journey. Why should not man be able to do the same thing, on a smaller scale?

Usually, man's thirst is adjusted to the restoration of his body water to its normal level and to keeping it there. Any excess taken in, whatever the reason may be, is rapidly excreted by the kidney. If a large quantity of water is ingested, it is usually absorbed within $\frac{1}{2}$ hour or an hour, and eliminated again in an hour or two. In the desert, however, this situation is slightly different. If, in the preceding period, urine production is low, the amount of antidiuretic hormone circulating in the blood is relatively high. A sudden water load, therefore, will not be excreted as rapidly as it would in a normal climate. In fact, if a man drinks a litre of water, which is about as much as he can take at once, and then starts out in the hot desert, water will be used so rapidly for sweating that the excess will have little effect on urine volume. In a test where men drank 1 litre immediately before starting on a desert hike only 15 per cent of the excess intake appeared as increase in urine volume while the remaining 85 per cent was used for sweat formation (69).

While water is usually both absorbed and excreted rapidly, isotonic saline solution is rapidly absorbed from the intestinal tract but is excreted quite slowly, over a day or so (317). Drinking of saline solutions does not give an immediate diuretic effect, and since the need for salt is increased anyway, this might be a more practical method of 'prehydrating' the body than drinking pure water.

Of course, it is simpler to carry a litre of water in the stomach than in a canteen. However, if the total needs for the day will be, say, 10 litres, it is obvious that a litre, whether fresh water or saline, will take care of no more than a small fraction of the demand. Man must have water in the desert, and in large quantities.

Can man reduce the amount of water used in heat regulation?

The notion that man can train himself to get along on less water in the desert is reasonable but not founded on observed fact. Roughly, the demand for water is dictated by the need for heat dissipation, which has two components, metabolic heat and heat gain from the hot environment. If either of these two components could be reduced, water expenditure could be reduced proportionately.

We know that metabolic heat production depends on the amount of work done, and hard work requires more water for heat regulation. It is obvious that avoiding work will save on water. We know, however, that the metabolic rate will not be reduced below the normal resting level, so there is no further saving to be gained here.

When it comes to the heat gain from the environment, the situation is more difficult to evaluate. It has been mentioned above (p. 16) that an increase in body temperature does reduce the heat load on the body. The comparison of groups of men who could drink freely with men who had no water to drink showed a small but significant saving in water by the latter (131). The reason for this difference is not well established, but it may be due to the greater increment in body temperature in the non-drinkers, thus reducing the heat load from the environment. However, since the difference was only 11 per cent no great saving was accomplished.

The evaporation from the lungs most certainly cannot be reduced, for all observations indicate that the expired air is saturated with water vapour. This makes no difference anyway, for water evaporated from the lungs binds heat, just as water evaporated from the skin. The small amounts of water lost with the faeces and the urine, about $\frac{1}{2}$ litre per day, probably cannot be reduced further. Even if part of this water could be saved the amount would be insignificant compared to the tremendous need for water in sweat formation. Thus, if we could expect any economy in the use of water, resulting in a reduced need for drinking, we should look for a reduction in sweat production. There is one such possibility which we have not yet discussed, the exclusion of external heat by insulation of the body surface.

The value of clothing. If a brick is placed out in the desert it rapidly gains heat by conduction from the air and radiation from the sun and the hot surroundings. Obviously, insulation around a cold body reduces the rate of heat gain in a hot environment, and if the brick is placed in a thermos bottle it heats up much more slowly. The same effect prevails in man. Adolph (3) found that subjects who wore light clothing and sat in the sun had a lower rate of evaporation (which represents heat gained from the environment) than men who were nude. As usual, the Rochester desert team later collected additional valuable information. The mean values observed during the summer in the desert showed that the men wearing light khaki clothing had the heat gain from the environment reduced to 55 per cent of that observed in nude men (227).

The value of clothing will vary with its nature as well as with external conditions. Based on the experiments published by Adolph, it is reasonable to assume that light dress on a hot desert day can reduce the water expenditure to about two-thirds of the value without clothing. The inescapable conclusion is that, as far as water economy is concerned, shorts and short-sleeved shirts are not the best dress in the desert.

It may seem paradoxical that clothing should be an advantage in hot surroundings. There are, however, several comments to be made. What we have just discussed was water economy, rather than comfort. In moderate heat it is indeed more comfortable for westerners to wear light clothing. On the other hand, I have found that the tendency to shed clothing is reversed when the temperatures are very high. When the Sahara Desert really heated up in June, it seemed unbearable to walk around in the very light clothing we had been using earlier in the year. We switched to long baggy Arab trousers and long-sleeved shirts. In the cool morning, while temperatures were moderate, it was comfortable to have the shirt sleeves rolled up, but as the baking heat of the mid-day approached the bare arms felt uncomfortable.

Of course, the insulation in the form of clothing cannot be increased indefinitely. Metabolic heat is still produced, and some heat gains access to the body from exposed surfaces and through the clothing. All this heat must be dissipated by evaporation of water, and clothing that interferes with evaporation is a disadvantage. Therefore, the ideal would be a type of clothing that does not impede evaporation from the skin, but still yields a maximum of insulating protection against conduction and radiation from the environment. Loose fitting garments are better than the tight clothing commonly used by western man, for they permit circulation of air so that sweat can evaporate from the skin, rather than soak through the clothing and evaporate from its surface. White clothing reflects more radiation in the visible spectrum, but its effect is not as great as may be supposed, for in the infra-red range, which contains about one-half of the total energy of solar radiation, even the whitest cloth acts as a perfect black body. The radiation of heat from the ground is in the far infra-red, and here again the whiteness of the clothing is insignificant, for all kinds of fabric (except metal surfaces) are black bodies.

The Arabian bedouins have developed clothing that fits the description given above. Their long white burnouses are made from wool and are worn winter and summer. In June one particular nomad impressed me as I saw him coming in from the desert with his camels. Upon his arrival at the oasis he shed two woollen burnouses and a jacket, revealing that he wore also a long-sleeved shirt.

The wide woollen garments of the nomad are also good protection against cold. During the winter the desert may be bitterly cold and when the bedouin sits on his haunches and sweeps his burnouse around him like a tent, he makes his own little micro-climate, and when he goes to sleep on the ground, at best sheltered by a tent open all along one side, the warm clothing is a welcome protection.

SUMMARY

Man is an excellent temperature regulator who can dissipate heat by sweating at a rate more than ten times the resting metabolic rate. Sweating rates may be as high as 12 litres per day, and, in short periods, 3 litres or more per hour.

One problem of high sweating rates is the danger of salt depletion. Sweat contains a variable amount of sodium chloride, but always enough to cause a considerable salt loss when sweat is produced in quantities. The most obvious symptoms, severe and painful muscle cramps, occur when water is taken to replace the loss, thus diluting the body fluids. A relatively high intake of sodium chloride is therefore necessary.

The need for water manifests itself as thirst and an urge to drink. Characteristically, man does not drink sufficiently to make up for the entire loss, even when water is freely available. Thus he incurs a voluntary dehydration which, during the day in the desert, frequently amounts to 3 to 5 per cent of his body weight. The tendency is to make up for this deficit during major meals. Man cannot drink at once much more than about a litre of fluid.

As the body is depleted of water, urine volume is reduced to a minimum value of somewhat less than $\frac{1}{2}$ litre per day. Renal function continues at this level until severe states of dehydration have been reached. Sweating seems to continue at the level demanded by the need for heat dissipation, in spite of increasing dehydration. As dehydration progresses there is considerable sign of circulatory failure. The plasma-volume is reduced more than indicated by its proportional share in the total water loss, and in consequence the viscosity of the blood is increased. The pulse-rate is increased and the stroke volume of the heart is reduced, but the cardiac output remains the same.

As dehydration becomes severe in a hot environment, the metabolic heat is not carried sufficiently fast to the skin by the circulating blood. Although sweating continues and the skin is cool, the deeper temperature rises rapidly or explosively. At this stage of dehydration, death in a hot environment is caused by an explosive heat rise as the body temperature rapidly reaches the fatal limit of between 41° and 42° C.

Man cannot store water and has little, if any, ability to be trained to use less water in the desert. The need for water is set by the need for dissipation of heat. The use of clothing, within limits, reduces the water expenditure by acting as an insulating barrier against the heat flow from the hot environment to the skin surface.

2

BASIC PROBLEMS. THE ADVANTAGE OF A LARGE BODY

HEAT BALANCE

ANIMALS do live in deserts. A good flashlight at night or a little patience during the day will reveal a variety of mammals, reptiles, birds, and insects.

In simple terms, there are three ways in which animals can arrange their life in the hot desert: they can evade the heat, they can passively put up with it, or they can actively combat it by evaporation of water.

Let us briefly examine these possibilities. The simplest way to evade heat is to go underground. A few inches down the tremendous temperature variations are smoothed out, and the temperature does not reach the extremes of the soil surface and the atmosphere (347, 294). The burrowing animals, the evaders, can come out in the cool night and lead a normal but nocturnal life.

Putting up with the heat by remaining on the surface during the day would, unless water is evaporated, inevitably cause the body temperature to rise. This would necessitate an increased tolerance to high body temperatures beyond the limit found in other animals. There is, however, no indication that any desert vertebrate has a temperature tolerance much higher than that of its relatives in more moderate climates. For insects and other arthropods the situation may be different. It is not unusual to see flying insects during the middle of the day when the air temperature is about 40° C; occasionally an insect is seen creeping over the hot surface of a sand dune, and often a scarab beetle is seen, pushing its little sphere of dirt along the hot surface of the soil. Unfortunately, we lack adequate information about their actual body temperatures, measured with reliable techniques. We can assume that if any animals are able to put up with the heat, insects are the most likely prospects.

Combating the heat by evaporation is efficient, as we have seen for man, but expensive in an environment where little or no water is available. While man depends on his cultural adaptations, animals must rely on natural resources. Where no open water is available, animals can still use the water contained in plants or the bodies of their prey. An increased need for water to combat the heat, however, emphasizes the extreme dryness of the desert and the scarcity of water. The large animals, such as desert sheep, gazelles, and camels, have no chance of hiding underground during the day, at best they can rest in the little shade they may find. Therefore, these animals are faced with the dilemma of spending their scant water resources for evaporation or virtually being cooked.

Environmental heat load and body size

If we put a large block of ice outside in the desert and a small piece next to it, the small piece will melt away long before the large block. If a small pebble and a big rock are taken from a cool room where they have acquired the same temperature, and are placed on the desert surface where the sun beats down, the pebble will be burning hot while the rock still retains some of its coolness. Another way of expressing this difference between small and large objects is to say that the large object has a greater 'thermal inertia'. (We assume, of course, that the two objects we compare have similar thermal conductivities and specific heat capacities.)

The reason that the small object heats up so much faster is its larger relative surface. If we imagine the rock or iceblock broken into many small pieces, many new surfaces, previously unexposed, will be in contact with the air and will receive heat and solar radiation. Thus, the same total mass of rock will now heat up much faster and the crushed ice will melt sooner.

The mathematical description of the relation between surface and mass is simple enough. If we assume that a given cube is cut into smaller cubes with the side of each 1/10 of the larger cube, the combined surface of all the small cubes is 10 times that of the original. If we cut the linear dimension in 1/100, the aggregate surface is now 100 times the original, and so on. The same rule holds for any other shape, provided that the general shape is retained. Thus, any small object will have a surface area which, relative to its weight, increases as the linear dimension decreases.

Inanimate objects gain heat from the environment in proportion to their surface, but the heat load on an animal in the desert consists of two components, heat gain from the environment and metabolic heat. The first component includes conduction from the hot air as well as the radiation from the sun and the hot ground, and since both types of heat exchange are surface processes, the environmental heat load will be directly proportional to the surface. It so happens that metabolic heat production in mammals also is nearly proportional to the surface, rather than to the weight of the animal.[1] Therefore the total heat load

---

[1] The metabolic rates of mammals have been thoroughly investigated and much material has been accumulated and carefully discussed (45, 67). The essence of the information is that heat production (or oxygen consumption) in animals as a function of body size is more closely related to surface area than to body weight.

If the metabolic rates (M) of mammals of various size, from the mouse to the

on an animal, metabolic and environmental, will also be approximately proportional to the surface, and the small animal with its larger relative surface is in a much less favourable position for maintaining a tolerably low body temperature.

Conduction of heat. The heat flow to a cool body in a hot environment follows the usual physical laws for heat exchange. The heat flow consists of two components, one caused by conduction of heat between two media in direct contact, and the other by radiation exchange between objects not in contact. When gases or liquids are involved, the conductive heat exchange is further complicated by convection in these media.

The flow of heat by conduction depends on the temperature difference and the conductance of the media, and, of course, the area of contact. For a given temperature difference, twice as much heat is conducted when the area of contact is twice as large. For most practical considerations of desert conditions conductive heating is therefore proportional to exposed area and, of course, to temperature difference.

Convection. If cool air is in contact with a warm body, the layer of air at the surface will be heated and rise. The movement in the air caused by the temperature difference is called *natural convection*, and it increases the rate of heat transfer beyond that caused by conduction alone. Convection occurs also in the reverse situation, a cool body in hot air, where the surface layer of air will tend to sink as it is cooled. The same situation prevails in liquids, but this does not apply to the problems of desert animals under discussion here.

Radiation. Heat exchange by radiation follows the Stefan-Boltzmann law. Radiation transfer between two bodies takes place in both directions, and the net transfer is proportional to the difference of the fourth power of the absolute temperatures of the surfaces and to the effective radiating area of the objects. Also, the reflectivity (or absorptivity) of the surfaces enters into the equation. Therefore, although the radiation exchange is a complex function, we have again the obvious fact that the amount of energy transferred is directly proportional to the exposed surface.

---

elephant, are plotted against body weight (W) on logarithmic co-ordinates, the points fall close to a straight line represented by the equation: $M = K \times W^{0.74}$, where K is a constant with a numerical value depending on the units used. This line is the noted mouse-to-elephant curve of Benedict. If the metabolic rates were exactly proportional to body surface, the equation would be $M = K \cdot W^{0.67}$ (assuming equal shape of the animals).

The equation has theoretical implications which have been the subject of much speculation, but this need not concern us here, for, at the moment, we are only interested in the magnitude of heat production relative to body size. We need an estimate of the heat load arising from within the animal, and as an approximation we will assume that the metabolic rate is proportional to the surface.

When we now sum up the environmental heat load in the desert, we find that the heat flow caused by conduction and convection, as well as by radiation, is proportional to the exposed area. Thus the overall heat load on an animal, consisting of the two components, metabolic heat from within and environmental heat impinging from outside, is approximately proportional to the surface. This gives us an excellent opportunity to compare animals of widely different body sizes. Owing to its larger surface, relative to the body weight, a small animal is in a much more difficult position than a large one, and a simple calculation should give us the magnitude of the difference between the two.

Estimated need for water

If an animal exposed to the desert heat is to remain in heat balance, it will evaporate an amount of water which corresponds to the total heat gain. In the preceding chapter, we saw that a sweat production of about 1 litre per hour is not unusual for a man in a hot desert. The 580 kcal dissipated by the evaporation of this 1 litre of water correspond to the sum of metabolic heat and environmental heat gain. If we assume that this is a representative figure, what would the situation be for smaller and larger animals if they had to stay cool during a similar exposure?

Few studies have been made of the heat regulation of animals under hot desert conditions. Because of the complexity of the environment with its variable air temperature, ground temperature, and solar radiation, it is virtually impossible to evaluate and compare results obtained in different places and at different times.

One of the most valuable studies in this respect was made by the Harvard group, headed by D. B. Dill, that worked in Nevada during the construction of the Boulder Dam (later renamed Hoover Dam) on the Colorado River. Although this group was mainly concerned with man and the many cases of heat prostration among the workers during the early construction period, they appreciated the value of comparative studies in giving perspective to the understanding of physiological mechanisms.

In the Boulder Dam experiments (2, 104), a donkey and a dog were taken on daytime walks in the desert, accompanied by a man. The exposure was prolonged by making several round trips on a 6·4-km-long course, and in this way it was possible to obtain a careful comparison of the performance of three different species, donkey, man, and dog, under similar conditions of exercise and environmental heat stress.

An interesting aspect of this comparison is that the dog is supposed to evaporate all water necessary for heat regulation from the respiratory tract by panting, while the donkey and man sweat. This makes it possible to estimate the relative merits of sweating and panting. If our pre-

vious considerations are correct water expenditure for heat regulation
should be fairly much the same, when related to surface area, irrespective
of the mode of evaporation.

TABLE I

*The evaporation from donkey, man, and dog during a hot summer day in the
desert of the south-western United States*

	Body weight, kg	Evaporation, per cent of body weight per hr	Evaporation, kg/m²/hr
Donkey	96	1·24	0·573
Man	79	1·41	0·60
Dog	16	2·62	0·657

I have combined in Table I the information gained from the desert
hikes. It is immediately apparent that the dog used about twice as much
water, relative to his body weight, as the larger man or donkey. If, however, we calculate the evaporation per unit surface area,[1] we find that the
water loss is much the same in the three animals. It is, of course, not
possible to predict accurately the water expenditure in much larger or
much smaller animals by calculations based on their surface area. It is
possible, however, to estimate the order of magnitude, for the small
animal has no way of escaping the simple laws of physics and its large
relative surface—what it can escape by going underground is the parch-
ing heat.

If small and large animals were exposed to the same conditions on the
surface of the desert in the daytime and could maintain heat balance by
evaporation of water, we could calculate their expected evaporation
directly from the estimated heat gain, which should be proportional to
their surface. The observations made by Dill and his collaborators were
from a desert which is much like hot deserts elsewhere, and we can use
their figures as representative for the heat load on an average hot desert
summer day.

The expected evaporation needed to dissipate the desert heat load is
an exponential function of body weight and on logarithmic co-ordinates
the curve will come out as a straight line. However, a linear scale (Fig. 5)
emphasizes the exponential increase in water expenditure required if the
small animal is to combat the desert heat by evaporation. Small desert

---

[1] For the estimate of surface area I have used the formula $S = 0·1 \times W^{0·67}$, where
S is the surface in m² and W the body weight in kg. This approximation is inaccurate
and disregards differences in shape and posture, &c., but suffices for the level of accuracy
needed here.

rodents are in the size range of 10 to 100 grammes in body size. If an animal weighing 100 grammes were to remain on the surface of the desert during the day, and if it had the physiological mechanisms to dissipate heat by evaporation, it would use water at the rate of some 15 per cent of its body weight per hour and a 10-gramme animal should use over 30 per cent. Obviously, owing to their small size alone, these animals could not become diurnal for the simple reason that in a few hours evaporation would have removed all their body water. As a con-

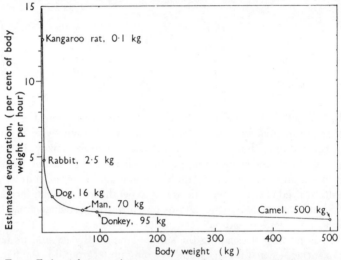

FIG. 5. Estimated evaporation necessary to maintain a constant body temperature in a hot desert environment for mammals of various body sizes. The curve is calculated on the assumption that heat load is proportional to body surface (see text). It shows the rapid increase in the theoretical cost of heat regulation in small mammals.

sequence small animals do not have the usual mechanism for active defence against overheating, they neither sweat nor pant.

A possible solution enabling the small animal to get away with exposure to daytime desert conditions would be an increased tolerance to elevated body temperatures. In this way the animal, instead of evaporating water to keep its body temperature down, could permit the temperature to rise beyond the limits usually tolerated by other animals. As far as we know, no desert mammal has taken advantage of this possibility, and it seems that mammals in general cannot extend the range of the body temperature beyond a maximum limit around 44° C.

If we look at the other end of the size range, we find that a very large animal, such as the camel, has some direct advantage, due to its body size. The benefit is, however, of diminishing magnitude as size increases.

If we calculate the advantage the camel derives from its size we find that, relative to its body weight, it should use half as much water as man does. If other circumstances were alike, this should permit the camel to live twice as long without water. As we shall see in the next chapter, other factors are not alike. A camel not only has a greater tolerance to loss of body water, it also has means to reduce the heat gain from the environment relative to that in other mammals.

WATER BALANCE—LOSS AND GAIN

Although animals, for short periods, can tolerate some depletion of their body water, they must in the long run remain in water balance. This means that all loss of water must be offset by an equal intake. The components of this simple account are listed below.

Loss	Gain
Evaporation	Drinking
Urine	Water in food
Faeces	Oxidation water

In the following chapters we shall repeatedly return to this balance-sheet and discuss its single components. The main difficulty in making the account balance in the desert is that the heat requires increased evaporation which is particularly difficult to meet by drinking, for usually no drinking-water is available. Therefore, many animals must rely on the second item on the gain side, water in the food. After rains, desert vegetation is lush, and the plants contain much water. As the dry season progresses, however, most vegetation dries up, and only a few plants such as cacti and other succulents retain a high water content and have a juicy pulp that serves as water-supply for many animals. Other animals can live on dry food, and for these the only water gain is that derived from the oxidation of the food, aside from the small amount of moisture absorbed in dry seeds and other plant materials. For these, water balance is particularly vulnerable, the extremely limited water intake must cover all needs, and the slightest increase in water loss upsets the precarious balance.

Oxidation water. The formation of oxidation water, or metabolic water, is important for many desert animals. For some this is virtually the only source of water. The oxidation of organic compounds leads to the formation of water from the hydrogen present, and when foodstuffs are oxidized in the metabolic processes, the yield of water depends on the hydrogen content of the metabolized food.[1] The amounts of water formed in the oxidation of the basic foodstuffs are given in Table II.

[1] A small amount of hydrogen is eliminated in the unoxidized form as part of organic compounds. In mammals the only compound of much significance in this respect is urea, which, owing to its composition, CH_4N_2O, removes appreciable amounts of unoxidized hydrogen. In birds, reptiles, and most insects uric acid,

Over the years there have been many statements to the effect that desert animals get along by having special mechanisms for the formation of water by metabolic processes, but the formation of water is, of course, the same whether an animal lives in the desert or not. There is no means whereby an animal could increase the yield of 'metabolic' water beyond that formed from the hydrogen contained in the metabolized compounds.

Another common misconception is based on the suggestion that animals could produce more water by increasing their metabolism. The net gain in water by no means equals the figures given in Table II, for the oxidation of foodstuffs requires oxygen. This necessitates ventilation

TABLE II

Formation of oxidation water, or metabolic water, when different foodstuffs are metabolized

The figure for protein is valid only when urea is the end product of nitrogen metabolism

	Gm H_2O formed per gm food	Litres O_2 consumed per gm food	Litres O_2 used per gm water formed
Starch	0·556	0·828	1·489
Fat	1·071	2·019	1·885
Protein	0·396	0·967	2·441

of the lungs and loss of water in the expired air in proportion to the oxygen uptake. Therefore, increasing the formation of oxidation water by increased metabolism is accompanied by a corresponding increase in evaporation from the lungs which usually will constitute a net loss, rather than a gain. Therefore, it would be of no avail to sit still and just turn up the metabolic rate to get water. As we shall see in a later chapter, however, a decreased metabolic rate in a dormant or aestivating mammal results in considerable advantages in water balance.

On the loss side of our balance-sheet we have already discussed the tremendous variations in the use of water for evaporation. Evaporation constitutes not only the greatest drain on the water resources of an animal, but is also the single factor that can vary the most. We have seen how this item can be reduced by avoiding the heat, and also that small animals have no choice and must avoid exposure in order to survive. Even if no water is used in heat regulation, a certain minimum or obligatory loss of water takes place from the body surface and, in particular, from the respiratory organs.

$C_5H_4N_4O_3$, replaces urea as the major end product of protein metabolism. The excretion of these hydrogen-containing metabolic products explains the relatively low yield of oxidation water in protein metabolism.

Small mammals have no sweat glands (except scent glands on the food pads), but there is still some water loss through the skin, variously called insensible perspiration, diffusion water loss, &c. The water loss from the scaly skin of snakes and lizards is supposed to be low, but these suffer the same problem as mammals with respect to the respiratory air. The expired air is saturated with water vapour, although the fact that its temperature usually is a little lower than the deep body temperature somewhat reduces its vapour content. As far as we know, no vertebrate has been able to escape from the need to keep moist the membranes where gas exchange takes place.

Insects are strikingly successful at living in dry places. The clothes moth that thrives on the dry wool of a garment in a centrally heated apartment in the winter lives in one of the driest desert climates and still obtains sufficient water for life and growth. Insects have an outer cuticle nearly impermeable to water, and their respiratory system consists of fine tubes where only the finest terminal ends seem to permit passage of water. Most amazing, some insects can extract from air some of the moisture it contains. No wonder insects are more successful at living in dry places than any other animals and form such an important part of the desert fauna.

The production of faeces and urine involves a necessary water loss. Even the driest faecal material contains some free water. The amount of water used by the kidney depends on the quantity of waste products to be eliminated and their concentration in the urine. Mammals secrete a liquid urine, and those that have a kidney which can produce a highly concentrated solution of the waste products have an advantage. Thus the water expenditure becomes dependent upon the efficiency of the kidney, and we find among desert mammals the most powerful kidneys of any.

Birds and reptiles excrete a semi-solid urine, for their main nitrogen-containing excretory product is uric acid. Uric acid and its salts are almost insoluble, and by excreting a paste of uric acid crystals, these animals use only small amounts of water in their urine.

Again, in the question of excretion, insects show the most extreme solutions to the water problem. Not only do they excrete uric acid, and withdraw virtually all free water from the intestinal contents, but some insects deposit uric acid in various parts of the body, thus completely eliminating the need for its excretion (352).

One additional item in the water balance-sheet has not yet been mentioned. In periods the female mammal nurses her young, and large quantities of water are required for the formation of milk. One possible way to reduce this drain of water would be to produce a more concentrated milk. It has been suggested that the very high fat content in the milk of seals and whales, 30–40 per cent as against some 2–5 per cent in most terrestrial mammals, should be viewed in the light of their life in an environment of relative unavailability of water (186), rather than as a means to provide concentrated food for the rapidly growing young. The only desert mammal for which we have adequate information regarding milk composition is the camel, which has about 4 per cent fat in the milk (24, 185). This does not show any particular economy in water expenditure, but whenever conditions of heat and drought put extra demands on the water resources, the young would be at least as much in need of water as the mother. It seems that the usual solution to the demand for water in milk production has been met by a timing of the reproductive period to coincide with the part of the year when temperatures are moderate and the chances for rainfall are greatest.

In the small mammal, however, where water is not used for heat regulation, the situation may be different. It would be a delight to know whether the mother kangaroo rat, who keeps her young in a cool burrow and manages her own water-supply almost exclusively on oxidation water, has arrived at the solution of using a concentrated milk to nurse her offspring.

SUMMARY

Animals that live in the desert could attempt to reach a solution to the rigorous environment in three ways: evade the heat, put up with it, or combat it by evaporating water.

The size of the animal is important. Small animals have virtually no defence against overheating—they do not sweat or pant. Owing to their large relative surface they would need too much water for heat dissipation and the only solution is escape. Small desert animals therefore are nocturnal and come out of their burrows at night. As far as we know, no mammal or reptile can put up with the heat by tolerating a greatly increased body temperature. Only large animals can afford to combat the heat by evaporation of water.

In the water balance of the animal, gain and loss must be equal. In an environment where water intake is limited, only animals that can reduce their output can survive. It is therefore valuable for a desert animal to have an efficient kidney that can secrete a highly concentrated urine and an intestine that can remove much water from the faecal material, and, if possible, to have mechanisms that can reduce the evaporative loss of water. Since evaporation is the largest single factor in the water balance, and also the most variable, the ultimate success of a desert animal hinges on the manner in which this avenue for water loss has been handled.

3

THE CAMEL

EXCITING tales have been told about the camel, making it the most famous animal of the desert. It can cross the scorching expanses of the Sahara, it can drink saline and bitter waters that poison man and other animals, and the bedouin who is out of water may save his life by killing his beast to drink the fluid he finds in its stomach. What is fact and what is fable in such remarkable reports?

The extraordinary attributes of the camel as a riding and pack animal have been appreciated by many a desert traveller. Reliable reports, however, are not as plentiful as the vivid descriptions which abound in popular literature on desert travel. The remarkably versatile explorer of the Sahara, Professor Monod of Dakar, has collected a list of well-documented treks where camels have travelled over distances exceeding 500 kilometres between watering-points (228). It is not surprising to find Monod's own travels on the list. In 21 days, from 12 December 1954 to 2 January 1955, he and his group traversed the waterless Empty Quarter of the Sahara which, as the crow flies, was 870 km. A calculation of the actual length of the march indicated a distance of 944 km, or nearly 600 miles. With this performance Monod has added a major accomplishment as a determined and inexhaustible desert explorer to his already distinguished career as a zoologist, botanist, geologist, and archaeologist.

Nearly all the travels in Monod's list were undertaken during the winter or early spring. This is the best and coolest part of the year in the desert. Rain may have fallen over scattered areas, bringing out fresh vegetation that helps the camel with moisture as well as feed. When summer comes the sparse vegetation dries up, and at the same time the heat imposes an increasing strain on the water resources of the animal. At this time of the year camels need to be watered more frequently, but the length of time they can go without water depends on many factors—the condition of the vegetation, the temperature, wind and sun, how hard they work, what load they carry, or how far they have to march.

There is no doubt that the camel is a very exceptional animal. It cannot escape the severity of the desert day by going underground like the burrowing rodents. How, then, is it possible for the camel to get along so remarkably well for long periods without water?

The puzzle can best be expressed as a series of questions. Does the camel store water, which is then used as need arises? Is the camel's temperature similar to that in other mammals, or can it tolerate body temperatures fatal to other mammals? Does its wool, whose insulating properties are renowned in cold countries, protect it from the heat of the environment? Has the camel an exceptional tolerance to depletion of its body water, so that cells and organs can function in spite of a high degree of dehydration?

The answers to these questions will help us to understand some of the most puzzling features in the physiological performance of this unusual animal.

DOES THE CAMEL STORE WATER?

When man drinks, he does so after a loss has occurred, to restore his water content to the normal. Does the camel drink in the same way 'for the past' to make up for a deficit, or does it drink 'for the future', making provisions for needs that may arise later? When desert travellers observe the huge quantities a camel drinks, and then its almost incredible performance on long marches, they may easily conclude that the tremendous intake constitutes a storage in anticipation of future needs. Further support for this hypothesis has been sought in the unusual structure of the camel's stomach.

The stomach

The camel, like other ruminants, has several stomachs, or, to be more precise, several compartments which precede the true stomach where digestive enzymes and acid are secreted. Ruminants in general have four stomachs, called the rumen, reticulum, omasum, and abomasum. Since most investigators seem to prefer to divide the stomach of the camel into only three parts, considerable dispute has arisen over which names should be used for these parts; unhappily, whatever the choice, one name would be left unused. This is of little concern to us here, for there is no dispute about the first section, the rumen. In the cow the rumen is a large, roundish sack which functions as a fermentation vat where bacteria and protozoa aid in the digestion of cellulose. The inside is smooth and even, there are no digestive glands, and all the fluid it contains is saliva swallowed with the masticated food.

The rumen of the camel is different, two areas in its wall contain diverticula which are separated into smaller chambers and sub-chambers by separating folds of the mucosa. The edges of the chambers have strong muscular bands, which some investigators have interpreted as sphincters. The whole structure has been supposed to constitute a system of water compartments or water sacs that could be kept closed by the 'sphincter' muscles to exclude the fermenting mass of feed in the rumen. The camel then should be able to release, when needed, pure water. This argument has been put forward without regard to the fact

PLATE 1

CAMEL (*CAMELUS DROMEDARIUS*)

This animal displays patches of long winter fur on its underside while on the upper parts much of the wool has been shorn, as can be seen from the clipping marks. The second camel, visible between the legs of the larger animal, illustrates how the legs are folded and virtually unexposed when the camel sits down

(*Photo, Dr. Beno Rothenberg, from* Land of Israel, *Schocken Publishing House, Tel-Aviv, 1962*)

that the muscular bands are straight and by no stretch of the imagination can be used to close the 'sacs'.

The 'water sacs' in the camel's stomach were known to Pliny who

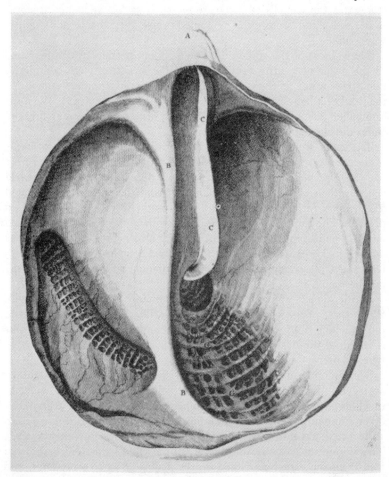

FIG. 6. In the year 1806 the peculiar structure of the camel's rumen was carefully described by Sir Everard Home, who concluded that the compartments or 'sacs' would be unsuited for water storage. Home's drawing is reproduced here from *Philosophical Transactions of the Royal Society*, 1806.

assigned to them the key role in the camel's ability to survive in the torrid lands of Africa. The intervening 2000 years have seen endless repetitions of this belief, in spite of several attempts to discredit it.

Early in the last century a careful dissection of a camel's stomach was made by Sir Everard Home who published an excellent drawing (Fig. 6)

(154). Home suggested that the volume as well as the structure of the sacs would be unsuited for any noticeable water storage. In spite of this and several later contributions which also raised doubts about water storage in the camel's stomach, terms such as 'water compartments', 'water sacs', and 'water cells' remained in use in textbooks and popular works alike.

The volume of the rumen diverticula is not particularly large, being in the order of 5 litres (199). Even if the structure were completely filled with water, it could by no stretch of the imagination suffice for the need of a large animal for day after day in the hot desert. We must remember that a man, for example, easily uses some 10 or 15 litres of water during a single day in the desert.

The water-storage hypothesis is further discredited when the contents of the sac-like structure are examined. Of the thirteen camels that I have had the opportunity to examine when they were butchered, not one had water in the sacs (300). The rumen itself contained coarsely masticated feed, which formed a semi-liquid mass with liberal amounts of fluid present. The sacs, however, were filled with more closely packed feed particles and contained less fluid. This was always the case, whether the animals had been grazing without water, had been kept in the oasis with feed and daily watering, or had been watered immediately before the butchering.

As mentioned, the main part of the rumen contained much liquid. When some of its contents were lifted out, liberal amounts of greenish, foul-smelling fluid would run down between the fingers. No doubt this is the fluid the desperate desert traveller can drink as a last resort to save his life.

The amount of rumen contents in the camels that we examined averaged 11 per cent of the body weight, with some individuals having as much as 15 per cent. This is the same order of magnitude as found in other ruminants. Cattle, for example, have been reported to have from 10 to 15 per cent or more of the body weight in rumen contents (276). The amount of water in the rumen is high. The semi-solid masticated feed from the camel contained on the average 83 per cent water, and the fluid that could be drained off in liberal amounts contained 98 per cent water. Ruminant digestion always requires large amounts of water, and the situation in the camel is what one would expect in any ruminant.

Further evidence that the fluid is nothing unusual comes from an analysis of its composition (Table III).

There is no significant difference in the composition of the fluid in the rumen and the liquid expressed from the contents of the sacs. Both fluids have a concentration of electrolytes not far from that of the blood, which makes it obvious that they are not stored water. The relative abundance of ions in the fluids is similar to that usually found in the saliva of ruminants. The rumen fluid is, however, slightly more dilute than the other body fluids, while the saliva in sheep is somewhat more concentrated than the blood (103).

The sodium concentration in the rumen fluid is high, potassium relatively low (part of the potassium may be derived from plant material), and the chloride concentration is low. Although we have no analysis for other anions, it is likely that the major constituent of the fluid is sodium

TABLE III

The fluids found in the rumen and the rumen sacs of the camel have a composition quite different from water

They have a total osmotic concentration approaching that of the blood, and a composition similar to saliva

Average figures from 13 animals, quoted from (300).

	Na, mN	K, mN	Cl, mN	Osmotic conc., $mosm$
Rumen fluid	106·9	17·6	17·6	281
Sac fluid	109·4	17·6	17·5	282
Blood-plasma	156·3	4·56	109·6	338
Water	1·4 to 1·9	(0)	1·46 to 2·34	

bicarbonate, the chief component in ruminant saliva, for the pH of the fluid was mostly around 7·6 to 8·0. The sodium bicarbonate serves to neutralize the large quantities of acid fermentation products formed in the rumen, and apparently the camel in this respect behaves like any normal ruminant.

If there is no water storage in the special sac-like structure, what is its function? While the rumen of other animals contains no glands, and this is true for the main part of the camel rumen, the bottom of the 'water compartments' does contain glands, first seen by Pilliet (259) and later described in detail (141). The number of the glands is estimated to be in the order of 100 million and it is likely that they produce much of the fluid in the rumen, a watery solution similar to ruminant saliva in composition and function. Thus, from the suggested role of these glands in digestion, they might be considered as accessory salivary glands. Anatomically, of course, they are not. Their location in the otherwise glandless rumen is curious. The division of the sacs into compartments and subcompartments, which has misled many writers into believing in the 'water sac' hypothesis, is probably a result of surface expansion to increase the total area of the gland-bearing mucosa. The second stomach of ruminants has a wall which is intricately divided into diverticula and subdiverticula—hence its name 'reticulum'. In the camel the structure reminds one of the glandular rumen sacs, and the walls contain similar glands. Although its volume is small (a litre or two) and the reticulum in other ruminants looks much the same, its sponge-like appearance has prompted a belief in further water storage. There is no evidence at all in support of this notion. The combined volume of all the stomachs below the rumen was from 3·5 to 8·5 litres in our camels, a small volume for animals weighing 300 to 500 kg.

To make sure that the intestine did not hold an unusually large volume we weighed the contents and found on the average 3·5 kg in the small and 7·7 kg in the large intestine. These amounts are somewhat smaller than those reported for cows.

In conclusion, we can say that there is indeed a large amount of fluid in the rumen; the only mistake is to assume that it is stored water. The liquid could serve as an excellent substitute for drinking-water in an emergency, in spite of its unappetizing appearance and foul odour. The thirsty man will drink anything, including his own scanty urine, and the rumen fluid is physiologically no worse than pure water. If anything, it may be an advantage that it contains some electrolytes, for the thirsty man in the desert is likely to have lost much salt in his sweat. (Probably not much nutrient can be obtained from the rumen fluid, for we found that its total content of solids was only about 2 per cent.)

The camel is not the only animal that has provided a drink for the desperate man in the desert. Other ruminants as well have copious amounts of digestive fluid, which are taken advantage of when occasion arises. The addax antelope (*Addax nasomaculatus*), the only larger animal that Monod observed regularly during his travels in the Empty Quarter, is hunted by the natives of the Sahara. To obtain fluid they place the rumen contents on top of a row of sticks arranged across the horns, keeping the skin of the animal underneath to collect the fluid that drips off (Fig. 7). Monod has described how the drained mass of half-digested plant remnants is afterwards fed to the camels who only reluctantly accept the extra ration (228).

Water from the hump

There is a widespread misconception regarding the role of the hump in the water metabolism of the camel. I am not referring to the nursery stories which tell that the hump is a water tank, for the hump consists of adipose tissue and contains mostly fat.

The misunderstood role of the hump arises from the knowledge that oxidation of fat yields more than its weight in water (1 gramme fat gives 1·07 gramme water). This means that a camel which walks into the desert with a hump of, say, 40 kg carries a potential water-supply of well over 40 litres. As the fat is oxidized in the energy metabolism, the corresponding amount of water is released. This has led to the deceptive idea that, in addition to supplying the usual storage of energy, the hump serves as a water reservoir as well.

As far as I have been able to find out, the idea that desert animals should get their main water-supply by oxidation of fat originated with

FIG. 7. To obtain the fluid from the rumen of the addax antelope native hunters of the Sahara place the stomach contents on a row of sticks arranged across the horns. The liquid then drips into the skin which has been placed underneath. (Reproduced with permission from Dekeyser and Derivot (102).)

Strohl (326). The thought is simple and tantalizing, and even competent biochemists have accepted it (20).

To begin with, all animals get the same amount of water from burning fat, so why cannot they all live in the desert? The hitch in the matter is that the oxidation of fat requires oxygen. This involves ventilation of the lungs, and since the expired air is saturated with water vapour, considerable loss of water ensues. The evaporation from the lungs is of the same magnitude as the quantity of water formed, and in very dry air it even exceeds the amount of oxidation water.

Some simple calculations will bring out this point (see Table IV). Let us assume that a camel has a metabolic rate of 10 000 kcal per day. If starch is used to provide the energy the amount of oxidation water formed is greater than if fat is the substrate. Furthermore, since the starch requires less oxygen for its metabolism, evaporation from the lungs will also be less in this case. If the inhaled air is completely dry, the water loss from the lungs will in both cases exceed the amount formed, but the net loss will be less unfavourable for starch.

TABLE IV

Water formation and estimated pulmonary evaporation in dry air at a metabolic level of 10 000 kcal

Whether fat or starch is metabolized, the evaporation from the lungs exceeds the water formed. The net water loss is somewhat greater when fat is metabolized

	Foodstuff used, kg	Oxidation water formed, kg	Oxygen used for oxidation of food, litre	Approx. evap. from lungs, kg
Fat	1·06	1·13	2130	1·8
Starch	2·39	1·33	1980	1·7

The conclusion of this simple calculation is that: (a) at a given metabolic level, starch yields more oxidation water than fat; (b) as water is formed, the use of oxygen results in evaporation from the lungs which, in dry air, exceeds the amount formed, and; (c) the net loss of water is lower for the metabolism of starch than for fat.

Although the hump is not a water store, either directly or indirectly, its value to the camel is considerable. In carrying its energy reserves in the form of fat, the camel is like other animals. Fat gives more energy per unit weight than other foodstuffs, and it is a valuable economy to carry the reserves as lightly as possible, in particular for an animal that may be without food for long periods of time.

Other water storage?

If neither the hump nor the stomach can be considered water reservoirs, is there any possibility of other water storage in the camel? Many excellent anatomists have examined camels, and some unusual structures have been found, but none that could be associated with water storage. To be of any help, water must be present in such quantities that it could hardly be overlooked, and in the many camels that I have dissected myself I have seen no evidence of water in unexpected places or unusual amounts.

It would, however, be easy to overlook the fluid if the general water content of the animal were higher than usual and the salt concentrations, &c., in body fluids lower. There is no evidence for such assumptions. The total water content of camels, when determined with the antipyrine dilution method, was in the normal range for mammals (78), and in all our own investigations in the Sahara we found concentrations in the body fluids similar to the usual values. Quite recently Macfarlane worked with my group in the Australian deserts and obtained similar results by using tritium for the determination of total body water.

One last possibility remains. It was suggested by Peck (247) that a 'physiological subcutaneous edema' occurred in camels within a few hours of watering, lasting for about 24 hours. This was in camels that had been given an extra ration of salt. In the area of North Africa where I have worked, I have seen no evidence of oedema in camels, with one single exception. One of our experimental animals was, for a period of time, given only salted water to drink. This camel had, after some days, gained weight beyond its normal. Its blood electrolyte concentration was as usual in camels but its total water content seemed increased. It was rather flabby and oedematous, and undoubtedly had a higher than usual water content. Whether this would do it any good, is, however, another question. Since this camel started with blood concentrations similar to those in other animals, loss of water by evaporation would result in increased concentrations. If the rise in salt concentration is deleterious in itself, this animal would not be much better off than others. It would probably be worth the effort to make further studies of the relation between salt and water intake in camels and observe the effects on ensuing dehydration.

PROBLEMS OF HEAT

The camel's body temperature

It has long been known that the body temperature of the camel is quite variable, and the animal has therefore gained the reputation of having a rather crude mechanism for temperature control (84, 310). It turns out that the camel has an even more variable temperature than reported, but at the same time it appears better regulated than has been assumed. Such a statement seems to contain a contradiction, because we are used to considering the much more constant body temperature of man as representing the ideal situation. As we shall see, an increase in body temperature has some conspicuous advantages for the desert animal.

When we speak about 'body temperature' we usually do not mean the average temperature of the body, but rather an imaginary average temperature of the deeper parts. It is customarily measured as the deep rectal temperature, and within a few tenths of a degree this is probably representative of the temperature of the body core.

The late H. C. Bazett, one of the grand old men of temperature studies, characterized the term 'body temperature' as a misnomer (40). However desirable it is to establish the true average temperature of the body, it is technically close to impossible. The skin is almost always cooler than the deeper parts, and temperature gradients extend inwards from the skin to a variable depth. In cool surroundings these gradients may be very deep, and an appreciable part of the total body mass may be at a much lower temperature than the core. An approach used by Hart for determining the average body temperature of mice consisted of killing the animal and immediately determining its heat content in a suitable calorimeter (146). This drastic method would be impractical for large animals, but since we need only an approximate estimate of the heat content for our considerations, we will assume that the core temperature is a suitable representation of 'body temperature', and the rectal temperature will be used as the closest approximation that we can obtain with reasonably simple techniques.

During the winter we found a diurnal variation in the rectal temperature of Saharan camels of about 2° C, between 36° and 38° C. At the same time the air temperature varied between approximately freezing and + 20° C. In our measurements the fluctuations in the camel's temperature were in regular diurnal cycles, rather independent of changing weather, sun, wind, rain, &c.

One of the reasons that the camel has gained a reputation for being a poor temperature regulator is that Sergent (310) found particularly low rectal temperatures, between 34° and .35° C, after rainy nights. It is indeed cold when the desert temperature approaches freezing and winds add to the chilling effect of the rain, but on three occasions when we had such weather, we observed no particular effect on our camels. They maintained their normal temperature for the particular time of the day when it was measured. There is no reason to doubt the observations made by Sergent, an experienced investigator from the Institut Pasteur; one can only note that our camels behaved differently.

In summer the variations in rectal temperature were much greater, with the temperature usually quite low in the morning and high in the afternoon. Morning temperatures were often between 34° and 35° C, and evening temperatures usually near or above 40° C. The greatest change observed in one animal in a day was from 34·5° C at 08.00 hrs. to 40·7° C at 19.00 hrs., that is, a rise of 6·2° C in 11 hours.

Several times we observed that the rectal temperature of the camel decreased particularly rapidly around 6 o'clock in the morning. Up until that time the skin was cool, but it suddenly became warmer as the drop in rectal temperature set in. The drop could not be caused by a cooler environment, for air and radiation temperatures were already increasing. More likely, the drop was due to a sudden vasodilation bringing cool blood from the periphery to the deeper parts. If this is correct the cooling power of the environment was greater than the camel utilized,

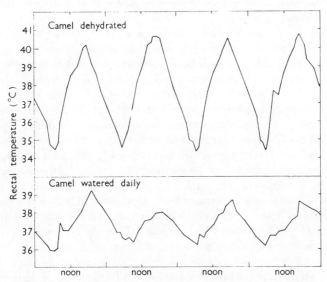

FIG. 8. When a camel is deprived of drinking-water its rectal temperature may show a diurnal fluctuation of as much as 5 or 6° C. When it is watered daily the fluctuations are much smaller. (Reproduced with permission from (301).)

and the lowest temperature obtained must have been at a well-regulated level.

Two representative temperature records are given in Fig. 8. A most conspicuous feature is that the temperature fluctuations were much greater in the animals when they were deprived of drinking-water. When they were watered every day, the fluctuations decreased to about 2° C per day, which is similar to the daily variations in camels during the winter. In the periods when they were deprived of water, however, the temperature not only reached a considerably higher daily maximum, but the morning minimum was lowered as well, as can be seen in the upper graph.

The lethal body temperature for a camel is not known, but in no case did we observe a rectal temperature in excess of 40·7° C. This seems to be an approximate limit to which the temperature can rise without harm, but in all probability the camel cannot tolerate any appreciable further increase. In man the upper limit of temperature for survival is about 42° C for the temperature of the brain (40). The effect of high temperatures depends on their duration, and it is likely that continued temperatures of 41° C may be dangerous and close to the upper limit of safety for man. The fact that we never observed temperatures in excess of 40·7° C in the camel, in spite of increasing environmental heat stress as the Saharan summer became hotter and hotter, suggests a well-regulated limit, and that any further rise beyond this point is prevented by increased heat dissipation. It would be extremely interesting to know more about the camel's tolerance to high body temperatures, and as opportunities for research improve in countries where camels are common, we can expect that careful and critical studies will give valuable results.

Advantages of a fluctuating body temperature. If the internal temperature is being kept constant as environmental heat impinges upon a body, all the acquired heat must be dissipated at the expense of water. If, instead, the body temperature is permitted to rise, all heat that goes into warming the body can be considered as stored. An example will illustrate the value of such heat storage. If the average body temperature in a 500-kg camel increases by 6° C, the stored heat will be about 2500 kcal (sp. heat $\simeq$ 0·8), and the dissipation of all this heat by evaporation would require almost 5 litres of water. Instead, the heat is dissipated in the cool night by conduction and radiation.

Thus, an increase in body temperature during heat stress can be considered as a means to store heat until it can be disposed of without expenditure of water. If the morning temperature is especially low, this increases the amount of heat that can be stored and postpones until later in the day the moment when the tolerable temperature limit has been reached and water *must* be used to prevent further rise.

The high body temperature during the day has another advantage as well. The flow of heat from a hot environment to a cooler body depends on the temperature difference, and if the difference is reduced, the heat flow will be less. Therefore, the rise in the camel's temperature to a level well above 40° C should have a considerable effect in reducing the heat flow from the environment. An exact estimate of the reduction in heat load and the saving in water is virtually impossible to make, because it is so difficult to establish the integrated environmental temperature and the conditions for heat flow to the organism.

When man and dog respond to dehydration with increased body temperature, this has been interpreted as evidence of inadequate peripheral circulation, so that heat from the deeper parts is not carried to the surface at a sufficient rate (9, 70). Facts supporting this opinion are the decreased efficiency of the heart in man (page 13) and the increment in rectal temperature of about $2°$ C for a water loss of 10 per cent of the body weight (285). In the camel, at least, it seems that the rise in body temperature is not a sign of failure in heat dissipation, but is an actively regulated pattern in the water-conservation mechanism.

Does body temperature affect metabolic rate? Within limits, the rate of most physiological processes increases with temperature. The change that occurs with a temperature increase of $10°$ C is commonly designated as the Q_{10}. If the increase is, say, twofold, the $Q_{10}=2$, if the increase is $2\frac{1}{2}$-fold, $Q_{10}=2\cdot5$, &c. Usually, little attention is paid to this effect of temperature in mammals, for their body temperature remains almost constant. There is, however, the usual temperature effect, which in man has a Q_{10} between $2\cdot3$ and $2\cdot9$[1] (67, 110).

If the Q_{10} in the camel were similar to that in man, the metabolism should increase by some 65 to 90 per cent when the temperature rises by $6°$ C from morning to afternoon. *A priori*, it might seem unlikely that the metabolic rate should increase this much. Firstly, a rise in metabolism constitutes a drain on energy reserves, and secondly, the increase in heat production would occur during high body temperature when an additional heat load is particularly undesirable. During recent studies on Australian camels, carried out in collaboration with Hammel, Rawson, and Crawford, we found that the Q_{10} for the camel's metabolic rate is actually in the order of 2. In other words, the camel's metabolism has a normal temperature sensitivity and is not suppressed at high temperature.

The fur as a heat barrier.

The amount of heat that reaches the body in a hot environment depends on the amount of insulation covering the surface. As we have seen in an earlier chapter dealing with man, even light clothes will cut down the heat gain and effect a considerable economy in the amount of water expended for heat regulation (page 20). Animal fur must have a similar effect as a barrier against the environmental heat, and since its insulation value is higher than that of light human clothing, one can expect a considerable advantage in the water economy.

It has been stated that the camel loses all its fur in the spring and becomes as naked as a 'scalded pig'. In zoological gardens I have seen mangy-looking camels with big, hairless patches, but in the desert I have never seen anything of this kind. Although the camel sheds

---

[1] It is, of course, not necessary to make the observations $10°$ apart; any convenient temperature interval will serve and the Q_{10} can then be calculated. If the temperature interval is small, the accuracy suffers accordingly—hence the uncertainty of the exact value for Q_{10} in man.

much of its wool in the spring, a rather thick and dense summer coat remains underneath.

The thickness of the camel's fur is appreciable, but as most arabs shear their animals in the spring to obtain the wool, it is difficult to get an accurate measure of the normal summer coat. I had one animal which I had kept through the winter and observed as it was shedding its winter coat during an extended period in the spring. When summer came its fur was still about 30 mm thick on the flanks, towards the back it gradually thickened to 50 to 65 mm in the midline and 110 mm over the hump,

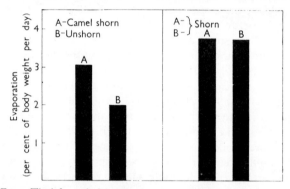

Fig. 9. The left graph shows that in summer a shorn camel (A) evaporates 50 per cent more than an animal with its natural fur (B). When the second camel is shorn, its evaporation increases to the same level as that of the first (right graph). This shows that the initial difference was due to the presence of the wool. (The difference between the level of evaporation in the left and right graphs is due to an increase in external temperature.) (Reproduced with permission from (301).)

with some of the coarse hairs as long as 140 mm. On the ventral surface and most of the legs the hair was straight and short, about 15 to 20 mm.

This was the only animal on which I could get a measure of the thickness of the natural fur. Another animal which I bought early in March was particularly attractive to me because it had not yet been shorn. The nomad who sold the animal declared that he could not let me have it for two days, although he would give no reason. His motives were apparent, however, when he returned two days later with an animal that had been shorn of its glorious fur. Complaints would have helped little, for the arabs were reluctant to sell their camels to begin with. However, the shorn animal, a huge male, turned out to be valuable anyway for it was used as a basis of comparison in establishing the fur as a heat barrier in the other animal.

The shorn camel had around ½ to 1 cm of fur left, but its water expenditure was still 50 per cent higher than in the animal that had its natural fur. (Total water expenditure was 3·0 litres per day per 100 kg body weight in the shorn animal and only 2·0 litres in the other.) To assure that this difference was due to the fur and not to individual differences between the animals, the unshorn animal had to give up its fur. I now discovered why my nomad friend had needed two days to complete his job. When I started the electric clippers brought along for the purpose of shearing camels, they were immediately jammed by the sand imbedded in the dense wool next to the skin. After a few tries, the clippers were completely useless, and I had to go about the tedious task of clipping a whole camel with a pair of laboratory scissors. Luckily, I am ambidextrous, so the blisters were evenly distributed on the two hands. The animal certainly was not beautiful, but the result was satisfactory, the evaporation of water had now increased to the same level as that of the other camel, demonstrating that the difference in evaporation observed earlier had been due to the fur (Fig. 9).

There is, of course, a limit to how thick the camel's fur can be and still be useful to the animal. Although an increased insulation will cut down on the heat flow from the environment, a limit is set by the need for dissipation of metabolic heat. The greatest biological value would be found in a fur thickness which gave a maximum reduction in the heat gain from the environment, and still permitted dissipation of the metabolic heat.

In this connexion it is also important in the water economy whether the sweat wets down the fur or evaporates from the surface of the skin under the fur and passes as water vapour through the wool. Since the heat is bound where water changes from liquid to vapour, there is considerable advantage if the sweat evaporates at the skin surface without wetting the fur. In the diagram to the left in Fig. 10 is indicated the situation when water evaporates at the skin surface. The skin surface will be the point of lowest temperature, and heat will flow to this point both from the body and from the outside air. The amounts of heat flowing will be in inverse proportion to the insulation value of the dermis and the fur respectively. In this system a thick fur will be advantageous as a barrier against environmental heat as long as it does not interfere with the passage of water vapour from the skin surface. A thin, highly vascularized skin will be an advantage because it will permit the easy flow of heat from deeper parts through the dermis to the site of evaporation.

If, on the other hand, the fur became wet and evaporation took place at its outer surface, the situation would be more like the diagram to the right in Fig. 10. Heat would be bound by evaporation at the outer surface of the fur, and since metabolic heat now must pass, not only through the skin, but also through the wet fur, the fur surface must be kept at a lower temperature than was necessary for the skin surface. The greatest disadvantage of this situation is that there is now no insulation between the hot surroundings and the coolest point in the system, and the heat flow from the air to the site of evaporation will increase tremendously.

It has many times been reported that camels do not sweat, but this is a mistake. Camels have sweat glands and do sweat, but no more than necessary to dissipate heat. The situation is that water economy is best served when no more sweat than necessary is formed, when all evaporation takes place from the surface of the skin, and the fur remains dry. A

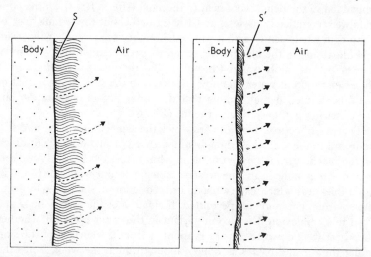

FIG. 10. Simplified diagrams of the temperature gradients in the skin and fur of a camel indicate the value of evaporation without having the fur wetted by perspiration. Evaporation indicated by broken arrows.

Left: If water evaporates from the skin surface (s) this is the coolest point in the system. The insulating dry fur is imposed between the hot air and the cooler skin surface and therefore reduces the heat flow from the environment.

Right: If the fur is wet and evaporation takes place from its surface (s′), the hot air has unimpeded access to the site of evaporation. Furthermore, the flow of heat from the body is now impeded by the intervening layer of fur. This means that much more water must be used to keep the site of evaporation sufficiently cool for the necessary heat dissipation.

camel usually does not sweat visibly, but if evaporation is prevented, e.g. under a pack saddle, the skin will be found to be quite wet on a warm day.

The same principle regarding the site of water evaporation applies to man as well. It is poor economy to sweat excessively, but man has little or no control over his sweating rates. However, a considerable economy can be obtained by using loose garments that permit circulation of air under the clothing and evaporation from the skin surface, rather than tighter fitting clothes which become soaked with perspiration that evaporates at the outer exposed surface.

It was mentioned above that there is some value in a thin well-vascularized skin through which the metabolic heat can easily be transported to the surface and dissipated by evaporation. A layer of subcutaneous fat would impede this heat flow to the surface of the skin. Perhaps the fact that stored fat in the camel is localized in the hump instead of being distributed in the subcutaneous tissue is of value in heat dissipation. A similarly localized distribution of fat is found in some other heat-tolerant animals, such as Indian cattle (Brahma or Zebu) and fat-tailed sheep. Perhaps even the Hottentot woman whose fat buttocks are considered a sign of beauty could have some advantage in the easy passage of heat to the surface of the body?

Estimation of heat gain from the environment

In the preceding pages we have several times referred to the difficulties in measuring reliably the heat load in a hot environment. An evaluation of environmental heat load would require the accurate estimate of all avenues of heat exchange. Let us for a moment outline what difficulties are involved.

If we first consider the animal, we find that its metabolic rate is variable, and so is its skin temperature. The area of skin is difficult to determine, and the fraction exposed to the environment varies with the position. The skin is covered with fur, and even if we could establish the specific heat conductance of the wool, the thickness differs all over the animal. Furthermore, the colour is not the same in various places, so the percentage of radiation that will be absorbed varies. The temperature of the fur surface on the back of a camel in the sun may be as high as 70 to 80° C (301). At the same time, the skin temperature underneath must be very close to 40° C, in other words the temperature gradient through the fur is more than 30° C. If we now want to use these measurements to calculate the heat flow, we will also need the thickness of the fur. But where is its geometrical surface? The radiometer used for measurement of the surface temperature 'sees' an integrated surface which remains undefined with relation to any geometrical plane. Consider now that the character of the fur, its colour, its angle relative to the sun, and relative to the radiation from the ground are all variable. If the camel sits down, part of the fur is also in contact with the ground, which may be warmer or cooler than the animal, and it is compressed by the weight of the body so that the heat transfer is altered.

The heat load from the environment consists of a number of components which change throughout the day. The solar radiation originates from a point source, and the number of calories falling per cm^2 can easily be measured. It even remains reasonably constant throughout several hours in the middle of the day, provided that the sky remains clear. Radiation exchange with the open sky is another matter which

changes throughout the day, and it may be positive or negative, depending on atmospheric conditions and cloud cover. Radiation from the hot
ground changes as soil surface temperature changes, and, of course,
reflected radiation varies with the intensity of solar radiation as well as
its incident angle.

Conductive exchange with the air has been saved until last because it
is the most variable of all. If the air is warmer than the body, heat will be
conducted from the hot air to the body surface. An increase in air movement increases the amount of heat transferred. This may seem to con-
tradict ordinary experience, which indicates that air movement has a
cooling effect. The reason for this impression is that when the skin is wet
air movement facilitates evaporation, and a breeze therefore feels plea-
santly cool. If the skin is dry, however, which frequently is the case in the
dry desert air, movement of the air is felt as an unpleasant increase in
warmth. High winds are extremely uncomfortable on a hot desert day,
and one instinctively seeks the protection of wide, loose-fitting clothing
which reduces the heat load.[1]

The difficulties in describing the heat exchange between the organism
and the environment are so formidable that not even for man under
constant conditions in the laboratory when air and radiation temperature are kept at the same constant level has it been possible to describe
adequately the complete heat exchange. This gives the proper perspective to the difficulties encountered in a natural environment with its
complexity and constantly changing conditions. If the problem is insoluble, why should we bother with this long introduction? The situation is that we can, by indirect means, get a very good estimate of heat
flow from the environment by measuring the rate of evaporation.

In Table V is assembled some information for a camel kept in the
Sahara in the early summer and watered daily, except for a period of 17
days. Water intake and output are accounted for, and we find that the
camel evaporates much less when it is being dehydrated than when it is
watered every day. As we have seen, the amount of evaporation represents dissipated heat, whether derived from the environment or
from metabolism. If the environment is unchanged, how can the camel
achieve a reduction in evaporation which must mean that it has somehow reduced the heat flow from the surroundings?

[1] In the humid tropics the situation is different. While a hot day in the desert may
have an air temperature of 40° C and a relative humidity of 10 per cent, a day in the
tropics may have an air temperature of 34° C and a relative humidity of 85 per cent.
The physiological strain on the organism is of the same magnitude, but the tropical
climate feels more uncomfortable because the skin remains wet in the high humidity.
If a breeze now springs up, evaporation is facilitated, but in addition, the air is slightly
cooler than the skin (which should be at about 35° C for a man to remain in heat
balance), and increased air movement therefore feels comfortably cooling.

Let us consider the figures for a moment. It is only during the hot day that there is a heat gain from the environment. In the night there is no need for evaporative cooling, but an obligatory evaporation from skin and lungs will continue, presumably at a basal rate similar to that in winter. We can therefore find that part of the evaporation which is due to heat regulation by subtracting from the 24-hour figure the evaporation at night. Temperature records indicate that the heat load of the day lasts for about 10 hours. In the dehydrated camel, the 24-hours' evaporation (1·43 per cent of the body weight) should therefore be reduced by the figure for 14 hours of obligatory evaporation (0·36 per cent), giving 1·07 per cent of the body weight as the evaporation which contributes to

TABLE V

The daily water output of a camel (last column) is much smaller when the animal is deprived of drinking-water

The other columns of the table give a detailed account of the various items in the total water balance sheet. All figures are litres of water per 100 kg body weight

		Daily intake				Daily water loss			
		Drinking	In food	Oxida-tion	Total	Faeces	Urine	Evapora-tion	Total
29 May to 5 June	Water	4·46	0·05	0·21	4·72	0·38	0·34	4·00	4·72
5 to 22 June	No water	1·99*	0·05	0·21	2·25*	0·30	0·52	1·43	2·25
22 to 27 June	Water	4·59	0·05	0·22	4·86	0·30	0·37	4·19	4·86

* Daily water intake for periods of water deprivation is calculated from the drinking at the end of the period when the animal drank to make up the incurred deficit (30 l).

heat dissipation. For the hydrated camel the corresponding figures are: diurnal evaporation, 4·10 per cent, 14 hours' obligatory evaporation, 0·51 per cent; giving 3·59 per cent of the body weight as water used for heat dissipation during the day.

The camel in which these determinations were made weighed 260 kg and the figures correspond to the dissipation by evaporation of 5420 kcal in the drinking camel, and 1620 kcal in the dehydrated camel. Thus the water expenditure for heat dissipation was less than one-third when the camel was deprived of drinking-water. How much of this represents an actual decrease in heat flow from the environment, and how much is due to the storage of heat in the form of increased body temperature?

The amount of heat stored in the body in the form of temperature increase is easily calculated from the increase in body (rectal) temperature, which was 2·1° C in the drinking and 6° C in the dehydrated camel. The specific heat of animals is about 0·8, and since the camel weighed 260 kg, the stored heat was 440 kcal when hydrated, and 1250 kcal when dehydrated.

Since the total heat gain is the sum of stored heat and dissipated heat, we get 5860 kcal for the drinking animal and 2870 kcal for the dehydrated (see Fig. 11), in other words, the camel can, when deprived of drinking-water, reduce the heat flow from the environment to about one-half. At least part of this reduction is due to the reduced gradient from the hot air to the body when the body temperature is elevated. Although this is probably the most important single factor in reducing the heat flow, it is not the only one. The dehydrated camel tends to expose as small an area as possible of its body surface to the radiation from the sun. It sits on the ground with its legs under its body, usually facing the sun (the

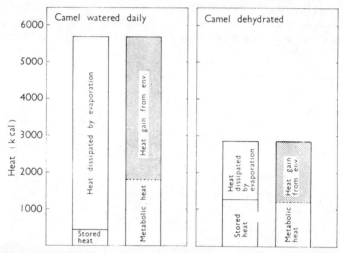

Fig. 11. The environmental heat gain of a camel is difficult to measure directly, but it can be calculated as the difference between total heat load and metabolic heat production. The total heat load is determined as the sum of stored heat and heat dissipated by evaporation (unshaded columns at left). The metabolic heat (unshaded portion of columns at right) can be subtracted from the total, leaving a fair estimate of the environmental heat gain (dotted area). In a dehydrated animal (right) the environmental heat gain was much smaller than in the same camel when watered daily (left). (Reproduced with permission from (301).)

well-hydrated animal frequently stretches out on a hot day), the body is oriented lengthwise to the direction of the sun's rays, and it remains sitting on the same spot from early morning, only changing its direction as the sun moves during the day. There is probably a considerable saving by sitting down in the morning, for later in the day the earth heats up to very high temperatures, and if the camel were to move to a different spot the heat flow from the ground to its underside would be considerable. Thus peculiarities of behaviour contribute in various ways towards savings in water expenditure beyond what is accomplished by the insulation of the fur and the rise in body temperature.

One very interesting aspect of the behaviour in camels was reported by

Pilters (261). During the summer in the Sahara she observed that camels would often rest during the hottest hours of the day, huddled on the ground in small groups, one animal pressed tightly against the next. Undoubtedly, there is less heat flowing from the next camel (actually none if their temperatures are identical) than from the environment if the same fur were exposed to the sun and its surface temperature rose to 70 to 80° C. In a way one could say that the clump of camels constitutes a social giant organism which minimizes its exposed surface to reduce heat gain—the same principle in reverse as young penguins employ when several hundred of them crowd together in a crèche on the Antarctic ice and thus reduce their heat loss (266).

THE MAJOR AVENUES OF WATER LOSS
Sweating or panting

Different physiological mechanisms can be employed in the dissipation of heat by evaporation of water. Man, for example, produces sweat from skin glands. Other animals, of which the dog is the best-known example, evaporate water from the moist tongue and mucous membranes of the mouth and upper respiratory tract.

Many ruminants, such as cattle and sheep, employ both sweating and panting in heat regulation. How does the camel compare to these? In a camel observed during the summer in the cool morning hours, the respiration rate varied from 6 to 11 with an average of 8 respirations per minute. In the hottest afternoon these rates were increased to 8 to 18 and averaged around 16 respirations per minute. There was no indication that the depth of respiration changed, and the observed change in rate must be completely insignificant in the heat regulation. Before panting becomes an efficient means for heat dissipation, much higher rates are necessary. In cattle exposed to heat, respiratory rates increase to 250 (122), and in the dog, where the entire burden of heat regulation is on the panting mechanism, the frequency during panting is between 300 and 400 per minute (150).

The slight increase in respiration in the camel is of the same order of magnitude or less than that observed in man. When work was performed at a constant rate in extremely hot environments Robinson found that pulmonary ventilation was increased by 25 to 50 per cent for each degree centigrade elevation of rectal temperature over the control values determined on the same men performing the same work in a cool environment (282). This increase is also completely insignificant in heat regulation, and Bazett (40) states that the respiratory response of man, which is most marked during rapidly rising temperature and levels off when the temperature is even, 'shows no indications of being directly concerned with cooling functions. It is entirely different in character from the panting reactions of animals.'

It should then be obvious that the camel must sweat. It has been reported that the camel has no sweat glands (199), but this notion has been proven wrong. Sweat glands are distributed over the entire body surface (194) and tests with indicating paper on the shaved skin show numerous gland orifices releasing sweat when the animal is exposed to heat. The statements that the camel does not sweat are due to the fact that the sweat evaporates from the skin under the fur. Therefore there is little or no visible sweating, except where evaporation is prevented in skin folds or under a saddle.

Kidney function

Urine volume. Quantitative information about kidney function and urine production in the camel is miserably poor. The few observations that have been made indicate that the urine volume may be quite low, but information sufficient to evaluate the role of the kidney in water balance is lacking. What is needed is a series of careful studies of the total energy and water balance of camels under well-controlled conditions, similar to what has been done for other domestic animals. As research facilities improve in countries where the camel is the most important domestic animal, such studies will undoubtedly be made. In the meantime we must make the best out of the few observations that have been reported.

As in other mammals the volume of urine in the camel is extremely variable. During the winter, when the vegetation is green and has a high water content, the water intake with the feed is high and urine output is correspondingly increased. At this time of the year little or no water is used for heat regulation, and the excess is eliminated by the kidneys. The urine volume will therefore be determined by the water content of the plants, and will depend primarily on how much the camel eats. In a single observation from such a period the urine flow reached 7 litres per day, which is rather less than one would find in a normal grazing dairy cow (299).

The volume of the camel's bladder is very small, and at high urine-flows it is emptied frequently. Spontaneously voided urine varies in volume from a few to several hundred millilitres. In a camel from which we obtained a total of 299 urine samples only one exceeded 400 ml and the largest sample we ever collected was 450 ml, which probably indicates the maximum functional bladder volume. The camel also has a peculiar way of emptying the bladder. The male has a fold of the preputium which makes it urinate backwards, like a female. Both stand up, and a rhythmic release of the sphincter causes the urine to be voided as a pulsation of separate small jets. A complete urination is slow and takes several times as long as in man. Whether the very slow discharge has any significance is doubtful.

Urine volumes observed on a number of camels in Morocco were all in the range of 1·5 to 5 litres per day. These camels were fed and watered normally, which frequently meant irregularly, and the figures therefore indicate some of the variation that can be expected (78). The lowest urine volumes, about 1·5 litres per day, were found in animals deprived of drinking-water (78). The camels in these observations weighed about 400 to 500 kg. Camels kept on different regimens of grazing and watering had daily urine volumes ranging from as much as 8 litres in the winter to less than ½ litre in the summer (200). One camel produced on the average only 0·9 litre of urine per day during a whole week although water was provided *ad libitum* (200). In animals observed during grazing in the Algerian Sahara, daily urine volumes were 1 to 4 litres. Unfortunately these last observations give no information about urination at night, or whether the night urine was voided and measured in the morning (261).

Our laboratory camels in the Sahara were fed on dates and dry hay that consisted of grass hand-picked wherever it could be found among the sand dunes. When watered every day a camel that weighed 300 kg produced on the average ¾ litre of urine daily. When it was deprived of water, the urine flow decreased to less than ½ litre per day. This is of the same magnitude as the minimum urine volume in man, although the camel weighed four times as much. The urine volume could be increased by giving extra sodium chloride in the diet, and would then be about 1 litre per day, even during the dehydration periods (299).

It is extremely difficult to give any interpretation of this meagre information. In any event the small volume of the bladder indicates that large quantities of urine are not normally formed, and the little information there is on urine flow indicates that the expenditure of water for urine formation may be low. It should be possible to gain some further understanding of the kidney's capacity to conserve water from information about the maximum concentration of the excretory products.

Urine concentrations. A high concentration of salts in the urine not only permits an animal to expend moderate amounts of water for excretion, but also permits it to drink waters with a relatively high salt content. There are numerous reports that the camel will eat the succulent plants in the dried-out river beds, the wadis, and these plants frequently have a very high salt content. A few analyses that we carried out in March and April showed that the concentration of sodium in particular was very high. In two of the plants the chloride was relatively low, but it was replaced by oxalic acid, which was present in quantities known to be highly toxic to cattle or sheep. In contrast to other desert

plants, those that grow in the wadis do not dry up much in the summer
—if they did they would contain a mass of salt crystals. Still, when
juicy, their salt content was far above that of sea water.

Camels are said to tolerate drinking salt or bitter water that is poisonous to man and other animals (74). 'Bitter' water usually contains relatively high amounts of sulphate, and sometimes also of magnesium.
Such water acts as a laxative for man, and even if the salt concentration
is relatively low, it will have a deleterious effect when ingested in quantity.
No information is available on what the camel can tolerate, with the
exception of a report that it feeds on marine algae along the coast of
Tunisia. Marine algae are usually in osmotic equilibrium with sea water

TABLE VI

*The major constituents of two highly concentrated urine samples collected
from Saharan camels*

	Na, mN	K, mN	Cl, mN	Urea, mM
Sample 1	834	77	970	229
Sample 2	11	902	492	1,415
Sea water	470	10	548	. .

and therefore high in salts, although the relative abundance of salts may
be different. If anything, the seaweed along the shore may have been
partly dried out, resulting in an even higher salt concentration.

If an animal is to drink sea water, which contains about 3·5 per cent
salt, it needs to have a kidney which can excrete a solution more concentrated than this. An ordinary white rat can produce a urine with a
chloride concentration of 600 mN, about the same concentration as in
the sea (4), but the magnesium sulphate contained in sea water produces
diarrhoea and a net loss of water. Even without the diarrhoea, producing
a urine equal to the sea water would, of course, result in no gain whatsoever. The kangaroo rat, which can produce a urine twice as concentrated as sea water, can utilize sea water for drinking, in spite of the
diarrhoea (292).

In our studies in the Sahara we probably did not find the maximum
concentrating power of the camel's kidney. The highest osmotic concentration in a urine sample was 2·760 osmolar while the plasma was a
normal 0·340 osmolar, and the urine therefore had a total concentration
eight times that in plasma (U/P ratio=8). This is twice as concentrated
as in man where the maximum U/P ratio is about 4.

The highest concentrations which we found of the commonest ions,
Na, K, and Cl, are shown above (Table VI).

It is clear that the camel's kidney can produce a urine considerably more concentrated than sea water. It is also interesting to note that when Na was high, K was low, and vice versa. In most urine samples the K was the dominating cation, and Na might be as low as 0·4 mN per litre, but when the camels had been grazing in the wadis, the Na excretion shot up (309). Unfortunately, we were unable to induce our laboratory animals to eat salty plants, and attempts to give salt in the drinking-water led to oedema instead of excretion of the salt.

There is another report in the literature of an even higher concentration than we found. Charnot (78) found a chloride concentration of 1068 mN per litre (37·87 grammes Cl per litre) in a camel which had been brought to Rabat from 120 km away. During the several days on the march it had neither eaten nor drunk, but before it started it had been given salty feed followed by watering. This was done to avoid the necessity for giving it anything during the voyage, and thus ensure that the meat during butchery would not exude water which would disqualify it in the eyes of the butchers. The importance of this observation is that it demonstrated a concentrating capacity of the kidney which permits the formation of urine almost twice as concentrated as sea water. This should indeed permit the animal to drink sea water and other salty waters, but it gives no information about how the animal can handle the more difficult ions, such as sulphate and magnesium. Interestingly, Charnot found that as the urine volume in a dehydrated camel went down from 5 to 1·6 litres, some of the urine concentrations were increased in a greater proportion (78). The chloride concentration remained constant, potassium about doubled, sodium went up ninefold, but the sulphate concentration increased more than sixteenfold. From being a very insignificant component of the urine in the hydrated camel, sulphate now became one of the dominating ions. This suggests that the camel's kidney has an exceptional ability to eliminate sulphate and indicates that further studies of its renal function might prove extremely rewarding.

Antidiuretic hormone (ADH). If desert animals regularly excrete a highly concentrated urine, it might be suggested that they should produce higher-than-usual amounts of antidiuretic hormone. Such reasoning is not necessarily correct. The maximum concentration of the urine depends on the capacity of the kidney to withhold water, but there is no reason to believe that a given kidney should need any unusual amounts of ADH in order to work at its own characteristic level. No excess of the hormone can make a kidney perform above its maximal ability.

A study of the amount of stored ADH in the neurohypophysis and adjoining hypothalamus of the camel gave total amounts similar to those found in oxen, although the distribution was somewhat different (1).

There was no evidence favouring a special role of the hormone in water conservation in the camel, but any future studies should include the circulating and excreted amounts.

Macfarlane infused ADH into camels that were dehydrated and therefore already had a low urine output. Instead of a further reduction in urine volume he found a severalfold increase in urine output (personal communication). This may seem paradoxical, but it is a result of an increased output of electrolytes caused by the ADH. As the electrolyte output goes up and the tonicity of the already highly concentrated urine remains within the same range, total urine volume must increase. Macfarlane has obtained the same effect of ADH in increasing the urine volume in sheep.

Concentration of urea. In 1925 Read (270) reported that he had found practically no urea in camel's urine. This was exciting news, for it suggested that the camel would have to use other compounds for nitrogen excretion. Since birds and reptiles achieve a considerable economy in water by excreting uric acid as a semi-solid paste, perhaps the camel had acquired the same excretory mechanism in the interest of water economy?

As could be expected, the master of comparative kidney physiology, Homer Smith, then located in Charlottesville, Virginia, immediately set out to obtain a sample of camel's urine. He succeeded when a circus came to town. In the evening when the circus parade went through the streets to advertise next day's show Homer Smith and his assistant Herbert Silvette marched successfully behind the camel, Silvette with a flashlight and Smith with a bucket. He found that this urine contained a normal amount of urea, amounting to approximately 60 per cent of the total urinary nitrogen (316). Similar results had already been published by Petri (252), who even concluded that the results recorded by Read had to be erroneous and suggested that they were due to an inactive urease preparation as well as a decimal error in the calculations! As we shall see, this turned out to be a case of jumping to conclusions.

One of the Saharan camels we worked with was a young 3-year old female. She was mature but, like horses, camels continue to grow after they reach maturity. The animal was deprived of drinking-water while fed on hay and dates for 17 days. We expected that as dehydration progressed, urine concentrations would increase. This had been the way we obtained maximum concentrations for the urine in other desert animals, and it seemed the logical procedure for the camel as well. However, to our surprise the urine concentration of urea decreased steadily day after day. At the end of the period the urea concentration in the urine (1·5 mM per litre) was below what it normally is in the blood of most mammals, including the camel (2 to 10 mM per litre), and the total amount of urea excreted in the urine in one day went down to less than 1 gramme.

As we obtained these results, Read's old report that the camel's urine was practically free from urea came to mind. There was a considerable similarity between one particular aspect of our animals, they were in need of nitrogen and it would be advantageous for them to reduce the loss of protein to a minimum. Read's camel, which was fed on sorghum leaves and sweet potato vines, was a pregnant female that needed all the protein that it could possibly save for the foetus, and ours was a young animal, still growing, that had been kept for 6 weeks on an extremely low-protein diet. This was not by design, it happened to be the only diet available; our animal was young and still growing for the simple reason that no native camel owner would sell a full-grown female. These were kept for breeding, and for our studies of kidney function it was mandatory to avoid males because they cannot be catheterized owing to an S-shaped loop of the urethra. Thus various circumstances of good luck brought us into a situation where we could confirm a report which had been considered erroneous by all 'sensible' scientists, including ourselves (296).

The low amounts of urea excreted in our camel corresponded to a metabolism of about 2·5 grammes of protein per day. There is no reason to believe that the actual protein metabolism of an animal as large as a camel would be this low. It is more likely that the phenomenon is based on the peculiar nitrogen metabolism in the rumen. If urea or ammonium salts are fed to cattle or sheep the microbes of the rumen synthesize amino-acids and protein. In this way livestock can be fed a large part of their nitrogen requirement in the form of urea. Since urea and ammonium salts are so much cheaper than protein, the utilization of this phenomenon in animal husbandry has considerable practical interest.

In the camel the situation must be about as follows. Instead of being excreted by the kidney, urea enters the rumen fluid where bacteria immediately use it in the synthesis of protein. Lower down in the digestive tract the bacterial protein is digested by the camel. In this way the camel has a special nitrogen cycle of its own, permitting the reuse of its nitrogen, over and over again, in rebuilding broken-down protein. In other mammals, once the amino-acids of the protein have been de-aminated, the nitrogen is lost to the body and excreted as urea.

An attempt to show whether urea could really be utilized in this fashion was made by injecting large quantities of urea in camels. On several occasions we injected intravenously amounts up to nearly 30 grammes (475 mM) of urea, but less than 2 grammes (30 mM) of this was recovered in the urine. The urea had apparently 'disappeared' as rumen microbes synthesized it into protein.

There is no reason to doubt that other ruminants can do the same thing, and this has been confirmed for the sheep (155). However, it is not likely to be found in a pronounced form unless the animal is in need of protein.

One of the important results of this study of urea excretion has been that it has given one of the major pieces of evidence that previous concepts on urea excretion were untenable. Since the urea excretion is high in animals that get enough protein, but is reduced to a very small fraction when the animals are in need of protein, it is clear that the renal excretion of urea in the camel must be actively regulated. The amount of urea excreted relative to the glomerular filtration rate may change fiftyfold, and this is not compatible with the concept that urea is filtered and merely diffuses passively back to the blood. A simple mechanical diffusion should be uninfluenced by the general needs for protein in the animal, and if the return to the blood were unregulated there should be a dependence on urine flow which we did not find (302).

Water in the faeces

Dry camel dung is one of the most commonly used fuels in North Africa and is sold in the markets for household use. This is not very surprising in a tree-less country, for the droppings of any herbivore have sufficient cellulose in them to burn rather well when dry. But even when fresh, the droppings of the camel seem almost dry to the touch.

The faeces of the camel consist of a large number of small, oblong pellets, each some 3 cm long or so. The pellet is very light, the outside is shiny and almost black, and when broken the interior falls apart as a mass of coarse almost dry plant fibres.

The amount of faeces eliminated varies with the composition and digestibility of the feed. One of our camels which was fed on dry dates and hay produced about 1000 grammes of dry faecal matter per day. Even when the animal had free access to drinking-water, the amount of water eliminated with the faeces was only 109 grammes per 100 grammes dry matter. This is a very low value, for the white rat excretes over 200 grammes of water per 100 grammes dry faecal material and a grazing cow over 500 grammes H_2O per 100 grammes.

This information is summarized in Table VII. It may seem unusual that the water content is being related to dry matter, instead of being given as percentage of water in the faeces. This, however, has a very good reason. The degree of digestibility determines the amount of undigested matter that passes the gastro-intestinal tract, and if we know the amount of water that accompanies each 100 grammes of undigested dry matter, it is simple to compute the water loss. Hence, all the figures used here express the water content in this way.

The water content in the faeces of the donkey is significantly higher than in the camel, but, as the data stand, they do not do full justice to the difference between the two animals. The donkey does not digest its feed as well as the camel, and for a given amount of food intake much more faecal material is formed. This lower digestibility brings the relative water loss for the donkey to about three to four times that in the camel.

TABLE VII

Water in the faeces of various animals expressed as grammes of water per 100 grammes of dry faecal matter

	g H_2O per 100 g dry faeces
Camel, hay and dates, no water	76 ± 2.5
Camel, hay and dates, daily water	109 ± 5
Donkey, hay and dates, daily water	181 ± 12
Kangaroo rat, barley, no water	83
White rat, barley, water	225
Man, mixed diet	200
Cow, grazing	566

Not only the amount of faeces but its water content as well depends on the type of feed and digestibility. When our camel had been grazing in the desert, the amount of water lost per 100 grammes of dried faeces was two to three times as high as when it was fed at the laboratory on dry dates and hay. The figures for water content that we obtained after grazing are in the same order of magnitude as those published by Charnot (78), which are the only other figures for water content in the camel's faeces that I know about. Charnot found a reduction of water content of the faecal material in the dehydrated camel, similar to what we had observed, although all her figures were at a higher level. In the dehydrated camel she found 168 grammes of water per 100 grammes dry matter, while in an animal with free access to water, the figure was 268 grammes water per 100 grammes dry matter.

It is really very curious that a mammal can extract so much water from the intestinal contents, and that water deprivation has such great influence on the amount of water remaining in the faeces. Presumably, the intestine should be unable to transport water against an osmotic gradient, and since the blood concentrations in the dehydrated animal are only moderately increased, this cannot explain the additional removal of water. Further investigations of the function of the intestine in the process of water conservation should prove interesting and would be well worth the effort.

TOLERANCE TO DEHYDRATION

One of the major questions to be answered about the camel is whether it has an exceptional tolerance to depletion of body water. Previous experimentation with other mammals has indicated that a water loss amounting to some 18 to 20 per cent of the body weight is fatal. As we have seen, when there is a simultaneous heat load, less water depletion is tolerated. When the water loss in a dog in a hot environment exceeds some 12 per cent of the body weight, the animal is in immediate danger of a fatal explosive heat rise. It may appear that other animals, rats and mice for example, can withstand considerably greater degrees of desiccation. When these animals are deprived of water they may live for about 2 weeks (depending on atmospheric humidity) and die with a weight loss of about 50 per cent of the initial body weight (290). Most of the weight loss, however, is caused by a loss of body tissues as well as water. When deprived of drinking-water most animals stop food intake, and the cause of death in rats on this régime is starvation. In the rats that died after 14 days of water deprivation, the percentage of water in the body had only decreased from 68·5 to 65·5 per cent. If the 50 per cent weight loss had represented water loss exclusively, the final percentage of body water should have gone down to 37. In order to separate the effects of water deprivation and starvation it is necessary to work with animals that can be dehydrated rapidly, in other words, they should be animals that use water for heat regulation. (Other means can be used, for example, inducing diuresis with osmotically active substances such as sucrose or mannitol, but these procedures introduce other complications.)

When we first deprived a camel of drinking-water for a considerable length of time, we found that the rate of water loss was much too slow to carry through our research programme in a reasonable time. After 17 days without water in January, our camel had lost 36·5 kg, or 16·2 per cent of its original body weight, 226 kg. During this period of time the camel had continued to eat at about the same rate as previously, some 2 kg of dates and ½ kg of hay per day. Since we knew little about camels, their food requirements and metabolic rates, we felt rather uncertain about where we stood. In order to find out we decided to give this animal water, and in 10 minutes it drank 40 litres of water, a trifle more than was required to restore its original body weight. To our amazement the camel showed no further interest in water, neither immediately after the drinking nor later in the day. Apparently it had ingested exactly what it wanted, and had no further interest in drinking. This was the first indication we had that the camel drinks to restore its original water content, rather than in anticipation of future needs.

This particular camel had, as we gradually learned from later experimentation, taken normal quantities of feed during the long period of water deprivation. From the biological viewpoint, it is of course most useful for an animal to maintain its appetite if it has to seek its food over large areas of land between widely spaced watering places.

At the end of the 17 days' dehydration period the camel was obviously thirsty, but no other ill effects were apparent. This established a tolerance to water depletion unmatched in other animals. However, weight changes (other than water loss) could have taken place during the long period of water deprivation, and we decided to postpone further experimentation until warm weather arrived and camels could be expected to lose water more rapidly.

We never did establish the maximum limit for water depletion that camels can tolerate. We did, however, keep camels without water during the hottest part of the summer until they lost appetite and appeared to be seriously debilitated by dehydration. How much longer they could have stayed alive remains unknown.

During the last days of June and early in July, when air temperatures exceeded 40° C over the major part of the day, we kept two camels without water for 7 days. The camels were sitting on the ground without any shade, fully exposed to the hot air and to radiation from the sun and from the ground, but they performed no work. During the week of observation they lost 26·5 and 27·2 per cent of their original body weights respectively. After the loss reached about 20 per cent of the weight, their appetites decreased and they almost stopped eating. When they were given water again, they drank huge quantities, but not quite enough to restore the initial body weight. There probably had been little loss of body tissue, for the animals made up for the difference the next time they were watered.

Since these animals tolerated a water loss exceeding 25 per cent of the body weight, even though exposed to the full heat load of the environment, they evidently escaped explosive heat rise and death when their dehydration was twice as great as the limit in other animals (12 to 14 per cent weight loss). How much more dehydration the camels could tolerate under the same hot conditions is anybody's guess, for when the explosive heat rise comes, it comes suddenly without much warning. How much more dehydration they could withstand in a cool environment is also uncertain, but it is probable that their limit is considerably beyond the point to which we took them.

Is water lost from intracellular or extracellular fluid?

Dehydration of man in a hot environment reduces the plasma volume out of proportion to the total water loss. Men who were dehydrated under desert conditions had a reduction in circulating plasma volume which amounted to 2½ times that expected if plasma water had been lost in proportion to the loss of the whole body (8). The reduction increases the circulatory strain, which in extreme cases ends in a fatal explosive heat rise as the circulation fails to carry the metabolic heat to the body surface.

The distribution of the water loss is different in the camel. In one Saharan animal which had been deprived of water for 8 days, the weight

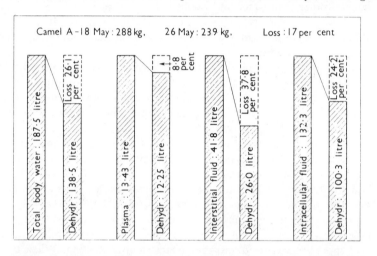

Fig. 12. A camel kept without drinking for 8 days in the summer lost 49 litres of water. This constituted 17 per cent of the original body weight and 26 per cent of the total body water (left bars). The greatest relative loss occurred in interstitial fluid, which had been reduced by almost 38 per cent.

loss was 17 per cent of the initial weight. If the original water content of the camel, before dehydration, was 65 per cent (a very fair assumption), the total volume of water had been reduced by 26 per cent (Fig. 12, left).[1] The percentage decrease in the volume of each fluid compartment

[1] The estimation of total body water in camels, using the anti-pyrine method, did not give reliable determinations. Since the dilution method requires that the exact slope be established for the decrease in plasma concentration and an extrapolation to zero time, a high degree of analytical accuracy is necessary. The difficulties we encountered seemed to be due to a slow or uneven rate of distribution, probably because of the large amounts of fluid in the rumen where equilibration is slow.

Other investigators have had difficulties with the antipyrine method in cattle (94) and sheep (209). However, Charnot claimed success for the method as employed in the camel (78). It is probable that the employment of another tracer substance, such as tritiated or heavy water, would be better. In the absence of determinations which we consider reliable, we have preferred to use an assumed 65 per cent of the body weight as the probable water content in the normally hydrated animal. This is in the order of magnitude determined for a number of mammals. Even if it should be wrong

shows that the greatest proportional loss took place in the interstitial fluid. The decrease in this volume was 38 per cent while the intracellular water had been reduced by 24 per cent. The smallest relative loss of water occurred in the plasma, which had been subjected to less than 10 per cent reduction. The plasma therefore carried less than its proportional share in the total water loss, a situation which should be highly advantageous in maintaining adequate circulation.

Although the interstitial fluid had the greatest proportional loss of water, the intracellular fluid lost a greater total amount (Fig. 13). Since

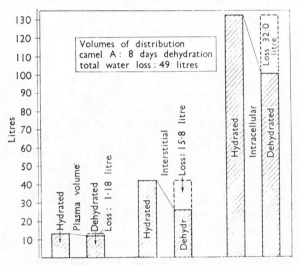

FIG. 13. In a dehydrated camel that had lost 49 litres of water the largest amount (32 litres) had been removed from intracellular fluid. Same experiment as in Fig. 12.

this compartment to begin with contains the overwhelming amount of the body water, it contributes about two-thirds of the total water loss, although its percentage loss was more moderate.

A much more accurate dissection of the water compartments was made by Macfarlane and Morris who joined our group during our studies in Central Australia in 1962. The preliminary results show that the total body water ranged from 65 to 75 per cent, with a fairly obvious relation to the amount of fat storage. During 9 days' dehydration the

by as much as 5 or 10 per cent, it would only slightly change the magnitude of the figures used in the tables and graphs presented here.

In our determinations of blood-volume we used Evans blue (T-1824), and for extracellular water the thiocyanate method. Interstitial water was then computed as the difference between extracellular and plasma water.

animals lost one-fifth of their body weight—that is, about 30 per cent of the total body water. The reduction in plasma volume was 13 to 24 per cent (average 20 per cent) and in thiocyanate space 12–21 per cent (average 15 per cent). This suggests that most of the water came from intracellular water and from the gut contents. Of the total water lost 50 per cent could have come from the gut, 30 per cent from intracellular, and 20 per cent from extracellular space. These results are somewhat different from our earlier results. In particular, a great loss of fluid from the digestive tract was not suggested in the African camels examined at butchery. There is, however, agreement on the relatively small loss of plasma volume in camels, where Macfarlane found a 20 per cent loss of plasma volume while equally dehydrated sheep would lose possibly one-half of the plasma volume (209).

Plasma volume. It would be interesting to know the mechanism that is responsible for the relatively unchanged plasma volume in the dehydrated camel. The curious aspect of this situation is that the maintenance of plasma volume could theoretically be anticipated and the reduction observed in man and other animals should not be expected.

This statement may require some explanation. For the sake of argument, let us consider an animal which has lost, say, 10 per cent of its water, with the loss equally distributed throughout the body water. All concentrations of soluble substances should have increased accordingly. Since salts and other crystalloids pass freely in and out of the capillary, they are of no consequence. However, since the capillary wall is impermeable to proteins, the increased plasma protein will tend to draw water from the extravascular space into the blood-stream. If the circulation, blood-pressure, and permeability of the capillary wall to protein remain unchanged, equilibrium is reached when the protein concentration and blood-volume have been restored to the original level. The amazing conclusion is now that when water is lost from the body, blood-plasma volume should tend to remain at its initial level, and all water loss should occur in extravascular space. Thus, the disproportionate loss in plasma volume in the dehydrated man is the phenomenon that requires explanation, rather than the tendency of the camel to maintain its blood-volume.

Of course, the situation is not as uncomplicated as indicated above. There is also an exchange of water between extracellular space and the cells, and since these have a high protein content as well as selective ion-transport mechanisms, the situation is not easily resolved by theoretical considerations. Further studies are needed of the actual movements of water, ions, and protein during dehydration.

We did observe one striking and perhaps important difference between the camel and other animals when we determined the blood-volume by means of Evans blue. This dye can be used for determining blood-volume because it is bound to the plasma proteins and therefore remains in the vascular bed for some time. It is gradually lost, however, at a rate which varies from animal to animal. In the dog the amount of circulating dye is reduced by about 10 per cent per hour (135), which means that the concentration of dye is reduced to one-half in about 6 or 7 hours. In man the average disappearance rate is lower, giving a half-life of some 12 hours (134). With this loss of dye the plasma gradually loses the blue colour which it has immediately after a determination of the plasma volume.

When we used the method for determining the plasma volume in the camel we found that the dye did not disappear as rapidly as in other animals. The half-life of the dye was in the order of 2 to 4 weeks. We could still make determinations of plasma volume, but the same animal could not be used for many determinations as the dye accumulated and built up to higher levels with each injection. This stability of the dye in the circulation could be due to a number of factors, such as a more stable binding to the protein, less metabolism and removal of the protein by the liver or tissues, or perhaps a capillary bed much less permeable to protein than in other animals. It certainly does indicate that somehow the plasma proteins behave differently from what has been experienced in other mammals, and although we do not understand the full significance of the difference as yet, it again points out the exceptional qualities of the camel.

RECOVERY FROM DEHYDRATION

Drinking capacity

When a man is very thirsty he can pour down his throat perhaps a litre of fluid in a minute. If he takes his time he can, in the next 5 or 10 minutes, probably down another litre or so, but it will prove increasingly difficult to drink, even if his intake does not yet cover his water deficit. Man simply requires several hours for complete rehydration.

A thirsty camel has a much greater drinking capacity. When our camels were moderately dehydrated, and we called it moderate when they had lost less than 20 per cent of the body weight, they would drink enough to make up for the entire deficit in about 10 minutes. On several occasions our camels ingested more than one-quarter of their body weight, and on occasion two camels took over 30 per cent of their body weight. One young female camel which weighed 201·5 kg when it started to drink, drank 66·5 litres of water, or 33·1 per cent of the body weight. The other camel, a large adult male, weighed 325 kg when dehydrated and drank 104 litres of water, or 31·8 per cent of the body weight. In the last camel the intake did not correspond to the estimated loss, which was 122 litres of water, but the difference was made up the next time the camel was watered.

A young student of animal behaviour, Hilde Pilters, who later married and published under the name Gauthier-Pilters, has collected some extremely valuable information about camels in the northern Sahara. She courageously followed and observed the grazing animals while she lived alone with desert nomads of the Shamba tribe. Her main objective was to obtain information on the grazing habits and how much the camels eat of various plant species. Much additional valuable information was gathered, including some interesting data on the drinking habits (260, 261).

In winter the camels were independent of drinking-water as the moisture content of the plants was high (70–80 per cent). They often walked 25 km per day, steadily nipping a bite here, a bite there, as camels usually do. Since they did not return to camp by themselves they had to be herded continuously from October–November to April–May.

In summer the plants contained less water, and the camels seemed to select and eat almost exclusively two particularly dry plants, *Aristida plumosa* and *Anabasis aretioides*, which contained only 10 per cent water. At this time the camels returned on their own to the nomads' camp to be watered, and therefore the shepherds were spared the arduous and dangerous duty of following the camels out into the hot desert. Camels grazing in the sand desert (erg) remained away for 3 to 5 days, but those on the rocky plains (hammada) returned in 2 to 3 days. If camels grazed in the dry river beds (wadis) where there is a rich vegetation of halophilic and juicy plants with enormously high salt contents, they were back in $\frac{1}{2}$ to 1 day. The animals that sought their food in the wadis had to drink even in winter.

When the animals returned to the wells for drinking, they would drink all they needed at once, provided this was less than 60 litres, but if the need was more they drank again some hours later.

After 3 to 5 days without water with air temperature of 40 to 45° C the camels would drink great quantities. The largest amount taken at once was 107 litres—by a lactating female which had been grazing for 6 days among the sand dunes. Some hours later she drank another 60 litres. The largest total quantity taken, 186 litres, was observed in a castrated male which first drank 94 litres and then 92 litres later in the day. This same large quantity was taken later again by the same animal.

Miss Pilters had no means for weighing the animals she observed. Judging from my own experience with animals from the same herds, a mature female would probably weigh 400 to 450 kg and a large male a little over 500 kg. If these camels really did not overhydrate, they drank in a day well over one-third of their normal hydrated weight, or about one-half of the dehydrated weight!

We always kept track of our camels and how much they drank. By weighing them we could establish the water loss, and we found that they regularly drank an amount closely corresponding to the estimated water deficit. We never found any appreciable overdrinking that could be interpreted as an excess intake or storage of water. The only exception to this was one camel, mentioned earlier, which was given large amounts of sodium chloride and developed considerable oedema.

Solutes in the body fluids, which increase in concentration during the dehydration, decrease again after water has been drunk. Thus the rate of distribution of the ingested water can be followed by following the plasma concentrations, for we can assume that there is equilibrium between plasma and other body fluids in their osmotic concentrations. Such studies indicate that even the largest amounts of fluid taken in by a camel are evenly distributed in 1 to 2 days.

As was indicated above, we found no water storage, and the large quantities of fluid in the rumen seemed to be nearly in osmotic equilibrium with the rest of the body. Other large compartments are non-existent, and it is difficult to imagine that body fluids in general should be able to maintain any osmotic differences—all available evidence indicates that water moves freely throughout the body. There is, however, some evidence that the concentrations of various solids do not change in the exact proportion that could be predicted from the water intake. But we had no reliable measure of total body water, which is necessary for such estimates to be precise. More accurate studies than we were able to do under field conditions in the Sahara were undertaken by Macfarlane during a recent expedition to central Australia.

SUMMARY

The camel's exceptional tolerance to heat and water deprivation does not depend on the storage of water. Although its stomach has a structure different from that in other ruminants, neither morphology nor function indicates that it plays any role in water storage. There is no evidence of water storage anywhere else in the camel's body. The hump contains fat, and the metabolism of fat yields an amount of water greater than the weight of the fat. Since oxidation requires oxygen the necessary ventilation of the lungs involves a loss of water vapour. This loss exceeds the amount of water formed.

The body temperature of the camel is quite variable, and when the camel is deprived of water, the daily fluctuations may exceed 6° C. These fluctuations are important in the water balance for two reasons. (a) As body temperature rises during the hot day, water otherwise used to keep the temperature down remains unexpended. The excess heat is stored in the body and is dissipated to the cool environment at night without use of water. (b) An elevated body temperature reduces the heat flow from the hot environment to the body, and therefore reduces the amount of water needed to prevent further temperature rise.

In a hot environment the fur is an important barrier against heat gain from the environment. When comparing animals with and without fur under otherwise identical conditions it is found that less water is used by unshorn camels.

The camel does not pant, but does sweat. Sweat is produced in moderate quantities, but the fur is not wetted and appears dry. Water evaporates from the surface of the skin rather than from the surface of the fur, an important factor in water economy.

The camel has a powerful kidney which can produce a concentrated urine. Adequate studies of the concentrating ability of the kidney are lacking. Under certain circumstances urea can be withheld from excretion and be resynthesized into protein by the microbial flora of the rumen.

The camel can withstand considerable dehydration. In a hot environment it can tolerate a loss of at least 27 per cent of the body weight, twice the dehydration that brings other mammals into lethal explosive heat rise. The limit for dehydration of the camel is unknown. When the camel becomes dehydrated the loss of water is not accompanied by a proportional loss in plasma volume. The maintenance of a high plasma volume facilitates circulation, which is one of the first functions to suffer during dehydration of other animals in hot environments.

The camel has an enormous drinking capacity. In a single drinking session it can ingest over 30 per cent of its body weight.

Conclusion: In the hot desert the camel exhibits a slow rate of water loss, mainly because of its fluctuating body temperature and the well-insulated body surface. This slow loss, in combination with an exceptional tolerance to dehydration of the body, permits the camel to withstand water deprivation for longer periods than any other mammal exposed to similarly hot conditions.

4

CATTLE AND THEIR PERFORMANCE IN HOT CLIMATES

ALTHOUGH cattle do not properly belong in this book about desert animals, they will serve a useful purpose of comparison, for they are the only animals about the size of camels whose reactions to heat and requirements for water are fairly well known. Our interest is primarily concerned with the basis for heat tolerance and we will attempt to gain some understanding of this phenomenon by examining the difference between more and less heat tolerant breeds. Although there is a wealth of excellent information about cattle and their reactions to heat much less is known about the effects of water shortage.

Cattle cannot be considered well adapted to arid conditions and they have no wild relatives in deserts or semi-deserts. Owing to the economic interest in milk and meat production, cattle have been introduced into most hot countries—with variable success. Most domestic breeds spring from two major stocks, the European, *Bos taurus*, and the Indian, *Bos indicus*, the latter being much better adapted to heat.

The origin of European breeds which have been domesticated for thousands of years is assumed to be the aurochs or urox, a bovine that persisted as a wild species in the deep forests of eastern Europe until late medieval times. The domesticated types are well adapted to cold, but do not thrive in hot climates, whether dry or humid. Indian cattle, which in the United States carry the collective designation, Brahman, are known in other Western countries as Zebu, a name that refers to the characteristic fatty hump over the shoulder. There are numerous breeds that have been under domestication far into prehistoric times. The general type is widespread, ranging westwards from south-eastern Asia and including many 'native' cattle of East Africa. They do well in tropical to semi-arid climates, and have lately been much used for the purpose of cross-breeding and upgrading the heat tolerance of European breeds. The latter have, in cooler climates, a desirably high productivity both of milk and meat, which deteriorates in the tropics. Attempts at combining the heat tolerance of Indian cattle with the productivity of European stock are proving worth-while, and success in the establishment of useful cross breeds is testified to in the now recognized breed of Santa Gertrudis cattle. These were developed from an existing shorthorn herd bred to a small number of highly select Brahman bulls for use on the King Ranch in Texas.

HEAT REGULATION

Body temperature

High air temperature influences the body temperature of cattle to a marked degree. The effect is greatest in temperate breeds and more moderate in tropical breeds. The normal rectal temperature of cattle is

TABLE VIII

The rectal temperature in various breeds of cattle maintained at 40° to 41° C and 65 per cent relative humidity

The last column indicates the extent to which the rectal temperature exceeded air temperature when measured directly with thermocouples (357)

	Rectal temp. °C	Rectal less air °C
Holstein	42·5	2·5
Brown Swiss	42·0	1·1
Jersey	41·6	1·6
Brown Swiss heifer	41·5	0·7
Brahman, lactating	41·3	0·7
Brahman heifer	41·0	0·4
Brahman, dry	40·4	−0·4

around 38° to 39° C. This temperature tends to increase when the ambient temperature exceeds the 25° to 30° C range; a corresponding rise does not occur in Brahmans until the air is about 35° C (357). As the rectal temperature reaches 41° C the distress is manifested in restlessness, panting, protrusion of the tongue, and profuse salivation. A rectal temperature of 42° C seems to be tolerated, at least for short periods. If high body temperatures are sustained for longer periods it has deleterious effects on milk production and growth, i.e. on the economic aspects of productivity.

The environmental temperature at which a given rectal temperature is reached varies with the individual animal and the breed. (It also depends on the humidity of the air and other circumstances affecting heat dissipation.)

A comparison of various breeds maintained at a constant environmental temperature of 40·6° C and 65 per cent relative humidity is given in Table VIII. There is a conspicuous difference between the breeds, the temperate breeds maintaining a definite hyperthermia while the Brahman kept closer to normal rectal temperatures, one of them even being able to keep its temperature consistently below that of the environment. This means that if body temperature is used as an indication of heat tolerance, the Indian cattle has a definite advantage above the European breeds. As far as productivity goes, this apparently is a correct viewpoint, and it has formed the basis for the Iberia Heat Tolerance Test which gives a numerical expression for the rise in rectal temperature during heat stress (272). On the other hand, as was shown for the camel, an increased body temperature has a considerable effect on water economy. Undoubtedly, if the European cows in Table VIII were able to maintain a lower temperature, more water would be used, and when the body temperature is above the ambient some heat is dissipated by conduction and radiation rather than by evaporation. Unfortunately no investigations have been concerned with the reactions of cattle which are subjected to dehydration and hence in need of maximum water economy. Therefore, the information we have about cattle is not easily compared to that about camels, but it will help clarify the importance of certain differences in the temperature regulation mechanisms.

Evaporation of water

Studies of the evaporation from European and Indian cattle reveal some very interesting differences (179). As the external temperature rises, European cattle show an increase in evaporation which becomes appreciable somewhere between 15° and 20° C and rapidly rises as the temperature goes higher. The most interesting aspect is that a maximum rate of evaporation seems to be reached before 30° C, and further increases up to 40° C bring no further rise in the water loss. In the Brahman cows evaporation is lower throughout the range and the rapid rise does not occur until somewhere between 25° and 30° C, but the increase continues up to 40° C. This difference in reaction to heat is clearly expressed in the poor performance of European cattle in hot climates where Brahmans maintain productivity and good physical condition.

Sweat glands. A popular explanation for the difference in tolerance to heat is that Indian cattle have sweat glands while European cattle have none. If this were true things would be simple indeed.

British workers at the Hannah Dairy Research Institute have found that cattle bred in temperate and tropical regions possess the same type and number of sweat glands, i.e. one to each hair follicle (123). Compared to the sweat glands in man those in cattle are small and poorly vascularized and do not seem very efficient. (Of course, histological investigations can only tell whether a gland appears to be capable of a high rate of secretion.)

The apparent similarity in the sweating apparatus of temperate and tropical cattle seemed less puzzling when it became known that Indian cattle had a higher density of hair follicles, and hence also of sweat glands. The average number of hair follicles per square centimetre skin surface was reported as Zebu, 1698; Zebu-shorthorn crosses, 1321;

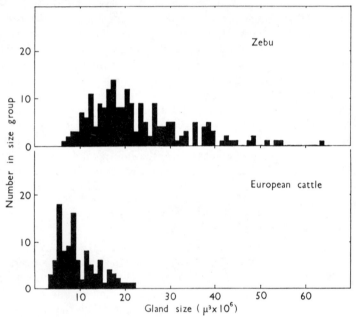

FIG. 14. The sweat glands in the Indian Zebu cattle are much larger than in European breeds. The total number of sweat glands per surface area is also somewhat higher in the Zebu. (Reproduced with permission from Nay and Hayman (234).)

Shorthorn, 1064 (107). Furthermore, a careful study of the size of the glands (234), with samples taken by biopsy from live animals, revealed that Zebus have much larger sweat glands than three European breeds examined (Fig. 14).

One reason for the earlier uncertainty on the number of sweat glands was that too few animals had been examined, for even individuals within a pure breed vary greatly in heat tolerance and presumably in sweat glands—another reason is that the sweat glands in preparations from butchered animals appear smaller than those in biopsy samples from living animals (125).

A structural difference that may be important is that Zebu have their sweat glands located much closer to the skin surface than do European cattle (108). The significance of this is not quite clear if sweat simply runs through a duct to the surface of the skin, but it has been suggested that water moves by diffusion through the sweat gland wall to the body surface. One reason for this belief is that in heat at high humidities the coat remains fairly dry (125). It should be noted that there is much uncertainty about this suggestion, and that many observers have reported

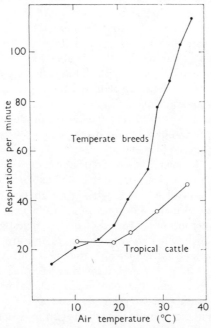

FIG. 15. Respiration frequency at high ambient temperature shows a much more moderate increase in heat-tolerant tropical breeds than in temperate breeds of cattle. (Reproduced with permission from Findlay (124).)

visible sweat in cows. It would be a tedious task to collect evidence to clarify the role of the sweat duct in cattle because individual, racial, and age differences would call for a large amount of material, but the study should be well worth-while.

One suggested reason for the better performance of Indian cattle in hot countries is an allegedly thicker hide, more resistant to attacks of flies, ticks, &c. It has been found, however, that both Zebu and Jersey cows have a relatively thin skin as compared to other breeds (108).

Panting. When cattle are exposed to hot environments, respiratory rates increase appreciably. The frequency of respiration may rise from a normal level of some 25 per minute to over 100 and even as high as 250 per minute (41, 52). The rise seems to be fairly uniform as the heat load increases, and there is no sudden shift from quiet, resting respiration to the high rates of panting (41). As the respiratory rate increases the work of the muscles of respiration should also increase. Thus the panting not only gives more cooling, but the exertion leads to an increased heat production as well. Since the response is less pronounced and begins at a higher temperature in Brahmans (see Fig. 15), this could be one of the reasons that these show less signs of heat strain at high temperatures. Another important difference is that Brahman cattle have an inherently lower metabolic rate than European cattle (357).

It has been widely quoted that the metabolic rate of cattle decreases at high environmental temperatures. This observation was made on lactating cows (180) and was explained by the precipitous decline in milk production and intake of feed in the heat. When heifers were similarly exposed, there was no change in heat production up to 38° C, and at 41° C there was only a slight drop. Some cows which displayed a considerable decrease in metabolic rate at 38° C showed a sharp increase again at 41° C (178) which could be interpreted as being due to the muscular exertion of panting. Since it is difficult to separate the many component factors involved in changes in metabolic rate at high temperature and since available information is insufficient, the problem of the energy cost of panting is in need of further investigations.

Rate of evaporation. The rates of evaporation in European and Indian breeds were compared by Kibler and Brody (179) in the temperature range from −15° to 41° C, and they found that all breeds (Jersey, Holstein, Brown Swiss, and Brahman) attained a maximal rate of surface evaporation or 'sweating' of 150 grammes of water per m^2 per hour. The evaporation from the respiratory tract due to panting reached a maximum of 50 grammes per m^2 per hour in the European breeds, while in Brahman cows the maximum rate was only about 30 grammes per m^2 per hour (all surface measurements indicate outer body surface). At the maximum heat stress, 41° C, the amount of heat dissipated by sweating was therefore similar in all breeds, while the amount of heat dissipated from the respiratory tract was somewhat lower in the Brahman cattle. In all breeds, the dissipation of heat from the skin was three-quarters or more of the total heat dissipation by evaporation of water (see Fig. 16). There was no evidence in these tests that Brahman cattle could sweat more per unit surface area than European cattle, but since their surface area per unit weight is about 12 per cent greater, this gives them an advantage in cooling.

There is no reason to review here the many investigations that show higher rates of evaporation in tropical or cross-bred cattle; they suffer from the same drawback as Brody's experiments—only a few animals have been examined, and both individuals and breeds differ greatly. It should be remembered that there are dozens of breeds of cattle in India (257) and a Brahman in the United States may be as different from a Zebu in Australia as a Black Angus from a Jersey. Suffice it to say that higher rates of evaporation have been observed in tropical cattle, such as 620 grammes per m² per hour in a cross-bred heifer after 3 hours at 48° C

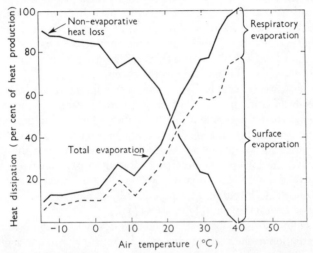

FIG. 16. The total evaporation of water in cattle increases with ambient temperature. Most of the rise is due to surface evaporation while the respiratory evaporation accounts for only a minor fraction of the increase. As ambient temperature approaches the body temperature, less and less heat is lost by conduction, convection, and radiation. (Reproduced with permission from Kibler and Brody (179).)

and 9 per cent relative humidity—more than four times the 140 grammes per m² per hour found for an Ayrshire (234).

The extensive skin folds of the dewlap under the throat and the navel flap increase considerably the surface for cooling. Interestingly, the dewlap has much fewer sweat glands than the midside, and it has been suggested that its function is not so much the production of sweat as the evaporating of that which trickles down from the neck (234).

Salivation. In cattle exposed to high ambient temperature one can frequently see a profuse salivation. In tropical cattle, however, the drivelling of saliva under similar conditions is imperceptible—again an expression of differences between breeds.

The saliva is not spread on the coat and most of it just drips to the ground. It therefore has little effect on heat dissipation. The amount of water lost as saliva may amount to 10 to 15 litres per day (65), a very considerable loss. Furthermore, the saliva has an appreciable content of minerals, mostly sodium and potassium bicarbonate, which represents a salt loss that may attain a noticeable magnitude.

Fur and insulation

The fur, as we have learned from the camel, may serve as an excellent barrier against environmental heat. In cattle this does not seem to be true. When exposed to hot room conditions cattle with sleek, summer-type coats have shown decisive superiority over those with deep winter-type coats. In the field, where heavy radiation is added to the heat load, the same is true (360). This is exactly the opposite of what we found for the camel, which benefits from a thick fur, and, as we shall see later, it is also the reverse of the situation in the sheep.

If a thick, woolly coat is disadvantageous, clipping of cattle should be beneficial. This is, in fact, the case (53, 360), presumably because the conditions for evaporation from the body surface are improved. It is worth noting that the coat in all breeds of tropical cattle is thin and sleek, and among European breeds those individuals that have the thickest coats have the lowest heat tolerance. Recent Australian work has indicated that heat tolerance is not necessarily the direct result of coat type, a short, sleek coat may be an indication of metabolic efficiency and a capacity to react favourably to stress (339).

The colour of the hairy coat is also of importance. A light coat reflects more radiation in the visible range, which carries close to one-half of the total energy of solar radiation. Most likely, in the infra-red there are no differences in reflectivity; all coats probably approach perfect black bodies in this range. But good spectrographic measurements should be carried out for the entire range of visible and infra-red radiation to obtain quantitative information on reflectivity at all wavelengths.

Among those investigations that have been concerned with coat colour (66, 271, 275), one particularly interesting observation stands out (323). The reflectivity of the coat of one and the same animal seems to be increased at higher temperatures. As the temperature was changed from 18° to 35° C over 16 weeks, the 'average hair reflectance' increased from 5 to 20 per cent in Brown Swiss cows, and from 15 to 40 per cent in Brahmans.

Reflectivity of the coat is of course of considerable importance in the field, although it cannot contribute to the differences found in the hot room.

The hump of the Indian cattle. In the preceding chapter it was suggested that the localization of adipose tissue in the hump of the camel is advantageous to heat dissipation. If the same amount of fat were distributed in the general subcutaneous tissue it would impede the flow of heat from the deeper parts to the surface of the body. The same argument can be applied to Indian cattle where the conspicuous shoulder hump is mostly adipose tissue and grows as the animal is fattened.

A hump is also prominent in the Sanga type of East African cattle, but in this case it is anatomically different, consisting of muscle tissue and serving a locomotory function (225).

The different pattern of fat deposition in European and Indian cattle has also been brought out as a partial explanation of the difference in heat tolerance in the following way: European cattle evolved in cool climates and the winter is the hardest time. In winter, fat is needed, (a) as food storage, and (b) as insulation against the cold. Indian cattle evolved in hot countries where the summer is the time of food shortage. The animals now need (a) fat for food storage, and (b) absence of sub-cutaneous insulation. It has been pointed out that the two types of cattle, when fattened, deposit the fat subcutaneously and intramuscularly respectively, in accordance with the thoughts above (193).

This idea will perhaps not stand careful scrutiny, but it suggests that while previous work has been concerned with transfer of heat from the surface to the environment, the transfer of heat inside the body may also deserve attention.

Dehydration and drinking. Apparently, nothing is known about the tolerance of cattle to dehydration, but there seems no reason to expect any unusual tolerance. The water consumption of cows in cool surroundings is high and increases with increasing temperature. The total water consumption in 'dry' (non-milking) cows was found to be 6 per cent of the body weight per day (334), which is four times the voluntary water intake of the camel in cool surroundings (about 1·5 per cent of the body weight, if watered daily).

There is some evidence that a reduction in water expenditure can be accomplished by infrequent watering. When Zebu cattle were watered for 1 hour at 2- or 3-day intervals, they drank 12·0 and 30·7 per cent less than if water was available all the time every day (127). Probably, the first result of such water restriction is to reduce a wasteful production of relatively dilute urine, but what further effects there may be on the economy of water expenditure is unknown.

One aspect that needs attention is the water loss in the faeces. While a well-watered cow produces large quantities of soft faecal material, the droppings of a cow that grazes the semi-arid ranges of central Australia are firm and almost dry. The water reabsorption in the intestine has not been studied in relation to water economy and it would probably prove a most rewarding subject.

Observations on the amount of urine formed during heat load in cattle show a peculiar difference from what we have learned about man. We have already seen that man does not readily drink enough to make up for water loss, and that the volume of his urine therefore decreases and its concentration increases. Cows, however, behave differently. As their water intake goes up at high temperatures there is a parallel increase in urine output with increased frequency of urination and decreased concentrations (334). Thus the water intake goes up more than could be required to cover the increased evaporation. In one cow the urine output went up from about 25 to 125 litres per day. It seems as if these cows drink, not to avoid dehydration, but to cool the body directly with the huge volumes of water, which in these experiments was at $15°$ C.

THE WATER BUFFALO

The water buffalo or carabao is interesting because it has few, if any, sweat glands. It has been stated that the number of its sweat glands is one-tenth that in cattle (358). It has a low tolerance to heat, and can be kept in hot countries only if allowed to wallow in water or mud. Because of its large size its metabolic rate should be low, and its relative surface small. In consequence, metabolic heat production as well as heat gain from the environment should be low.

The water buffalo is mostly kept for its milk, which has a high fat content (7·5 per cent) and is peculiarly white, apparently lacking carotenoids. Some buffaloes are used for draft purposes, but they are too slow, and cattle are preferred as work animals. They are mostly used in tropical environments where the heat load is not as severe as in deserts. Temperatures in the humid tropics are much lower than in the desert, but owing to the high relative humidity, conditions for evaporative cooling are poor.

No information exists about heat or water balance in the water buffalo, and investigations should prove very interesting. The famous temperament of the animal might add additional excitement.

SUMMARY

Cattle are not particularly adapted to hot, dry conditions, but Indian cattle are more heat tolerant than European breeds. The difference is probably due to higher sweating rates, larger relative body surface, and, under field conditions, the lighter colour in heat-tolerant breeds. Evaporation from the body surface is important. Although panting is pronounced in cattle, the amount of heat lost from the respiratory tract is less than a quarter of the total heat dissipation. It has not been established whether the mechanical work of panting causes a significant rise in metabolic heat production, but heat-tolerant cattle pant less than other breeds.

Usually, water intake and urine output are high in cattle. The actual tolerance to water deprivation and dehydration is unknown. Important functions that should be studied in this connexion are fluctuations in body temperature, plasma- and blood-volume, explosive heat death, urine concentrations and renal function, and reabsorption of water from the intestinal contents.

5

THE DONKEY

THE sure-footed little donkey is one of the most enduring of beasts. It has an extraordinary capacity for finding food in the most barren places, is a quick walker, can carry tremendous burdens, and will walk patiently hour after hour on the hottest and driest of trails. In countries where donkeys are commonly used, one will often see a man riding ahead on a donkey with his dangling legs almost touching the ground, his wife walking behind with whatever load there is to carry. The donkey has some of the best qualities of both bicycle and wheelbarrow, being a convenient and easy form of transportation, excellent for moving heavy loads, and costing almost nothing to feed.

The wild asses, the African *Equus asinus*, and the Asiatic *E. hemionus*, are steppe animals that extend their range into the arid parts of the continents. In his report on the living animals of the Gobi Desert, Roy Chapman Andrews reported that the wild asses are found in greatest abundance 'in parts of the deserts where there is no water whatsoever' (13). The wild donkeys have never been studied from the viewpoint of how they can live in places where there is no water, and of the domestic variety seemingly only two individuals have been under the scrutiny of physiologists. One was used by Dill's group in Nevada in the 1930's as a comparison for studies of man (2, 106), the other was studied by my own group in the Sahara in the 1950's for comparison with camels (301). Thus, in a way, both were studied as a sideline to other investigations, but they yielded much interesting information. Although it is undesirable to make generalizations from studies of one or two animals, we now have a fair idea of how donkeys react to heat and dehydration, and of the qualities that make them particularly suited for hot and dry countries.

Both the donkey used by Dill and our African jackass were small animals, barely 100 kg when well fed and watered. Some breeds are larger, for example the so-called Spanish donkey used for breeding mules, but the small animals are probably closer to their wild ancestors than any other type. It would be reasonable to expect that the wild asses have similar physiological reactions to heat and lack of water, but perhaps to a more extreme degree.

BODY TEMPERATURE

When we took hourly temperature measurements in the donkey, we found diurnal fluctuations similar to those in the camel, but by no means as pronounced. During hot periods, when the donkey was watered once a day, the rectal temperature varied by two degrees, between 36·4° C in the morning and 38·4° C in the evening. The animal was kept outside, fully exposed to heat and sun, and the air temperature regularly exceeded 40° C during the day. In winter the rectal temperature of the donkey varied within the same limits as in the summer, with a minimum around 36° C and the maximum slightly over 38° C. Evidently the donkey was an excellent heat regulator, quite capable of maintaining a normal body temperature during cold as well as heat stress.

How about a donkey that has to work? During the research at Boulder Dam in Nevada Dill had obtained for study a young female donkey, or 'burro' as it is called in Spanish. Dr. F. G. Hall, a member of the party, has told me that the donkey was a pet and the property of a garage man who, among other things, also sold beer. The animal was fond of beer, and the man let this be known for it induced the tourists to stop and buy the donkey a bottle of beer. This was good advertising and increased the sale tremendously. The donkey would take hold of the neck of the bottle with her mouth, turn the head up and let the beer run down her throat. In the main experiment each of five members of Dill's party in turn took her on a 2-hour walk, covering about 6·4 km in each round trip. The donkey had not been watered for the preceding 24 hours and now covered about 32 km without water. Her rectal temperature, which was measured at the end of each round trip, slowly rose from 38·5° to 39·6° C. Even though this donkey carried no load, 32 km is a long walk on a hot summer day in the desert, and the donkey seemingly had no difficulties in keeping cool.

When we deprived our Saharan donkey of drinking-water, the daily temperature fluctuations increased in magnitude. The morning minimum was irregular and perhaps a degree below what we had seen before, and as dehydration progressed the maximum rectal temperature increased somewhat. There seemed to be an upper limit of 39·3° C, beyond which the donkey would not permit the body temperature to rise. This maximum was one degree above the usual daily maximum, but 1·3° C lower than the maximum normally reached by the dehydrated camel. It seems unlikely that the donkey should be unable to tolerate a body temperature above 39·3° C; it is more likely that variations in body temperature are not used in water conservation with the same efficiency as in the camel. The low morning temperatures undoubtedly accomplished some saving in water by permitting part of the heat gained to be stored in the body as it is in the camel. At the high end of the range the donkey is more like man, who usually keeps his temperature from rising, but who, when dehydrated, displays a moderate rise in rectal temperature.

We have, on one occasion, observed a temperature above 39·3° C in the donkey. This was on the fourth day of a dehydration period in the summer, and in the afternoon the rectal temperature began to rise rapidly as the animal showed increasing signs of distress and restlessness. When the temperature reached 39·8 C it seemed that the donkey was on the verge of explosive heat rise; it was given water to drink, the temperature went down immediately because the water was cool, and a few hours later the animal seemed completely normal and recovered.

WATER LOSSES

The sweating mechanism. The donkey has sweat glands all over the body surface, it is a nose breather, and it does not pant. Not much is known about the sweat glands, but the amount of water evaporated from the skin surface has been measured by strapping small cups containing a water absorbent to shaved areas and determining their weight gain at intervals (269, 301). This and similar methods have some disadvantages, primarily that they interfere with the normal exchange of air over the area being measured, and that the temperature of the skin itself is changed. The cup method has the advantage that it is simple and convenient, and in spite of its drawbacks it gives useful information.

We made determinations of this kind on the upper shoulder of the animal, where the fur was shaved off to permit the cup to be placed directly against the skin. This location was chosen because it was the only place on the donkey where the cup could be strapped on easily so that movements of the animal would not change the position of the cup or admit air at its edge.

The evaporation increased at high air temperatures, but there was not a very consistent relationship between the two. This is not surprising, for air temperature is not a good expression for total heat load, which should include the heavy radiation from the sun and ground. The best expression for the integrated heat load that we could obtain was the black-bulb temperature, measured with a thermometer placed with the bulb in the centre of a blackened copper sphere, similar to the so-called globe thermometer (42). This black-bulb temperature, in still air, gives a reasonably good measure of total heat load. If there is wind the temperature of the black bulb decreases while the actual heat load on the animal increases (a black-bulb thermometer which shows 50° or 60° C will be cooled if air at about 40° C passes over it, but in the same situation more heat is conducted from the hot air to the cool animal surface).

The results of plotting evaporation against black-bulb temperature are shown in Fig. 17. At low temperatures there are too few determinations to establish a reliable difference between the donkey and the camel. Above a certain breaking-point evaporation increases linearly with the heat load. This critical point seems to be about 30° C in the donkey but between 35° and 40° C in the camel. The highest evaporation measured in the donkey was about 0·6 mg per cm² per minute and 0·4 mg per cm² per minute in the camel. There is no indication that the maximum capacity of the cooling mechanism had been reached. For comparison, it is interesting to note that the maximum rates of evaporation from the skin of cattle determined by the Missouri group was estimated at 0·25 mg per cm² per minute (179), a value reached at much lower heat loads.

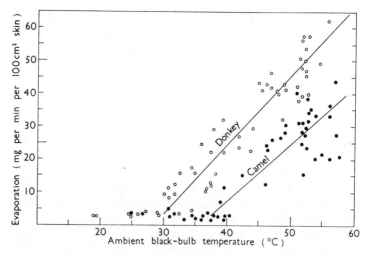

FIG. 17. Evaporation from the shoulder skin of a donkey (open circles) and a camel (black circles) in relation to black-bulb temperature. Under the given conditions the black-bulb temperature gave an approximate measure of environmental heat load. (Reproduced with permission from (301).)

Urine volume and concentration. Information about the urine volume in the donkey is inadequate. The animal we had was a male and rather cantankerous when he did not approve of our activities. A donkey turns very quickly and, if he can, he hits with both hind feet at once. The only practical way we found to get urine samples was to hire a small arab boy to sit ready with a beaker.

For almost a week the boy stayed alert, and the average daily urine output of the donkey was estimated to vary between 1·2 and 1 litre when it was watered daily. In later periods of dehydration we obtained occasional samples that were reliably timed, and one of these indicated a rate of urine flow of 451 ml per day, the lowest we measured with certainty. These volumes were of the same magnitude as the total urine volume in the camel, but since the camel weighed about three times as much, the relative urine volume was three times as high in the donkey.

The urine concentrations revealed nothing very unusual about the donkey's kidney. In general, K concentrations were high and Na low, but feeding a ration of salt would reverse this. The most concentrated urine samples are listed in Table IX. Some of them were obtained from a dehydrated animal, but similar samples were often found when the donkey could drink freely.

TABLE IX

Composition of the most concentrated samples of donkey urine collected in periods of dehydration

Cl, *mN*	Na, *mN*	K, *mN*	Urea, *mM*
529	272	230	315
346	340	312	261
466	1·1	465	158
376	210	283	559

Although these concentrations of electrolytes are considerably higher than the maximum concentrations in man, they do not indicate a very exceptional kidney. Many desert animals can produce a much more concentrated urine, and many non-desert animals such as the dog and rat reach the same concentrations as the donkey. Of course, a closer study of the kidney function of the donkey may still reveal interesting capacities.

Water content of the faeces. The faeces of the donkey have a higher water content than those of the camel. On the laboratory diet, when the animal could drink, the donkey's droppings contained 180 grammes of water per 100 grammes dry matter, while camel droppings contained only 109 grammes. Unfortunately, no determinations were made of the water content of the faeces in the donkey that was deprived of drinking-water.

In addition to the higher water content, the total amount of faeces in the donkey is greater. For a given amount of food, the less-efficient digestion of the non-ruminant leaves more undigested material to be eliminated. The donkey produced per day about 720 grammes dry faecal matter per 100 kg body weight, containing 1300 grammes H_2O. The camel produced daily only 370 grammes dry faecal matter per 100 kg body weight, containing 410 grammes H_2O—in other words, the faecal water loss, when related to body weight, was three times as high in the donkey.

The rate of total water loss

When the donkey was watered every day in the winter while being given only dry feed, its daily water intake averaged 3·52 per cent of the body weight. Under the same circumstances a camel drank 1·47 per cent of the body weight per day. In other words, the donkey drank, when it could take what it wanted, over twice as much as the camel.

When the animals were deprived of drinking-water and eating the same dry feed, the total daily water loss was about 2·5 per cent of the body weight in the donkey, and only 1 per cent in the camel. In winter no water is used for heat regulation, and the figures mentioned therefore indicate the basic minimum water expenditure for the two animals.

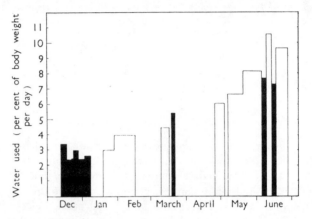

FIG. 18. The rate of water expenditure in a Saharan donkey increased considerably from winter to summer. When periods of water deprivation (dark bars) were interspersed between periods of daily watering (white bars) it became evident that dehydration caused only a moderate decrease in water expenditure. (Reproduced with permission from (299).)

If we assume for the moment that both animals have the same degree of tolerance to desiccation of the body, for example, 30 per cent weight loss, the time they should be able to go without water in the winter would be 12 days for the donkey and 30 days for the camel. This rough estimate assumes that water loss continues at the suggested rate, that only dry food is eaten, and that cool conditions prevail.

In nature the vegetation usually contains some moisture, particularly in winter, and the camel can probably remain in water balance and go indefinitely without water. If succulent vegetation is available the donkey can do the same. If he needs, say, 2 kg of plant material (dry weight), and the plants contain 70 per cent water, the amount of free water in the food exceeds 4 litres. It is presumably for this reason that the wild asses of the great Asiatic steppes and many other animals are independent of drinking-water during winter. When summer comes and the vegetation dries up, and the necessity for temperature regulation places additional demands on the water stores, both the camel and the donkey have to drink.

In summer the need for water increases greatly and the donkey's daily requirements now amount to some 8 to 10 and up to 12 per cent of the body weight per day (see Fig. 18). The expenditure of water when the donkey was not allowed to drink was a little lower than if it was watered daily, but the difference was not as conspicuous as in the camel, which could reduce its water expenditure to about one-half when it was dehydrated.

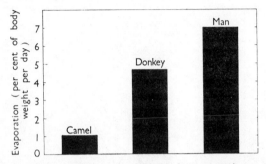

FIG. 19. Water used for heat regulation in summer, in excess of that used in winter, in animals fully exposed to direct sun in Sahara in June. The figures for camel and donkey are from periods in which the animals were deprived of water. (Reproduced with permission from (299).)

Water used for heat regulation. By subtracting from the total daily water expenditure the amounts used for formation of urine and faeces, as well as the amount that is the obligatory evaporation from lungs and skin during the cool hours, we are left with an amount of water which is used to dissipate heat. Such a calculation gives the amounts of water plotted in Fig. 19. The graph also contains evaporation for heat regulation in man, information obtained in the United States deserts (5) under conditions which were similar but probably not identical to those in the Sahara. We can now see that the donkey uses four times as much water for heat regulation in the summer as the camel does, but apparently less than man. When Dill compared the donkey with a man, walking in the hot Nevada desert, the evaporation was 1·33 per cent of the body weight per hour for the donkey and 1·47 per cent in man (106). Since these figures were obtained in the same experiments their validity is good.

Part of the difference in water expenditure between the camel and the donkey is due to the donkey's smaller body size and larger relative surface. The two animals weighed about 270 and 95 kg respectively, so the relative surface in the donkey was about 40 per cent larger than in the camel. Thus, the water loss relative to the surface area was still three times greater in the donkey. This difference in evaporation must be ascribed primarily to two factors, the donkey has a much thinner coat of fur than the camel, and it does not utilize fluctuations in body temperature for water saving to the same extent. A further difference is that our donkey mostly remained standing while the camel was sitting on the ground throughout the day, thus reducing the amount of exposed surface.

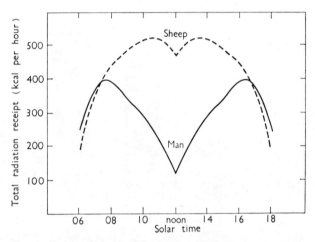

FIG. 20. Estimated receipt of direct solar radiation in an animal with horizontal posture (sheep) as compared to vertical posture (man). Calculated for the summer at 30° latitude. (Reproduced with permission from Lee (197).)

The similarity in water expenditure in donkey and man has some interesting aspects to it, for it is the result of two major differences working in opposite directions. The donkey has a fur which, although thinner than the camel's, is a better protection against heat gain from the environment than the thin clothing used by man. In fact, a delightful picture in Dill's book (106) shows, walking with a donkey, a man who has pulled off his shirt, exposing the upper part of his body to an unobstructed heat gain. This difference works in favour of the donkey, but another factor works in the opposite direction, the contrast in posture between man and donkey. The effect of posture on the area exposed to solar radiation as the height of the sun changes during the day was estimated by Lee for man and sheep (197), but we can just as well use the result for man and donkey (see Fig. 20). During the time of the day when solar radiation is strongest, the difference is to the disadvantage of the animal with a horizontal posture, cancelling out much of the advantage gained from the better insulation. These two factors, working in opposite directions, explain why the donkey and the man come out so relatively close in their expenditure of water for heat regulation.

Tolerance to dehydration

The donkey showed about the same tolerance to depletion of body water as we found in the camel. Both animals seemed rather unaffected by water losses of 12 to 15 per cent of the body weight, a degree of dehydration which would result in explosive heat rise and death in many other mammals. They lost their appetites and looked increasingly distressed at weight losses of 20 per cent or more.

On two occasions the donkey was kept for 4 days without water in the summer and lost 30 per cent of its body weight. From the general condition of the animal, and from the fact that it once seemed to be on the verge of explosive heat rise, the donkey seems to have been close to its limit of tolerance to water depletion. In any event, this value of 30 per cent is remarkably high compared to other animals, including man. Other animals die after a water loss of probably 17 to 20 per cent of the body weight when they are merely dehydrated, but if they at the same time are exposed to a hot environment, they are likely to go into explosive heat rise at a weight loss of about 12 per cent (6).

Volume changes during dehydration

In the experiment where Dill dehydrated a donkey by walking it for 20 miles in the desert, he found that the plasma chloride concentration increased by 12·4 per cent. This corresponded very closely to the water loss, which indicated that extracellular and intracellular fluid had been depleted of water to about the same extent. Predicting from the effects of dehydration in man, Dill expected that the plasma water should be reduced relatively more than the remaining body water, and this notion is compatible with the chloride findings, for salts pass freely through the capillary wall. He was surprised, however, to find that there was no rise in plasma protein as would be expected from a decrease in plasma volume. The explanation suggested for this was that in the donkey 'protein evidently moves with freedom in and out of the capillary' (106). There is, however, another possible and more probable interpretation.

It is, to begin with, very improbable that any animal has capillaries highly permeable to protein, and in my opinion the absence of change in plasma protein merely indicates that plasma volume was maintained at its normal level. Since chloride moves freely in and out of the capillary, its plasma concentration should equal that in the extracellular fluid, and be a fair indication of total water loss. In an animal in good physiological condition the plasma proteins should serve to maintain an unchanged plasma volume, as was explained for the camel (p. 66), and Dill found exactly what should be expected. His figures do not permit any further estimate of relative losses in extracellular and intracellular volumes, but a pattern of water loss such as outlined for the camel seems more likely than a capillary freely permeable to protein.

Another interesting finding in Dill's results was that the plasma chloride, which had increased during the dehydration period, returned to the initial level after rehydration. This indicates that the sweat must be relatively chloride free, at least as compared to man. During the long periods in the Sahara when we fed hay and dates to our donkey without any extra ration of salt, our experience was much the same. There was no indication of any appreciable loss of salt in the sweat, judging from the continued normal chloride concentrations in the blood even after periods of heavy sweating (after rehydration had taken place). Collection of sweat samples for analysis is not as easy in a furred animal as it is in a man, where the investigator usually has the added advantage of a co-operative subject, but if the salt losses in the sweat were appreciable, one would expect incrustations of salt on the skin. When man sweats heavily in the desert, he may not actually get wet because the sweat evaporates so fast, but the skin gets covered with small crystals of salt.

A plant-eating animal, which usually gets little sodium chloride in its natural food, simply could not afford to produce large volumes of sweat if the salt concentrations were high. It is likely that herbivores, if they sweat at all, usually produce a sweat with a low salt concentration so that an undue drain on the sodium and chloride is avoided.

The plant-eater could, of course, produce a sweat where potassium replaces sodium. The cutaneous elimination would then lighten the load on the kidney by removing one of the major excretory products, but the amount removed this way must be small for one does not find salt incrustations in the fur. In one of our camels sloughed-off epidermis could be removed from the skin surface with a forceps. One gramme of this material contained: insoluble (mostly epidermal cells) 743 mg, chloride 127 mg, sodium 41 mg, potassium 80 mg, undetermined 9 mg. Thus, some salt was found on the surface of the skin, with sodium and potassium in the molar ratio of $1:1.5$, and both of these as chlorides.

DRINKING CAPACITY

After a 20-mile walk in the desert and 36 hours without water, Dill's donkey drank 12·2 litres of water within 5 minutes. This is about ten times as much as a man can drink in the same time, however thirsty he may be. Our Saharan donkey, which was about the same size, could easily drink 10 litres in 70 to 80 seconds, taking time out for only one or two respirations. The fastest drinking of which we have a record was 20·5 litres in 150 seconds, and the first 10 litres of this went down in 73 seconds.

The donkey always seemed to drink an amount closely corresponding to the water lost during the preceding dehydration period, and water losses as great as 20 per cent of the body weight were made up for in less than 2 minutes. If more water was available the donkey would be completely disinterested in drinking, whether this water was presented

TABLE X

Water consumption in a donkey after 4 days of water deprivation in June

Days without water	Weight before dehydr.	Dehydr. weight	Weight loss		Drinking	
			kg	per cent of body weight	litres	per cent of dehydr. body weight
4	107·0	74·5	32·5	30·4	20·5 (23·5)*	27·2 (31·5)*
4	104·1	73·0	31·1	29·9	20·3 (26·9)*	27·8 (36·8)*

* Figures in parentheses represent total amount of water consumed over 2 hours. Water taken immediately, in less than 5 minutes, is given without parentheses.

a few minutes, half an hour, or several hours later. Thus, the animal seemed to have an amazing ability to rehydrate to its original volume, neither over-drinking nor remaining in a deficit. Since there is no time for absorption of water into the blood and dilution of body fluids during the short drinking session, the intake of water must be accurately metered by some neurological mechanism connected with the drinking, the peristalsis of the oesophagus, or, more likely, the filling of the stomach. Much fine work on the factors that control the intake of fluid in dogs and other animals has been done in Adolph's laboratory, and perhaps someone will feel tempted to continue these studies using donkeys as well.

When the donkey had been exposed to extreme degrees of dehydration, with losses of body weight amounting to 30 per cent, it was unable to drink immediately sufficient water to make up for the entire loss. On the two occasions this happened, the donkey drank first, within a few minutes, 20·2 and 20·3 litres of water respectively (see Table X). Thus the donkey could drink more than a quarter of its body weight of water. When additional water was offered during the next hour or two, the donkey could again drink more, but it did not take enough to make up for the entire weight loss. This probably was because the animal had lost its appetite and had stopped eating during the 2 last days of the dehydration period, for it rapidly went back to its original weight as it was fed and watered regularly.

An amusing little incident showed us that the donkey which drank 20·3 litres took exactly as much as it could hold. When it had ingested this huge volume of water and took a few wobbly steps, it could not hold on to it all and a small amount, perhaps 50 ml, spurted out of its anus. This was quite unexpected to us, but since the donkey happened to be on a concrete floor we could obtain a sample of the fluid it had lost. The analysis of the water gave a low salt content, not much higher than in the drinking-water, which shows that it could not be any body fluid. It seemed that the donkey had filled its entire gastro-intestinal tract all the way out to the anal sphincter with as much water as it could hold. As it took the first few steps it could not quite hold on to it and lost a small amount of the precious fluid.

The rapid dilution of blood and body fluids which occurs when such large amounts of water are introduced into the body must be a considerable strain on the animal. The fact that the water is in contact with the entire gastro-intestinal surface gives an extremely rapid absorption and precipitous falls in concentrations of the body fluids. Such dilutions should cause severe water intoxication and death in other animals, but it is difficult to make a direct comparison since other animals could not withstand such high degrees of water depletion to begin with. In the donkey there seemed to be no ill effect whatsoever of the sudden rehydration, and complete distribution of the ingested water seemed to take place in less than 8 hours, judging from the change in plasma concentrations.

There must be a tremendous biological advantage for an animal to be able to drink rapidly and to its full capacity. Predators are likely to lurk at water holes and an animal that can drink its fill in a minute or two and then get away has a great advantage. The drinking capacity in the camel was of the same magnitude as in the donkey, but this animal took more time, and frequently spent a leisurely 10 or 15 minutes with the water, taking pauses and looking around between drinks. Evidently, the domestic camel in its behaviour is farther away from its wild ancestors, or it has never needed to be afraid of predators to the same extent as the smaller herbivores.

SUMMARY

The donkey has not been much used as an experimental animal and the generalizations given below are tentative because they are mostly based on observations of a single animal.

The donkey has, when no water is used for heat regulation, a rate of water expenditure of about $2\frac{1}{2}$ times that in the camel. In summer, when water is used for heat regulation, the rate is 3 to 4 times as high as in the camel.

The main reasons for the higher rate of water loss in the donkey are (*a*) the fluctuations in body temperature are smaller than in the camel, (*b*) the fur coat is thinner, and (*c*) the behavioural adaptations which reduce heat gain are not as extreme.

The donkey, like the camel, has an exceptional tolerance to dehydration of the body, being able to withstand a water loss of 30 per cent of the body weight.

The donkey eliminates rather large amounts of faeces because the food is not as well digested as in ruminants. The water content of the faeces is also relatively high, resulting in a faecal water loss some three times that in the camel. The urine volume is also higher than in the camel.

The available information indicates that plasma volume is relatively well maintained as dehydration progresses. This may be one of the explanations for the high tolerance to water depletion.

The drinking capacity of the donkey is impressive, it can ingest in a few minutes more than one-quarter of its body weight in water. The drinking seems adjusted to a restoration of the water content to the normal level, and over-hydration has not been observed.

6

SHEEP

DOMESTICATION of sheep began perhaps 8000 years ago in Asia Minor (117). At the present time various breeds of sheep are used from the cold Atlantic climate of Iceland to the hot arid climate of central Sahara. Of the many varieties only a few have been the subject of systematic investigation, mainly by Australian and British workers. Naturally, such studies centre around breeds that are of particular interest as wool and meat producers. Virtually nothing is known about the physiology of the less well-defined breeds, the short-haired Saharan animal, the fat-tailed sheep of Egypt, or the fat-rumped breeds of the Near East. Many of these varieties are kept in marginal areas of low productivity and high aridity, and in all probability they are more tolerant to inadequate feed and water than European breeds. The same probably holds for a breed kept by Indians in the hot arid south-western United States, the Navajo sheep, which has had a shorter existence than the old world types, but still can be expected to be well-adapted to arid conditions.

Racial differences between sheep probably are considerable, even among the closely related European breeds. For example, at high temperature merino sheep drank less than half of what some other European breeds consumed when kept on the same diet (95). Interestingly, the merino is a breed developed in the arid parts of Spain, in Andalusia. It also has long wool, similar to sheep in the Scottish highlands and other cold north Atlantic countries. It would be most fascinating to have comparative information about some of the short-haired tropical and desert varieties, including the fat-tailed and fat-rumped ones.

It is worth notice that relatives of the domestic sheep are mountain animals, rather than steppe or desert dwellers. Still, among sheep, we probably find some of the most drought- and heat-resistant of any medium-to-large size animal, outdone only by the camel and some wild antelopes and gazelles.

TEMPERATURE REGULATION IN SHEEP

Lee (196) exposed a variety of domestic animals to high temperatures and concluded that sheep had the greatest tolerance to heat of them all. Merino sheep withstood for 7 hours a room heated to 44° C when the relative humidity was 65 per cent, although the same sheep had been unable to tolerate 41° C and 75 per cent relative humidity. During the test the respiratory rate increased from less than 30 per minute to about 240, and the rectal temperature rose from about 38° to over 41° C. As the rectal temperature exceeded 41° C the closed-mouthed breathing would change to open-mouthed panting, and a rectal temperature slightly below 42° C seemed to be the limit for continued existence as an integrated organism. The pulse-rate showed amazingly little change, increasing from about 40 at low temperatures to around 50 per minute at the highest temperatures. Furthermore, there was no significant difference in the pulse-rate with variations in the supply of water to the animal.

Sheep exposed to hot arid conditions in Queensland in the summer showed only moderate diurnal variations in the body temperature, about 1·5° to 2° C (209). This is a more moderate fluctuation than found in the camel, and this relative stability is achieved by evaporation of water, mainly through panting. Later studies of merino sheep at Julia Creek in central Queensland gave an average of 40·1°±0·1° C for the rectal temperature in mid-summer, while the average mid-winter temperature was 39·6°±0·3° C. Although the difference between the hot summer and the cool winter is statistically significant, it is not very great. Sheep standing in the sun in summer at air temperatures between 41·6° and 43·0° C had rectal temperatures up to 41·6° C. In winter, afternoon rectal temperatures did not go above 40° C. (210).

These relatively small variations in rectal temperature indicate that sheep keep their body temperature fairly constant under a variety of external conditions, both hot and cold.

Heat regulation in relation to feeding level. While we are discussing heat regulation, there is an important difference between domestic and wild animals that merits mention. Domestic stock is selected and bred for high productivity, and for economic reasons this productivity is desirable the year around, not excepting the hottest summer. To be productive, animals should be well fed, and a high level of feeding has an unfavourable effect on heat tolerance. For wild desert animals the summer is usually also the most difficult time with a scarcity of food and lack of water. But, if they can get through this period, the more bountiful pastures of the desert winter give the needed foundation for reproduction and growth of the young. The scarcity of food in the summer might even work to their advantage.

The effect of the feeding level on the metabolic heat production in sheep is evident in Fig. 21. At low temperature these sheep (which were closely shorn) showed an elevated heat production which was necessary to maintain the body temperature. The feeding level made no difference, the amount of energy required to keep the body warm without the protection of wool was the same in either case. The interesting differences were found in the other end of the temperature range, at the high environmental temperatures. Here it appeared that a high level of feeding resulted in an increased heat production, while the sheep at the low level of feeding had a steadily decreasing heat production at the highest ambient temperature. A sheep in the latter situation is, in a way,

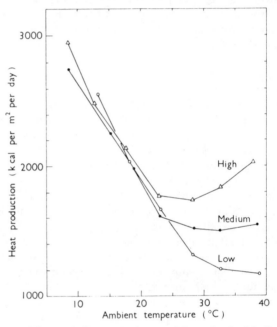

FIG. 21. The metabolic rates in sheep at different levels of feeding are identical at low temperatures. However, at high ambient temperature the metabolic heat production is higher in the well-fed sheep. (Reproduction with permission from Armstrong *et al.* (16).)

most like the desert animal in the summer when feed is scarce and of low quality. The lack of good feed in itself leads to a decrease in internal heat production, and consequently to a reduction in the amount of heat that must be dissipated by evaporation of water.

The fleece as a protection against heat

In the sheep the heavy wool acts as a protection against the heat of the environment, much as it does in the camel. When the sheep stands in the sun the surface of the fur gets very hot, with temperatures at the tip of the wool as high as 87° C (209). Although these temperatures were measured with small glass thermometers, I believe that the measurements could be reasonably precise, for we frequently observed surface temperatures in the camel's wool of close to 80° C when measured with a radiometer. The greasy wool of the sheep gets much dirtier and darker than the camel's fur, and it could readily absorb a greater proportion of the solar radiation in the visible range.

With the high temperature at the tip of the wool, the skin temperature was 42° C, in other words, 4 cm of wool sustained a gradient of 45° C between tip and skin. Obviously, the thickness of the fleece must be an important factor in reducing the flow of heat over this steep gradient.

TABLE XI

Shearing the wool of sheep removes much of the insulation against the hot environment and the animals must now pant at a much higher rate (last column) to keep the rectal temperature from rising

Observations made under field conditions with the sheep fully exposed to the sun. From (210)

	Wool length mm	Reflectance	Wool tip temp.	Skin temp.	Rectal temp.	Resp. rate
Unshorn	35 to 40	0·18	76	42·5	40·2	108
Shorn	5 to 8	0·36	53	45	39·8	230

The simplest way to test the protective role of the wool is to remove it. At more moderate temperatures, with the environment below the body temperature of the sheep, dissipation of heat by conduction and radiation should be facilitated by the absence of the fleece. This was also observed, as expected, at an environmental temperature of 30° C. Sheep that had been shorn so closely that only about 1 mm of the fleece remained, evaporated one-half the amount of water evaporated by sheep with 10 cm fleece. At an environmental temperature of 38° C, however, the evaporation in the shorn and unshorn sheep was the same (57). This is precisely the temperature where external and body temperature are about equal, that is, there is virtually no heat flow through the wool and evaporation should equal the metabolic heat production.

At higher environmental temperatures the protective value of the wool becomes important, and the unshorn sheep is better off. This has been shown with convincing results by a number of investigators. For example, Lee (197) found that the presence of the fleece helped reduce the rises in both rectal temperature and respiratory rates when sheep were exposed to the high temperatures of the hot-room.

In a study under field conditions with the sheep fully exposed to the sun, conspicuous differences were observed (see Table XI). The shearing of the wool removed the dirty surface so that the reflectance of the fresh, clean wool underneath was greatly increased. Accordingly, the temperature at the tip of the white wool was much lower in the freshly shorn sheep, but because the layer of wool was thinner, the skin temperature was higher. The rectal temperature showed no significant difference in the two groups, but the shorn sheep had to pant at more than twice the rate to keep the temperature down to this level.

If sufficient water is available, shearing of the sheep may make little difference, but if they graze on a range with sparse and scattered vegetation, it is to their disadvantage to remove the wool and increase the need for water. Long and frequent walks to the watering-places require energy and take time away from grazing, and it may be profitable to review the practices of shearing in view of water economy and productivity. In fact, the same considerations apply to the camel, for the nomad has the habit of shearing his animals in the spring. This practice is definitely not in the interest of water economy during the summer.

THE MAIN USES OF WATER

Panting or sweating

In the preceding discussions we have assumed that the degree of heat stress is reflected in the rate of respiration. However, it is known that sheep also possess sweat glands. We therefore encounter the same problem as we had with cattle—what is the relative importance of evaporation from the respiratory tract and from the skin?

This question has been discussed many times (68, 196, 274). One report on a Corriedale ewe (a breed not particularly heat resistant) suggested that the cutaneous water loss was about twice the respiratory loss at $40°C$ (184). Later investigators have not been as optimistic about the role of the skin in heat dissipation. First of all, since reliable observations of skin temperatures (under the fleece) show these to be higher than the simultaneous body temperatures (209, 210), heat must of necessity flow from the skin towards the body, not in the opposite direction. If the sheep are to maintain heat balance, which they actually do during the hot summer, the evaporation from the respiratory tract must dissipate the metabolic heat as well as the heat coming from the skin.

Although skin temperatures in excess of body temperatures mean that no metabolic heat can be moved to the skin for dissipation by sweating, water can still evaporate from the skin and remove some heat. In fact, this is exactly what happens, for part of the heat flowing through the fleece is dissipated at the skin surface, and only a fraction of it penetrates farther to the body itself.

The best determinations of water loss from the skin that have come to my attention were recently made by Brook and Short (68). These investigators determined the total evaporation from the skin areas in various breeds of sheep, and as control animals they used four merino sheep which were congenitally deficient in sweat glands. This permitted the investigators to establish how much water normally passes through the skin of the sheep at high temperatures when no sweat glands are present, and by subtracting this value from the total skin evaporation in the other sheep they were able to establish with reasonable certainty the amount of water appearing on the skin as a result of the activity of the sweat glands. The results were summarized in a very instructive table which looks as follows (Table XII).

TABLE XII

A comparison of the function of sweat glands in sheep, cattle, and man points out vast differences in their activity

Values for rates of sweating of cattle and man are the highest reported in the literature. From (68).

| | Sweat glands | | Rate of sweating | | Ratio of |
	Number per cm^2	Volume of secretory part (mm^3)	Sweat per gland (mg/hr)	Total sweat $(g/m^2/hr)$	sweat/gland/hr to gland vol. $(mg/hr/mm^3)$
Sheep	290	0·004 (0·001 to 0·008)	0·01	32	2·5
European cattle	1000	0·010 (0·006 to 0·015)	0·06	588	6·0
Man	150	0·003	1·3	2000	433

The efficiency of the panting mechanism is corroborated by the many observations of high respiratory rates during heat loads. Some measurements (196) indicate that the respiration at the same time becomes much more shallow so that the actual renewal of the air in the lungs is not greatly increased. This permits an efficient ventilation of the upper respiratory tract, where most of the evaporation takes place, without undue over-ventilation of the lungs themselves. The high and seemingly well-regulated respiratory rates are evident from Fig. 22.

With the information currently available, it seems that sheep primarily rely on panting for heat dissipation at high temperatures. In this respect they are different from the camel, which, although it has a thick wool, uses primarily sweating for heat dissipation. The respiratory rates in the camel exposed to heat remain low, between 10 and 18 respirations per minute, while the rates in sheep may exceed 270 (59), and in lambs 400 respirations per minute (210).

Kidney function

Urine volumes. In the use of water for excretion the two essential factors are the volume and the concentration of the urine. Although numerous studies have been made on food intake and elimination of faeces and urine, studies under hot arid conditions are few. Field work is difficult to carry out with complete and quantitative collection of excreta,

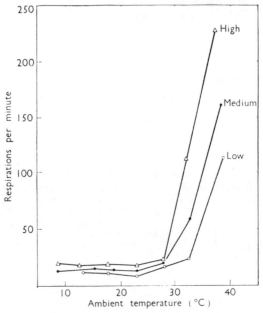

FIG. 22. The frequency of respiration in sheep increases sharply at high ambient temperature. The greater increase in sheep on a high level of feeding is a reflection of the higher metabolic heat production in these. (Reproduced with permission from Blaxter (56).)

and since food intake and productivity have been major concerns in most investigations, purely physiological studies of sheep under extreme climatic conditions have been more in the background.

Many Australian workers have realized the importance of a broad knowledge of basic physiology for the understanding of the performance of domestic animals. Macfarlane is one who has had the opportunity to carry out his investigations without the need for immediate practical results, and he and his group have contributed much information about the basic physiology of the sheep under desert conditions.

Under hot field conditions Macfarlane (209) found that sheep deprived of water for 5 days produced an average amount of 1680 ml of urine, or 336 ml per day. The urine volume was higher (585 ml) when the experiment started, and declined to 130 ml per day by the 5th day. In all probability, this last figure represents the minimum urine volume consistent with normal physiological function. The average weight of the sheep was 50 kg and on a weight basis the urine production was therefore of the same magnitude as in one of our laboratory camels which weighed about five times as much and produced around $\frac{1}{2}$ litre of urine per day when dehydrated. One difference is that the camel, even when it was watered every day, did not increase its urine volume much, while sheep produce several times as much urine when they are watered regularly.

Under field conditions, when water was available to merino sheep that received dry rations, urine flows were $1\cdot34 \pm 0\cdot65$ litre per 24 hours in winter and $0\cdot73 \pm 0\cdot39$ litres per 24 hours in summer. In other words, daily urine volumes in summer were only about half of those in winter (209). These sheep, in spite of free access to water, had a relatively reduced urine volume during the season when active heat regulation by evaporation is necessary. An interesting contrast is provided by results obtained on cross-bred sheep in Scotland. When kept at $38°$ C, these showed greatly increased urine volumes, up to several times as much as at lower temperatures (56). This result is similiar to the over-drinking observed in some cows at high temperature (see p. 79), and suggests that the sheep attempted to keep cool by ingesting amounts of water far above the needs for excretion of urinary solids and for vaporization. It is, however, difficult to give a convincing explanation for the difference between the Scottish sheep and the Australian, for in addition to the temperature of the drinking-water, the level of the feeding (which greatly influences water intake), the breed of the sheep, and many other factors may be important.

An interesting case of differences in urine volumes that seems to be genetically determined has been reported by Evans (119). Among Scottish Blackface sheep some, designated LK, have a lower potassium content in the red blood-cells than the usual high potassium, HK, sheep. The LK and HK are genetically determined, and Evans reported a significantly different urine volume in the two types when fed and watered alike, 524 ml per day in LK and 734 ml per day in HK. Evans suggested that a study of inheritance may be of value in relation to sheep populations subjected to periodic drought or life in semi-arid environments. His observations were made on sheep that could drink freely— it remains unknown whether the minimum urine volume would be similarly related to genetic traits.

Urine concentrations. The highest osmotic concentration determined by Macfarlane in the urine of dehydrated sheep was 3·19 Osm. The simultaneous plasma concentration was slightly elevated, 0·42 Osm. The ratio between the concentrations in urine and in plasma, the U/P ratio, was therefore 7·6. This indicates the degree to which the urine was concentrated above the plasma, and shows that in the sheep the kidney is a quite efficient organ. In man the osmotic U/P ratio may be 4·2, but in the extremely efficient kidney of the sand rat it may reach about 17 (see p. 181). The sheep kidney by no means approaches this record, but must still be considered an organ well suited to eliminate excreta with a relatively small loss of water. (In a later chapter the concentrating ability of the kidney will be discussed in greater detail.)

Studies of the renal function of sheep in hot environments showed some interesting peculiarities (207). The glomerular filtration rate was about twice as high in summer as in winter. The greatest change in a single animal was from 138 to 40 ml per minute. This difference could not be ascribed to an acute effect of high temperature, for exposure to heat for 4 hours had no effect on the filtration rate. On the other hand, if the heat exposure was accompanied by dehydration, it depressed the filtration rate, but this is in the opposite direction of the natural summer change.

While the filtration varied conspicuously with the season, there were no changes in the renal plasma flow. Usually, sheep urine has a low concentration of sodium and a high of potassium. This is reasonable, for a plant-eater consumes food high in potassium and low in sodium. Sodium concentration in the urine may be less than 1 mEq per litre (209). Potassium is actively secreted by the renal tubule, which, again, is reasonable for a plant-eater.

As the respiratory rate increases during heat load, there is a progressive increase in the excretion of sodium, and the sodium:potassium ratio rises (211). This is opposite to the situation in man where sodium is retained by the kidney during heat stress. Sodium excretion during heating therefore seems linked to the method of evaporative cooling. In man, who produces a salty sweat, sodium is retained while in the sheep, which pants and evaporates without losing salts, sodium is excreted.

The tubular secretion of para-amino hippuric acid (PAH) was found to be high, twice that observed in other mammals. This is not at all surprising, for many plants contain benzoic acid and related compounds which are excreted as hippuric acid and its derivatives. The large amount of hippuric acid in the urine of the horse is precisely the reason that this compound was first isolated from horse urine (and named accordingly), and it is understandable that the kidneys of herbivores handle this substance more efficiently than those of carnivores (cat and dog) or man.

Tolerance to saline water. Recommendations made by various Australian authorities concerning the mineral content of water for livestock reveal considerable discrepancies in maximally allowed limits (249). Almost all authorities consider sheep more tolerant to salty water than other livestock, which are listed in approximately the following order: sheep, cattle, horse, swine. The recommendations vary from place to place, but the highest permitted concentrations of salt seem to be about 2·5 per cent sodium chloride for sheep, 2 per cent for cattle, and 1·5 per cent for horse and swine.

When an animal uses water for heat regulation, the entire concept of a maximally permissible limit for minerals in the drinking-water must be modified. If part of the ingested water is distilled off, the minerals remain and must be excreted with a reduced volume of water. For example, if half of the water is evaporated the other half must be used for excretion of the minerals in twice the concentration in which they were ingested. Since the limit for minerals is set by the concentrating ability of the kidney, the important consideration will be the ratio between the original volume of water ingested and the amount that remains after some has been used for evaporation. Thus, if evaporation is high in summer, a relatively low mineral content in the water may be intolerable, while in winter, when no water is evaporated in heat regulation, it may be perfectly acceptable and harmless to the animal.

The mammalian kidney cannot, to any appreciable extent, be trained to produce a more concentrated urine. It is therefore unlikely that an animal can 'learn' to eliminate excretory products with greater efficiency than characteristic for the particular species or breed. On the other hand, we have virtually no information about a possible increase in the amount of salt eliminated in the sweat. There seems to be a general agreement that very little, if any, salt is lost from the skin in the sheep, and the same is generally held true for cattle. There are, however, no quantitative investigations of cutaneous elimination of salts in domestic animals. We do know that the salt content of human sweat changes tremendously with a number of factors, such as degree of acclimatization, rate of sweat production, heat load, temperature of the skin, &c., and the relative proportion of the different ions can also change appreciably. The sweating mechanism in man is so different from that in most domestic animals that it is impossible to draw any conclusions by analogy, and the possible role of cutaneous elimination of salts should be studied in both sheep and cattle.

The long-term tolerance of sheep to drinking-water containing sodium chloride, sodium sulphate, and magnesium sulphate has been systematically studied (248, 250, 251). In experiments that lasted for 15 months 1 per cent sodium chloride had no ill effect, 1·5 per cent was detrimental to some sheep, and 2 per cent was detrimental to all. The general reaction of the sheep was to increase the volume of drinking with increasing salt concentration, and some sheep took in as much as 170 to 230 grammes of sodium chloride each day for 1 to 10 weeks. The increased drinking has one advantage: if the amount of water evaporated is of a given magnitude, it will constitute a smaller fraction of the total volume. The larger the ingested volume, the smaller is the increase in concentration due to evaporation. The kidney is much better able to handle large volumes of moderately concentrated urine than to excrete a small volume of highly concentrated urine.

Additions of sodium sulphate and magnesium chloride to the water had some adverse effect, and diarrhoea occurred occasionally. The most concentrated sulphate solution, which contained 0·9 per cent sodium chloride and 0·5 per cent sodium sulphate, had no adverse effect on the sheep. It seems that a careful study of the renal excretion of sulphate in the sheep, as well as in the camel, would be an interesting undertaking.

Dehydration and tolerance to water depletion

In field experiments carried out by the Macfarlane group in the hot arid regions of central Queensland, sheep were deprived of drinking-water for 5 days. As they stood in the summer sun they were given full rations of feed, so the additional strain of walking around to seek the food was absent. In these sheep the average body weight decreased from 50·3 kg to 38·5 kg, a loss of 23 per cent (209).

Macfarlane has told me that there was a considerable difference in tolerance to heat between animals investigated in his laboratory and similar sheep studied in the field. An exposure to 41° C for 3 days and a weight loss of 20 per cent was all the laboratory sheep could take, but in the field, weight losses could exceed 31 per cent. Of course, the conditions are not fully comparable, for the constant laboratory conditions give a time distribution of the heat stress entirely different from the daily cycle in the field, which includes a heavy radiation load during day and a cool night. Part of the weight loss undoubtedly is due to a simultaneous loss of tissue. The sheep is a relatively small animal and its metabolic rate is high enough to give an appreciable loss of body substance in a few days of starvation.

The daily weight loss in the Queensland sheep was of the same order of magnitude as that of the donkey in the Sahara, but an accurate comparison is not possible because we lack adequate information about their environments during the water deprivation. In all likelihood the heat load in the Sahara was more severe than in Queensland. The donkey could withstand 4 days without water with a weight loss of 30 per cent, but it could certainly not have lasted for another day or

perhaps two. Whether the difference between the sheep and the donkey
is due to the less severe climate in Queensland or to a slower loss of
water in the sheep cannot be evaluated at this time. My guess is that
both factors are involved, because the sheep, owing to the thickness of
their fleece, should have an advantage in a slower heat gain from the
environment. A disadvantage for the sheep is its smaller size. The
relative merits of heat regulation by sweating and panting could perhaps
be studied profitably in these two animals.

The statement that the sheep performs much like a camel (210) is only
partly true. The sheep certainly is one of the most tolerant domestic

TABLE XIII

*Changes in fluid compartments and in solute concentrations in sheep kept
without water for 5 days. From (209)*

	Initial	5 days without water	Per cent change
Body weight, kg	50·3	38·5	−23
Plasma vol., litre	3·16	1·74	−45
Extracellular fluid, litre	13·3	7·3	−45
Plasma Na, mEq/l	144·1	157·0	+ 9
Plasma Cl, mEq/l	111·0	142·0	+28
Plasma Osm. conc., mOsm.	314	420	+34

animals investigated so far, but it does not match the extremely low rate
of water loss of the camel. As we have seen before, the camel uses less
than one-quarter of the amount of water that the donkey uses for cooling
during the hot day under otherwise comparable conditions, and even if
the sheep should prove better than the donkey, it will not equal the camel.
Although it has a similar protective wool there are other differences
from which it cannot escape; the sheep is smaller and has a larger relative
surface, it does not utilize a fluctuating body temperature for temporary
heat storage, and it may be less tolerant to depletion of the body water.
Presently we shall see how it differs radically from the camel in the
distribution of a water loss between the various fluid compartments of
the body.

Plasma volume in dehydration. The most conspicuous change in fluid
distribution in sheep, when deprived of drinking-water for 5 days, was
the tremendous decrease in plasma volume which was reduced to almost
half of its initial value (see Table XIII). This is in sharp contrast to the
camel which suffered little loss of plasma volume in dehydration. Human physiologists have considered as very serious decreases in blood-
volume much smaller than those displayed by the sheep, and have

regarded them as the main cause of explosive heat rise and death in the hot desert. When we discussed the camel we suggested that one of the reasons for its excellent tolerance to water depletion was its ability to maintain plasma volume. In the sheep we now have an animal whose tolerance to heat and water depletion exceeds what is 'normal' for mammals and approaches that found in the camel, and still it shows a decrease in plasma volume which is quite amazing. There is a discrepancy in interpretation that needs clarification. Is it possible that the determinations of plasma volume with Evans blue are wrong? This does not seem to be the case, for the plasma protein concentration rose by 60 per cent during dehydration and the hematocrit by 39 per cent. Both these changes indicate that the measured reduction in plasma volume had actually taken place. In man the serious effect of reduced plasma volume is readily explained by the greatly increased blood-flow to the skin during heat exposure, and the tolerance of loss of plasma volume in sheep may partly be due to panting being the main mechanism of heat dissipation.

The volume of extracellular fluid shows a change similar to the plasma volume, but since it was determined by the thiocyanate method, it is more difficult to interpret the figure. Thiocyanate space is not well defined and it is unknown how dehydration might influence the distribution of the thiocyanate ion, and consequently the measured volume. The plasma sodium concentration showed a very moderate increase, considering the large amount of water lost, probably because part of it entered the cells. The plasma chloride, on the other hand, showed an increase which was close to the increase in the osmotic concentration of the plasma (34 per cent change), which probably is the best indication of the change in water content of the entire organism among the methods used so far. Of course, more detailed studies of water content and distribution of losses should involve determinations of total body water using isotope tracers (deuterium or tritium).

It is amazing that the reduced blood-volume does not have a dramatic effect on circulation. In fact, during actual exposure to heat the sheep showed less change in heart-rate than was observed in other animals similarly exposed. In sheep kept at 41° C for 7 hours, the heart-rate went up from normal rates of around 40 per minute to around 50 per minute (196). Unfortunately no information is available on heart performance as dehydration progresses to a more severe degree in hot surroundings, a subject that should be most interesting.

Drinking

Earlier in this book it was stated that the animal which drinks occasionally at a water hole where it may fall prey to a carnivore must drink fast and get away fast. Accordingly, the sheep should be able to drink their fill in a short time. When Macfarlane's sheep were offered water after 5 days, they drank 7 to 9 litres 'at once' (209). This is around 18 to 23 per cent of the dehydrated body weight and similar to the drinking capacity of camel and donkey. Since the average weight loss was 12 kg, and some fraction of this was due to loss of tissue, it seems that sheep drink to restore their water content, and do so rapidly. Unfortunately no timing of the drinking has been published by Macfarlane, and the data are insufficient for a careful evaluation of the degree of rehydration.

TABLE XIV

When sheep are watered at 3 or 4 days' intervals their water consumption is significantly lower than in sheep watered daily. From (82)

	Average water per day	Control sheep, daily watering
Water every 2 days	1·8	1·8
3 days	1·5	2·4
4 days	1·3	2·4

Withholding of water from sheep seems to have a 'sparing' effect on expenditure. In experiments where water was available for only 1 hour every other day, sheep drank as much as if watered daily, but the water consumption fell if the intervals were increased to 3 or 4 days (see Table XIV). These experiments were made in the late spring in South Africa with moderate air temperatures ranging up to 36° C. They suggest that a dehydrated sheep may be able to reduce its water expenditure, although they give no hint of the possible mechanism involved.

SUMMARY

Some breeds of sheep are highly resistant to hot arid conditions. The best investigated breed is the merino, which is widely used in Australia, but certain African and Asiatic sheep should be better adapted to semi-desert conditions.

The sheep keeps its body temperature relatively constant, and in hot surroundings excess heat is dissipated by panting. Some evaporation does take place from the skin.

The thick fleece is an excellent protection against heat flow from the environment. Its removal greatly decreases the tolerance to hot conditions.

The sheep has an exceptional tolerance to dehydration. A conspicuous feature in the distribution of the water loss is a drastic reduction in plasma volume to which the sheep does not appear as sensitive as could be expected.

7

CARNIVORES

THE carnivores are in a favourable position since the body fluids of their prey provide appreciable quantities of water. Furthermore, the water content of the food remains about equally high in summer as in winter. As a practical approximation one can say that two-thirds of the animal organism is water, a proportion that changes little with the seasons. It could therefore be suggested that carnivores should be independent of drinking-water, at least if no water is used for heat regulation. An indication that this may be so has been reported by Marais who, during an extensive drought in South Africa, noticed that the wild hunting dog (*Lycaon pictus*) was the only large animal not perceptibly inconvenienced by the absence of drinking-water (214).

The commonly known carnivores of deserts and arid lands are jackals, hyenas, coyotes, and foxes. The lion, which we associate with steppes and savannahs, was formerly common, but does not now extend into the Sahara proper. It is not known whether this is for lack of water or the lion's need for a more ample population of large herbivores than is now found in this vast desert area.

In the great Sahara Desert there are fourteen species of carnivores. All of these, with one exception, the small, fox-like fennec (*Fennecus zerda*), are found near water or oases, or are directly associated with them (102). Since carnivores move rapidly over long distances they can include a watering-place in their forays, especially if their drinking can be limited to intervals of several days.

Of the physiology of these wild animals, virtually nothing is known. The domestic dog, on the other hand, has long been a favoured subject of experimentation and is better understood than most other mammals. A discussion of its heat and water metabolism will reveal many interesting aspects which are probably more or less characteristic of carnivores in general.

THE DOG

The nomad in the central Sahara always has dogs around his camp. Together with camels, sheep, and man, they survive the hot summer, evidently able to tolerate the most extreme conditions of desert heat found anywhere. Almost 200 years ago, Dr. Blagden of the Royal Society took a dog with him into a room heated to 115° C. The dog was

PLATE 2

FENNECS (*FENNECUS ZERDA*)

This delightful fox-like animal from Sahara is the size of a small cat. The adults have even larger ears than these young animals

(*Courtesy, Zoological Society of Philadelphia*)

kept in a wicker basket so that it would not burn its feet and came out of the experiment completely unharmed. When Dill took his dog for walks in the Nevada desert, its feet were blistered by the hot sand, and to protect them he tied several cotton tobacco bags over each foot. The dog was then able to follow him on extended walks in the hot desert. Many desert animals have an advantage the dog lacks, they have foot soles covered with stiff hair that makes it possible for them to move with ease over the scorching desert surface (170).

In hot surroundings the dog depends on the evaporation of water for keeping his body temperature within reasonable limits. Most of this evaporation takes place from the moist surfaces of the tongue, the mouth, and the upper respiratory tract. The large tongue hangs out of the open mouth, increasing the exposed area, and the saliva flows freely, often dripping to the ground. The air movement is increased by a very rapid shallow respiration, known as panting.[1] The characteristic panting is entirely for purposes of heat dissipation, and is different from the increase in breathing that occurs in connexion with exercise. If a dog swims in cold water, ordinary breathing through the nose supplies enough oxygen for the needs, and there is no panting whatsoever (273).

The most characteristic aspect of panting is a very high respiratory frequency, often between 300 and 400 respirations per minute. In dogs in cool surroundings the respiratory rate is about 10 to 40 per minute, and when panting starts the frequency increases, usually abruptly, to rates in excess of 300 per minute. Intermediate rates are unusual, and Hemingway (150) observed no panting with respiratory rates less than 200. Dogs that are exposed to a moderate heat load often pant for a brief period, intermittently with periods of normal breathing. If observations are made over a period that includes both types of breathing, the average respiratory rate is intermediate, but such average rates do not represent the true panting frequency.

The panting of the dog occurs as a response to an increase in body temperature, whatever the cause. It is therefore possible to produce panting experimentally in various ways, by having the dog run on a treadmill in the laboratory, by exposing it to high air temperatures or radiation from light bulbs or other heaters, or by the application of diathermy. In every case panting occurs as an unequivocal response which counteracts the rise in body temperature. Diathermy has been particularly valuable because it permits the application of accurately measured and constant heat loads so that the response can be studied with great precision from the quantitative viewpoint. A number of valuable investigations, employing this technique, have come from Hemingway, who has also applied diathermic heating directly to the

[1] Early work on panting has been reviewed by Bazett (39).

hypothalamus, thereby demonstrating that the panting reflex is associated with the temperature of this part of the brain (151).

How efficient is panting in heat regulation?

Apparently, panting is a good way of dissipating heat. Many investigators have exposed dogs to hot atmospheres and found that they are excellent temperature regulators. The dog was included among the domestic animals that were systematically tested for heat tolerance by Lee and his collaborators (278). When dogs were kept for 7 hours in the hot-room, they proved tolerant to 41° C. At 44° C and high humidity (65 per cent) they had to be removed after 3 or 4 hours with a rectal temperature of almost 42° C. At lower humidities, however, they could tolerate 43° C room temperature for the full 7 hours without any significant elevation in rectal temperature. It is therefore evident that the panting mechanism is quite efficient for cooling at low humidities, but it suffers from the same disadvantage as all other evaporative cooling in that it becomes increasingly ineffective at higher atmospheric humidities.

Advantages and disadvantages of panting

One of the most obvious beneficial aspects of panting is that the animal provides its own ventilation of the cooling surfaces. Another advantage is that the panting animal avoids the salt loss which may be serious when man sweats. It has also been pointed out, although incorrectly (see page 111), that when evaporation takes place from the respiratory tract rather than from the skin there is an economy in circulation because blood that is sent to the lungs is both oxygenated and cooled.

One main disadvantage of panting is that the increased respiration, unless it is very shallow, gives a greater exchange of air in the lungs than desirable, causing the removal of excess carbon dioxide from the blood and severe alkalosis. Another disadvantage is that the increased frequency of respiration involves increased muscular work, which not only requires energy but also adds to the heat production of the organism.

Since panting is such a unique form of heat regulation, these various aspects deserve further discussion. Some points will take only a few sentences, but others will require a more detailed treatment.

The salt loss. As we have seen the salt loss in the sweat of man may be a serious and completely incapacitating phenomenon. There is reason to believe that this does not hold for other sweating animals, for probably both the donkey and the camel have minimal salt losses in their sweat.

The panting dog can frequently be seen with saliva drooling from the mouth, but the amount of fluid lost is only a small fraction of the amount evaporated. An excess flow of saliva is, of course, no necessity for the cooling mechanism to be efficient. Different animal species apparently differ greatly in their salivation response; sheep show no tendency to excess salivation and dripping (197), while in cattle the drooling of saliva may amount to a loss of as much as 18 litres per day (65). Since drooling is physiologically unnecessary, panting need not involve any salt loss at all. Sweat, on the other hand, will always contain some salt, although there is no biological necessity for the salt loss to reach the magnitude often encountered in man.

Air movement over the cooling surface. At the low humidities in the desert man does not require any extra air movement for the sweat to evaporate. Usually, evaporation is so fast that the skin seems dry although the sweating rate may be as high as 1 litre or more per hour, and additional movement of the hot air over the surface merely increases the heat load. In the dry desert, therefore, the cooling mechanism of the dog does not give it any obvious advantages over sweating animals in this respect.

At lower temperatures the situation is different. Dill (104) has pointed out the superiority of the dog over man in dissipating heat produced by exercise under ordinary laboratory conditions. Here, the dog has a great advantage in providing his own ventilation over the cooling surface, while a man who does hard work requires air movement for comfort. Unfortunately we lack adequate quantitative information about the relative merits of sweating and panting at various temperatures and humidities. Studies of this problem are difficult because of the many complications involved with animals different in so many other respects, including body size and surface insulation. It would, however, be extremely interesting to see a broad comparative study of the relative efficiency of sweating and panting.

Is there an economy in circulation? When heat is dissipated from the skin of man this requires a considerable cutaneous flow of blood which is diverted from its usual function of carrying oxygen. It has been pointed out that one of the outstanding physiological advantages in panting is that it places no additional burden on the circulation because the blood must pass to the respiratory system in any event. This argument would be correct if the evaporation took place from the lungs, but all available information indicates that this is not so.

Apparently evaporation takes place mainly from the large hanging tongue and the moist surfaces of the mouth, with the upper part of the air passages contributing only to a minor extent. The strongest indication that heat loss from the lungs themselves is insignificant is gained from the fact that there is no measurable temperature difference between the blood in the pulmonary artery and the pulmonary vein. If the blood coming from the lungs were able to cool the remaining parts of the body to any appreciable extent, it would have to be considerably cooler than the blood coming to the lung. When the dog breathes normally at 20° C air temperature the difference across the lungs is 0·01° C, and at −18° C the difference is increased to 0·03° C, i.e. when the inspired air is 56° C cooler than the body (and virtually completely dry), it still does not cool the blood in the lungs appreciably (222). This does not prove that pulmonary cooling is insignificant in panting, but it makes it extremely unlikely that the shallow breathing could have any effect on deep lung temperatures. We can therefore assume that in the dog the lungs play no measurable role in heat dissipation. In cattle blood temperatures have been measured at high air temperatures, and whether the animals breathe normally or pant heavily there is no measurable temperature difference (58). Neither in man has any temperature difference been demonstrated across the lungs (115).

If there is no evaporation in the lungs, the cooling surfaces must be higher up. Since they have no function in gas exchange, they will require a blood-supply of the same magnitude as necessary when evaporation takes place from the skin. This is corroborated by the finding that the blood-flow to the tongue of the dog was increased sixfold when the rectal temperature was 42° C, and the rise in tongue blood-flow began about the same time as the onset of panting (113). In other words, the suggested economy in circulation in the panting animal is not a reality.

Gas exchange during panting. It is a common textbook statement that during panting respiration becomes so shallow that the gas exchange in the lungs is not increased, in spite of the high frequency of respiration (111). This belief is not supported by actual studies of the panting animal, provided the experimental approach does not introduce errors.

The simplest way to establish whether or not there is an alteration in air exchange in the lungs is to measure the carbon dioxide tension of the arterial blood. Since this is in equilibrium with the alveolar air, the composition of the alveolar air can be accurately determined from the blood sample. The advantage of this approach is that the information is gained without any kind of interference with the breathing of the animal. The application of a mask with valves to obtain gas samples or to measure tidal volume involves an increased resistance to air flow, increased dead space, and other interferences with free breathing. Therefore, blood sampling is not only the simplest but also the most reliable way that information can be gained about the ventilation of the lungs. In the panting dog the carbon dioxide content of the blood is decreased, sometimes to as little as one-quarter of the normal value, showing a tremendous over-ventilation of the lungs.[1] In the absence of panting, the carbon dioxide content of the alveolar air remains exceedingly constant, both at rest and during work (14, 126, 273). A change in the alkalinity of the blood with a decrease in its carbon dioxide content has also been observed in panting cattle, although these animals, as we have seen, depend mainly on their sweating mechanism for the dissipation of heat (51).

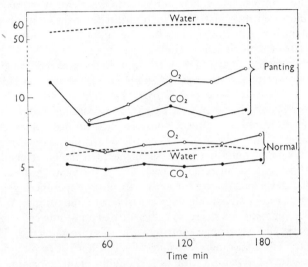

FIG. 23. Changes in respiratory gas exchange and in evaporation in a panting dog. Note the broken ordinate for evaporation, which increased about tenfold during panting. O_2 and CO_2 in ml per kg body weight per minute, H_2O in mg per kg per minute. (Reproduced with permission from Shelley and Hemingway (313).)

As carbon dioxide is removed from the blood there is a considerable change in the pH of the blood in the alkaline direction, and the panting dog, which has lost three-quarters of its blood CO_2, exhibits a degree of alkalosis which would be intolerable to man. When a man removes carbon dioxide from the blood by voluntary hyperventilation, the alkalosis is sufficiently severe to bring him to the stage of beginning tetanic cramps and loss of consciousness when one-third of the total carbon dioxide has been lost (314). Part of the physiological mechanism of panting, therefore, must be an unusual tolerance to alkalosis.

Many of the changes which occur in connexion with panting can best be discussed by reference to Fig. 23. In this particular experiment the

[1] It is possible that CO_2 is lost from the tongue. This would change the conclusions regarding ventilation of the lungs, but the statement regarding tolerance to alkalosis would remain unaltered.

evaporation of water from the respiratory tract was increased tenfold, from about 6 mg H_2O per kg per minute to between 50 and 60. The increase in gas exchange was reflected in the release of carbon dioxide at an initial rate of more than twice the normal, a rate that subsided somewhat during the following hours. The oxygen consumption, in the control dogs 6 ml per kg per minute, was over 8 ml early in the experiment and gradually increased to 12. This rise in oxygen consumption is important but, unfortunately, it is not clear to what extent it was caused by the increased muscular work involved in the panting itself, and to what extent it was due to the fact that the animals became more active and restless at high air temperatures.

The respiratory quotient (RQ), the ratio between carbon dioxide release and oxygen taken up, was very high during the early period of the experiment, as could be expected from the high release of CO_2 without a corresponding increase in oxygen consumption. Later, the RQ gradually decreased and after 2 hours reached normal values. At this time, therefore, the release of CO_2 corresponded to the oxygen intake, and the alkalosis would not progress further. On the other hand, with the large excess amounts removed early during the panting, the alkalosis which had developed during the early part of the experiment persisted.

One observation on panting dogs is particularly interesting. Although the tidal volume did not decrease sufficiently to prevent over-ventilation of the lungs, another change contributed in this direction (150). During panting the chest was more expanded than in normal respiration, and there was, therefore, an increase in the amount of air remaining in the lungs at the end of each expiration. The volume of air inhaled during inspiration would therefore constitute a smaller fraction of the air already in the lung and give less 'washout' of CO_2 than would occur with a normal residual volume.

The work of panting. The increased work of the respiratory muscles adds to the metabolic heat production and thus to the heat load. To some extent this is a vicious circle: the greater the need for heat dissipation, the more heat is generated. This raises the question, what is the actual cost of panting, and what does it mean in the over-all heat balance?

Unfortunately, the direct measurement of the heat production during panting cannot be used as a measure for the cost of the panting mechanism, for other factors are involved. It was mentioned above that the additional activity of the animal at high temperature is responsible for part of the increase in oxygen consumption, and since there is likely to be some increase in body temperature, this factor also contributes to an increased oxygen uptake not forming part of the cost of panting.

The energy requirement for the ventilation of the lungs of man has been carefully worked out by Otis, Fenn, and Rahn (242). In all probability these calculations do not apply to the increased respiration in the dog for the reason that panting apparently takes place at the resonant frequency of the respiratory system.

It has been pointed out by many investigators that the dog changes abruptly from resting respiration to panting, and that there are no intermediate rates of respiration. Although each dog seems to have its

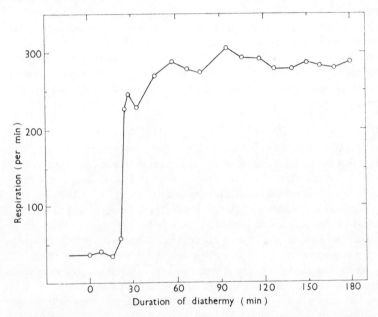

FIG. 24. When a dog begins panting the respiratory frequency rises abruptly from normal values of 20 to 40 per minute to characteristically high rates of several hundred respirations per minute. Intermediate rates usually do not occur. (Reproduced with permission from Hemingway (150).)

characteristic response, they all follow a similar pattern with a sudden increase to a characteristic high frequency, without intermediate rates (see Fig. 24). Crawford interpreted this response as a means to reduce the work of the respiratory muscles (91). If the dog pants at the same frequency with which the respiratory system oscillates naturally, the energy necessary to keep it going will be a small fraction of what would otherwise be required. To test whether the panting takes place at the resonant frequency, Crawford first determined the mean panting-rate in 10 dogs and found it to be 320 $\pm$ 42 cycles per minute. The resonant frequency of the same animals was then determined and found to be 316 $\pm$ 18 cycles per minute. These findings seem to support the idea that the dog minimizes its heat production by utilizing the natural resonant frequency of its respiratory system.

If the dog were to breathe without taking advantage of the elastic rebound, the energy requirement for the work of breathing could be calculated from the equation of Otis, Fenn, and Rahn (242). Crawford showed that, according to this calculation, the heat generated by panting, if added to the basic metabolic heat of the animal, would make it difficult to evaporate enough water to keep a dog in heat balance in an environment of $35°$ C and 50 per cent relative humidity. This obviously leaves no excess cooling power for external heat loads or increased heat production by exercise. If, on the other hand, dogs make use of the phenomenon of resonance, cooling can be achieved with a more moderate increase in internal heat production, thus economizing with energy as well as with water.

Sweat and sweat glands

It is commonly stated that the skin of the dog contains no sweat glands, but this is probably based on the observation that no sweat secretion is visible on the skin of a dog which is under obvious heat stress. There are numerous microscopic examinations of the skin of the dog which point out the presence of sweat glands, these being found in almost all areas of the skin, most numerous on the back, fewer on the neck and sides, and least on the ventral surface (83). These skin glands apparently do not secrete much fluid in response to a general heat stress. The panting mechanism is very efficient in heat dissipation, and evaporation from the skin seems insignificant in general heat regulation.

The skin glands can, however, secrete fluid, and they will do so in response to the injection of pilocarpin (116). Do these glands have any normal function in heat regulation? This question was investigated by Aoki and Wada (15) who found no general response of the sweat glands in dogs that were sufficiently heated to produce pronounced panting. However, dogs subjected to heating in a wooden cabinet with four 100-watt electric bulbs exhibited some local sweating in skin areas directly exposed to the radiant heat, the threshold skin temperature for sweating being from $38·4°$ to $38·7°$ C.

The presence of a sweating mechanism which is not controlled from the central nervous system, but which responds to local temperatures in the skin, can be interpreted as a protective mechanism against local overheating of the skin. In a dog, where essentially all dissipation of heat is accomplished from the respiratory tract, the skin will attain a high temperature when the animal is exposed to sun. A slight amount of sweating in the skin can, to some extent, offset such local overheating. It seems, however, that the major part of the heat which flows towards the skin must be absorbed by the blood and transported to the cooling surfaces of the respiratory tract. The sweating can, however, be essential if there is an immediate threat of over-heating to such an extent that tissue damage may be involved. Further studies of the quantities of heat that can be dissipated by evaporation from the skin as related to the thickness of the hairy cover should give information as to whether or not the mechanism has the importance suggested here.

The dog in the desert

Heat exchange. To a dog, life in the desert is rather different from the experimental hot-room in the laboratory, mainly because of the intense radiation from the sun and from the hot desert surface. Since the dog does not sweat much, his skin should become quite hot. The surface layer of the fur should attain temperatures similar to that of the ground, which may be 70° C and, depending on the insulation value of the fur, there should be a variable but appreciable flow of heat towards the body.

It should not be overlooked that the high skin temperature, although it causes a flow of heat from the skin towards the deeper parts of the body, is an advantage in the heat balance of the animal. This statement may seem paradoxical, for a superficial consideration may lead to the impression that a flow of heat from the deeper parts towards the skin, as in man, would be more advantageous.

If we, for the moment, consider only the exchange of heat between the surface of the organism and a typical hot environment, with the air at 40° C and the ground surface at 70° C, we have a situation roughly as follows (cf. Fig. 25).

In man the average skin temperature is maintained somewhere around 35° C by the evaporation of sweat. This dissipates the metabolic heat that flows to the surface from deeper parts, but in addition the surface receives heat by conduction and radiation. The conductive heat flow from the air (40° C) to the skin surface (35° C) is over a gradient of 5° C. The radiation exchange between skin (35° C) and ground (70° C) gives a net flow towards the skin over a gradient of 35° C (this exchange is in the far infra-red and therefore independent of visible surface colour). The radiation heat gain from the sun is virtually independent of the skin surface temperature (the portion of the visible light absorbed depends on the reflectivity of the skin, but in the infra-red all energy is absorbed, irrespective of coat colour).

In the dog the fur surface absorbs radiation from the sun, independently of surface temperature (the fraction of visible light absorbed again depends on reflectivity). Since the surface of the fur may be nearly as hot as the ground, the difference in temperature between the ground and the fur surface will be small, and the net radiation flux towards the

skin will be greatly reduced relative to that in man. (Adequate measurements of fur-surface temperatures of dogs in a desert environment are
unavailable—hence the vague statements.) The most important difference between man and dog is that in dog the surface temperature is
higher than the air temperature, therefore there will be a loss of heat by
conduction from the surface to the air. What happens is that part of

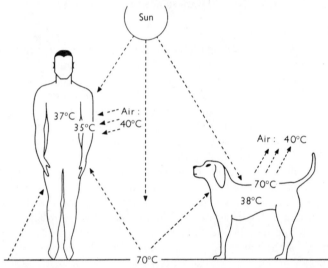

FIG. 25. In the hot desert the heat exchange is different in man and dog. Due
to the low surface temperature in man there is an appreciable heat flow from the hot
air to the cooler skin as well as radiation from the ground to the skin. In the dog,
however, where skin temperature is higher, heat is lost by conduction from the skin
to the air, and furthermore, radiation from the ground is less than in man. Since the
radiation gain from the sun is independent of skin temperature it is of similar
magnitude in the two. (By wearing clothes man shifts his heat exchange in the
direction of that of the dog, and thereby reduces the environmental heat load, cf.
page 20.)

the heat which is absorbed in the form of solar radiation is dissipated by
conduction to the air, instead of being removed by the evaporation of
water such as in man.

It is worth noting that exactly the same principle applies to the camel
and other fur-bearing animals. Part of the absorbed radiant heat is
dissipated by conduction to the air, a situation that is inevitable when
the temperature of the wool surface exceeds the air temperature. Thus,
this is not a characteristic of the panting animal, the dog, but a consequence of an insulating fur whose surface can attain temperatures far
above those tolerated by the nude skin of man.

Performance in the desert. Some very instructive comparisons between
man and dog were made by Dill during his studies at Boulder Dam,

Nevada (104, 106). Preliminary observations indicated that the dog was not as well adapted as man to desert conditions, particularly when sunlight was intense. The dog preferred to remain inactive in the shade, and if taken for a walk in the sun, it soon became uncomfortable. In one experiment the man and the dog walked for 3·2 km out into the desert and returned over the same route, requiring 70 minutes for the round trip of 6·4 km. The dog made four such trips, covering about 26 km, and the man five, covering 32 km. At the end of each round trip, observations were made of rectal temperature, body weight, water intake, and the properties of the blood. The major aspects of the water exchange are summarized in Table XV.

TABLE XV

Water exchange of man and dog in the Nevada desert. From (104)

	Man	Dog
Gross water loss, per cent of body weight per hour	1·74	2·61
Net water loss, per cent of body weight per hour	0·59	0·1
Total gross water loss, per cent of body weight	12·4	15·2
Total net water loss, per cent of body weight	4·2	0·7

The comparison of the amount of water evaporated per hour by the man and the dog (top line of the table) shows that the dog used about 50 per cent more water. But, as was discussed in Chapter 2, the heat load in the desert consists of two components which are both approximately proportional to the body surface, metabolic heat and heat load from the environment. It would therefore be reasonable to recalculate the evaporation in relation to the surface of the two organisms, and we then find that the evaporation per m² body surface was 0·73 kg per hour in the man and only 0·66 kg in the dog. Thus, both species evaporate at nearly the same rate when exposed to exactly the same conditions of temperature and exercise in the desert.

The small difference in favour of the dog which was observed is not sufficiently well documented to be used for a detailed evaluation of what advantages a dog may possess. One obvious advantage to consider is the insulation value of the fur; a disadvantage is the horizontal position of the body which exposes more of the surface to the sun than in the erect man. Depending on coloration, the reflection of visible solar radiation may be higher or lower than in man. Further studies under actual desert conditions would be highly desirable.

The fact that the dog used a little less water than man, relative to his surface area, should not detract from the fact that he used more water in proportion to the body weight. Since death from dehydration occurs when the depletion of body water reaches a critical limit, it is the water loss relative to body weight that is significant to survival. This determines how long the animal can continue using water from its body resources when none is available for drinking.

In Dill's experiment both man and dog drank as much as desired at the completion of each round trip. The striking difference that appeared was that the dog would drink an amount almost equal to the water loss, while man underwent a considerable voluntary dehydration. This is indicated as the net water loss in the second line of Table XV.

TABLE XVI

Changes in plasma chloride and protein concentrations in man and dog after 5 hours' walk in a hot desert.

Same experiment as in Table XV. From (106)

	Man	Dog
Initial plasma chloride, mN	102·6	111·5
Final plasma chloride	103·5	113·2
Initial plasma protein, g/100 ml	7·35	6·35
Final plasma protein	8·79	6·32

During the entire experimental period, nearly 5 hours for the dog and 6 hours for the man, the total amount of water evaporated (3rd line of table) was 12 per cent in the man and 15 per cent of the body weight in the dog. The last line, giving the total net water loss, indicates that the expenditure of water in the dog had been virtually completely covered by drinking, with the exception of 0·7 per cent of the body weight, so little that it could not be measured with accuracy. The man, however, although he had been in the position to drink as much as he wanted, had incurred a voluntary dehydration of 4 per cent.

Dill suggests that the explanation for this difference lies in the salt balance. The man was losing salt continuously in the sweat, and drank only enough to maintain the normal plasma chloride concentration (see Table XVI). The dog, on the other hand, lost virtually no salt, and would therefore maintain an unchanged plasma concentration if he drank exactly as much as he evaporated. This should then lead to the maintenance of an unchanged plasma volume in the dog, while man should become increasingly dehydrated. This simple explanation for the voluntary dehydration in man does not hold true, however, for if the plasma chloride is kept up by drinking salt solutions, man still does not drink sufficiently to make up for the loss. The plasma protein concentrations observed by Dill indicate that the plasma volume remained unchanged in the dog, while in man plasma water provided a disproportionate share of the water loss, such as observed later by many other investigators (see Chapter 1).

Drinking

The dog has been the subject of a number of excellent investigations concerned with the physiological regulation of drinking (354). The feeling of 'thirst' or an urge to drink normally occurs in response to a relative water deficiency in the organism, and since the water intake, in the long run, is accurately adjusted to the needs, there must be some regulating mechanism. When a thirsty animal drinks it is satiated within a few minutes, long before the water has left the stomach and replaced the deficiency in the blood and tissues. How does the animal know how much to drink, is the satiation a result of the moistening of the mouth, is the water 'metered' as it passes down the oesophagus, or does the degree of distension of the stomach tell the organism when to stop?

By providing dogs with oesophageal fistulae, the act of drinking can proceed without water reaching the stomach. Such dogs continue 'drinking' and swallow two or three times the real water deficit and take in as much as $4\frac{1}{2}$ litres in 10 minutes before they are temporarily satiated (43). This indicates that when the water does not reach the stomach the animal's ability to measure its intake is seriously impaired. If the stomach is distended with a balloon, the sham drinking is reduced in volume, and distension of the stomach is therefore clearly a regulating factor. If the balloon is kept distended the dog will start drinking again, for it is still as dehydrated as it was before, but the sham drinking will again be at a reduced level, both in volume and frequency.

Although dogs vary in their individual responses, the experiments indicate that satiation of thirst includes an immediate temporary effect which depends on the amount of water passing the oesophagus as well as upon the distension of the stomach. A subsequent permanent satiation follows the absorption of water from the intestine and dilution of the body fluids. In the absence of the dilution which follows the uptake of water, sham drinking continues at short intervals (21, 43, 335). This is in complete accord with Andersson's studies of the drinking in goats where it was shown that the urge to drink is controlled from a 'thirst centre' in the hypothalamic region of the brain (12).

The water balance of a meat-eater

From the viewpoint of water balance, the most characteristic features of the diet of the carnivore are the high water content and the relatively large amounts of protein in the food. In mammals, the protein is metabolized to urea, which requires considerable amounts of water for its excretion in the urine. The problem is whether the water contained in the food is sufficient for this excretion as well as the inevitable evaporation from the lungs and the loss with the faeces. If this account can balance, it permits a carnivore to remain in water balance and frees it from the necessity of drinking, as long as the need for heat regulation does not impose additional demands on the water reserves.

In principle the problem of the water balance in a meat-eater has been solved by a study made by Irving and his collaborators of the water metabolism of the seal when it feeds on fish (164). The calculations were

TABLE XVII

Water available to a carnivore that eats a rabbit weighing 1 kg.

(*Composition of rabbit quoted from (243).*)

	Food component, g	Oxygen used, litre	Water formed, g
Protein	181	175	72
Fat	78	157	84
Free water	692		692
Total		332	848

made on the assumption that the seal does not drink sea water. They showed that after losses through evaporation from the lungs and with the faeces have been covered, ample water still remains for the excretion of the salts contained in the food and the urea formed in its metabolism. Of course, the seal needs no water for heat regulation, and for the terrestrial animal in this situation the problems are fundamentally the same. The amounts of free water, oxidation water, urea formed, and salts are of the same magnitude in the two cases. The total amount of water available if a dog eats a rabbit weighing 1 kg, is, according to Table XVII, 848 ml. Can this cover the needs?

The evaporation from the lungs can be calculated from the pulmonary ventilation. The uptake of 332 litres O_2 requires a ventilation of 6640 litres (standard conditions, $0°$ C and 760 mm). This air is inhaled relatively dry and exhaled moist. When this air is heated to $35°$ C (temperature of expired air) its volume increases to 7400 litres. If we assume that the average dry desert air has a relative humidity of 10 per cent at $30°$ C, it contains 3 mg H_2O per litre. To bring this air to saturation at $35°$ C (39 mg H_2O per litre) 36 mg H_2O must be added per litre, or 269 grammes for the total volume of air. The protein yields 62 grammes of urea in metabolism, and if excreted as a 12 per cent solution this takes 475 ml H_2O. (The concentrating ability of the dog kidney is similar to that of the rat; see Table XXVI, page 181.) The electrolytes from the rabbit body are no worry when the urine volume is this high, the concentration in the urine will only be some 50 per cent higher than in the rabbit fluids, and the dog can concentrate the urine electrolytes more than twice as high again.

The volume of faeces in a carnivore is relatively small, and it is safe to assume that no more than 50 grammes H_2O will be lost this way (on a mixed diet man loses 100 grammes H_2O per day with the faeces) (320).

The total account therefore gives a combined loss of 794 grammes H_2O against the 848 grammes available, and, if all assumptions are correct, the dog should be able to remain in water balance, provided no water evaporates from the skin. On this point available information is inadequate, and this makes the entire calculation uncertain. If cutaneous loss is very low, and particularly if atmospheric humidity is higher than assumed, thus reducing pulmonary evaporation, it should be feasible for a carnivore to remain in water balance on its normal diet. If, however, there is need for a large surplus to be used for temperature regulation, this most certainly cannot be provided without other sources of water.

Tolerance to dehydration

As far as I know no study has been made of the water balance of dogs on a diet of animal food only. If they are fed an ordinary laboratory diet, the situation is different, the water content is lower and salts often higher. If they are now deprived of drinking-water they will stop eating, and the ensuing weight loss will be a combination of water loss and the result of starvation. Therefore, it is difficult to make any evaluation of water balance from such experiments.

If dogs are exposed to high temperatures the evaporation of water leads to rapid dehydration, which, as we have seen, can take place at a rate of between 2 and 3 per cent of the body weight per hour.

Such exposures to heat have been used to study the effects of extreme dehydration in the dog (9). When dogs were exposed to air at about 50° C, they promptly started to pant. If no water was given they lost weight by evaporation at the rate of about 1·5 per cent of the body weight per hour. Progressively the same changes appeared as seen in man: increased pulse-rate, rising rectal temperature, increased plasma concentrations, and gradually some reduction in the amount of saliva that dripped from the hanging tongue. The frequency of panting was maintained, but when the dehydration reached 10 to 14 per cent of the body weight, the animal's rectal temperature started to rise explosively. At this stage the animal could be saved if it was removed from the hot atmosphere, or if it received water to drink. If the rectal temperature was 41·7° C the dog would recover without complications and, occasionally, animals that had temperatures as high as 42·0° C survived. It is worth noting that this is very close to the critical rectal temperature observed for a number of other mammals as well.

If the explosive heat rise was prevented, the dogs could survive greater degrees of dehydration. In a cool atmosphere dogs would recover rapidly after dehydration that amounted to as much as 17 per cent of the body weight. What is the reason for this difference?

Evidently the dehydration makes the dog intolerant to heat. There are two main possibilities to explain this phenomenon: (a) evaporation from the respiratory tract decreases and the cooling mechanism breaks down as the progressing dehydration makes water unavailable; or (b) although evaporation continues there is a circulatory failure which makes it impossible for the blood to carry metabolic heat at a sufficient rate to the cooling surfaces. The first of these possibilities can be eliminated, for the mouth is still moist and the membranes cool as the dog enters the stage of explosive heat rise. The other possibility, that of circulatory failure, is a more likely possibility. The heart is already strained by a high pulse-rate, and while an increased circulation is needed to the cooling surfaces, blood-volume is reduced due to dehydration and a disproportionate decrease in plasma volume, and the viscosity of the blood is increased as the protein concentration goes up with the water loss.

The picture is very similar to the breakdown which occurs in circulatory shock, and the causes are much the same. There is, in the dehydrated dog, the conflict between the increased need for blood-flow to the cooling surfaces and the reduction in blood-volume which, at some point, makes it impossible to meet the demands on the circulatory system. Once the capacity of the compensatory mechanisms is exceeded, the animal rapidly enters irreversible circulatory failure, which in hot surroundings results in the explosive increase in deeper temperatures as heat transport is eliminated.

THE CAT

When cats are exposed to hot atmospheres under laboratory conditions they exhibit a tolerance which is close to that of the dog. The 7-hour exposure which was used as a standard test of domestic animals by Lee and his group could be tolerated by the cat at 41° C air temperature and 65 per cent relative humidity (277). A temperature of 43° C could be tolerated for only 2 hours, and the cat had to be removed with a rapidly rising rectal temperature. At lower humidities, however, the cat could tolerate this high temperature for almost 7 hours.

The main burden of heat regulation in the cat is carried by panting. Respiratory rates in Lee's experiments changed from initial values around 60 to panting rates very close to 240 to 250 respirations per minute. At the three highest temperatures, 38° C, 41° C, and 43° C (actually 100°, 105°, and 110° F) the respiratory rates remained within 240 to 255 per minute, in spite of the tremendous difference in heat load at these three temperatures. It therefore seems likely that the cat utilizes a well-defined respiratory frequency, probably corresponding to the natural resonant frequency of the respiratory system, such as was demonstrated for the dog by Crawford (91).

In addition to the increased respiration during heat stress, the cat makes use of its saliva by spreading it over its coat. This method of increasing the cooling is adopted by the cat when the body temperature rises to 40° C or more (277).

The cat is the first animal of those we have discussed so far in which the saliva is purposefully used for cooling the outer surface. This type of cooling is, however, widespread among marsupials, such as will be discussed in a later chapter. A number of small rodents, which normally are not exposed to heat and do not use water for heat regulation, have an emergency reaction which consists of a copious salivation and wetting of the fur when the body temperature approaches the lethal limit (296).

Cats can withstand somewhat higher rectal temperature than dogs, probably slightly above 43° C (9). This was also reported by Prouty who found that they tolerated rectal temperatures between 43° and 44° C and tended to coat accessible parts of the skin with saliva at the high temperatures (267).

Tolerance to dehydration. Since cats evaporate water for heat regulation, they can be dehydrated rapidly so that weight loss due to starvation is not a complicating factor in the evaluation of the effects of water loss. They can withstand acute dehydration slightly better than dogs, with water losses reaching as much as 20 per cent of the body weight (9). Similar results have also been obtained in earlier experiments, where the weight loss ranged from 18 to 26 per cent when the animals died from exposure to temperatures above 38° C. This degree of dehydration was reached in from 20 to 27 hours (93).

The ability of cats to live without water has been tested in rather extensive experiments (75) which, however, are difficult to interpret because it is uncertain when weight was due to water loss or decreased food intake. This shortcoming was carefully avoided in the work of Wolf and his collaborators (265, 355). These workers demonstrated that cats could be kept successfully without drinking on diets of cod fillets, fresh frozen salmon, or ground round beefsteak. In these studies it appeared that the concentrating ability of the cat's kidney is quite high, somewhat above that of rat and dog. The highest concentrations observed were 2550 mM urea and 3·25 Osm total osmotic concentration.

If the fish or meat had been partly dehydrated by the removal of some of the water, the cats were unable to maintain themselves, they lost weight, and had increased plasma concentrations. If sea water was given to drink with this diet, which in itself was too low in water content to sustain the cats, they would thrive and maintain water balance, and even overcome previously incurred water deficits. This finding can perhaps be explained most easily by a hypothetical example. Let us assume that a cat has formed 20 grammes urea and that 100 ml H_2O are available for excretion. The necessary 20 per cent urea concentration is above the capacity of the kidney, but with the aid of 100 ml sea water the urea can be excreted with 200 ml of water as a 10 per cent solution. The 3·5 grammes salt in the sea water in combination with the smaller amount of salt from the fish can also be handled with ease by the kidney when the urine volume is 200 ml.

This is an example of how sea water can be utilized with advantage, even though urine salt concentrations cannot reach as high as those in the sea water, when some water is available from other sources. In the starving animal, or for the castaway on a raft without food, sea water cannot be of any such benefit, and its ingestion will merely lead to faster dehydration.

WILD DESERT CARNIVORES

Virtually no information exists about wild desert carnivores. In all probability, they can combat heat by panting, similar to dogs and cats. When water is not needed for heat regulation they should be able to remain in water balance on the water supplied from the body fluids of their prey plus that gained from oxidation.

The larger desert carnivores probably depend on access to drinking-water, at least during the warm part of the year. The only Saharan carnivore that seems entirely independent of drinking-water is the fennec (*Fennecus zerda*). Monod (228) found that this little fox-like animal, which weighs less than a kilogramme, is one of the commonest mammals of the Empty Quarter of north-western Sahara. The fennec lives on a mixed diet consisting of insects, lizards, rodents, and more plant material than is commonly consumed by carnivores. The animal digs rather deep burrows so that exposure during the hot day can be kept to a minimum, and probably very little water need be used for heat regulation.

The young fennecs are born in the burrows in the early spring, and the arabs frequently dig them out and sell them to the settled population in the oases, where they are fattened to be eaten when they grow up. The young looks very much like a small grey kitten with a short stubby tail and small rounded ears. As they grow the ears grow out of proportion, and the adult animal seems to be mostly ears. I had two of these delightful animals as house pets in the Sahara, and later was able to have them in my home in the United States. During the summer in the Sahara they would pant in characteristic dog fashion if they got overheated from playing on a hot day. It is therefore evident that they do have the characteristic panting response and can use water for heat regulation. Obviously, if they live in areas where no drinking-water is available, they cannot rely on this mode of heat regulation to any great extent, and burrowing and nocturnal habits are a necessary part of the water-conservation mechanisms.

My tame animals were given anything they liked to eat, small scraps from the table, meat, bread, various vegetables, and fruits. They had a particular liking for sweet, juicy fruits such as peaches and strawberries, but they refused to touch strawberries bought in grocery stores, perhaps because these had been treated with chemicals that retard spoilage. On this mixed diet, with all the water the animals cared to drink, as well as frequent drinks of milk, urine concentrations were often quite high.

In one such sample the urea concentration was 2620 mM, or close to 16 per cent. This is higher than the highest urea concentration found under the most extreme experimental conditions in cats, and since the fennec probably can concentrate its urine much further, it is likely that it can sustain its water balance better than a cat, which can manage on fresh meat or fish. This suggests that the fennec should be able to excrete the urea derived from the metabolism of its carnivorous diet and easily remain in water balance. The importance of the water contained in the vegetable components of its usual diet in the wild, when much plant material is included, and the extent to which water is used in heat regulation will remain unknown until further studies are made of this delightful little animal.

Although not true carnivores, a few other carnivorous animals deserve mention. These are a rodent, the grasshopper mouse (*Onychomys*) (page 185); an insectivore, the desert hedgehog (*Hemiechinus*); and a marsupial, the mulgara (*Dasycercus*) (page 202). All three live in arid countries where they subsist on a predominantly carnivorous diet, and in the laboratory we have maintained them on meat without drinking-water. The grasshopper mouse and the mulgara are discussed in some detail in the chapters on rodents and marsupials, respectively. The desert hedgehogs (*Hemiechinus auritus aegypticus*) have, in our preliminary studies, given some suggestion that they may be able to subsist on meat with a lower water content than the grasshopper mouse will tolerate.

All the three animals mentioned above, as well as the fennec, have underground retreats where they can avoid severe heat. In general we can therefore say that small carnivorous desert animals manage their water balance without much difficulty on the water contained in their food.

SUMMARY

Two representative carnivores, the cat and the dog, are able to withstand air temperatures higher than the body temperature when the humidity is low. The dog, in particular, is a good heat regulator. Both species depend on panting and evaporation of water from the respiratory tract for dissipation of heat at high temperatures. A detailed examination of the panting mechanism has been made only in the dog.

During panting respiration is shallow, but nevertheless brings about an increased ventilation of the lungs and a wash-out of carbon dioxide from the blood, which results in pronounced alkalosis. The panting dog seems able to tolerate this alkalosis without much difficulty.

One advantage of panting is that it does not produce salt losses to the extent which is characteristic for sweating in man. Another advantage is that the animal provides its own ventilation of the cooling surfaces, while the sweating animal has to rely on natural or forced convection of air.

The dog suffers if exposed to extreme desert conditions. He can, however, prevent undue rise in body temperature while walking in the desert fully exposed to the hot air, the sun, and the radiation from the ground. Compared to man under the same conditions, the dog evaporates more water, but if the evaporation is considered relative to surface area, it is equal or slightly lower in the dog.

Carnivores characteristically eat food with a high water content which should be sufficient to cover all needs for water, including that needed for the excretion of urea formed in protein metabolism, provided that water is not used for heat regulation.

In cool surroundings the tolerance to dehydration in the dog is between 17 and 20 per cent of the body weight, but at a more moderate water loss, 10 to 14 per cent of the body weight, the dog becomes intolerant to high temperatures. The events leading to death under these conditions involve an explosive rise in body temperature, apparently caused by a breakdown in circulation, rather than inability to continue evaporation from the respiratory tract.

The cat is, in principle, similar to the dog in its heat regulation, but it is somewhat more tolerant to dehydration of the body, and can also tolerate a slightly higher body temperature.

Wild desert carnivores have not been studied in any detail, but the sporadic knowledge which is available suggests that their physiological reactions are similar to those found in the domestic dog and cat.

8

RABBITS AND JACK RABBITS

ONE of the most conspicuous animals of the arid south-western United States is the jack rabbit, an animal which in spite of its common name is a hare (*Lepus*). While rabbits are good diggers and usually excavate their own tunnels and burrows, most hares remain above ground and have no underground escape. The jack rabbits are no exception; they do not have burrows and may be seen in the desert at any time of the day, although on hot days they are more inactive and tend to rest in shade. The most prominent feature of the jack rabbit is its tremendously large ears, which are completely out of proportion, even for a hare. Large ears are a feature of many desert animals; for example, the Saharan form of the widespread *Lepus capensis* is distinguished by ears much larger than relatives in more moderate climates (256).

The great physiological interest in these animals, which weigh about 2 to 3 kg (17), is that in theory they are too small to use water for heat regulation, but since they have no burrows they are not typical 'avoiders' like rabbits and small rodents. The tremendous ears of jack rabbits are also a puzzling feature. They look like excellent heat radiators, but would they not on a hot day increase the heat load by exposing such a large surface?

The two common jack rabbits, *Lepus californicus* and *L. alleni*, have been carefully studied because of their economic importance as competitors with livestock in the semi-arid south-west (345). Apparently they need water, for if they are kept in captivity and given a variety of dry plant material from their usual habitat, they will lose weight and condition (17). In nature, however, the range of jack rabbits is so small that they cannot possibly move to open water to drink, and there is no evidence of their going to available water holes or drinking-places for livestock where these exist (345). They do, however, drink in captivity if water is provided (347).

Jack rabbits eat a fair amount of green and succulent food. After rain, when there is fresh grass, this constitutes the major part of the diet. At other times of the year they eat the green leaves of the mesquite (*Prosopis*) and other shrubs, and during the dry part of the year cactus is of importance as a source of water. It has been estimated that the over-all intake of green and fresh food is some 80 per cent of the total. In captivity they live well on a mixture of dry feed and green plants without drinking-water. Such a diet provides sufficient water for normal needs, but hardly enough if evaporation is the main element in heat regulation.

One reason that little experimental work has been done on jack rabbits is that they are extremely difficult to capture and keep in captivity. If a wild animal is put in a cage it incessantly throws itself against the screen until it kills itself. This difficulty was circumvented by Arizona investigators who performed caesarean sections on pregnant females shot in the field, and followed this by the arduous and time-consuming task of hand-rearing the young. It is quite possible that the use of tranquilizers would be a successful means of subduing captured adults until they adjust to captivity. It would be well worth while to attempt this in place of the troublesome upbringing of unborn young.

Since virtually nothing is known about the physiology of jack rabbits, it will be necessary to discuss what is known about a distant relative, the rabbit. The wild rabbit (*Oryctolagus cuniculus*) has been introduced to Australia and thrives in arid regions, but it is unable to subsist under very dry conditions. Rabbits kept in an enclosed area of their natural habitat, but without water, lived well as long as green vegetation was available. In the summer, however, when the vegetation dried up, they lost weight and died after some 2 months.At the time of death the weight loss was about 50 per cent and the animals were extremely emaciated although food was available (148). This indicates that the wild rabbit is unable to endure true desert conditions, but that they can suffer through long periods of drought to regain condition when rain brings out fresh vegetation.

The domestic rabbit has been the subject of some excellent studies of heat regulation. On this basis it should be possible to discuss more intelligently the possibilities for jack rabbits in an apparently impossible situation where it seems that water must be used in heat regulation although little is available.

THE DOMESTIC RABBIT

Temperature tolerance. The domestic rabbit is not very tolerant to high temperatures. When white angora rabbits were tested in a hot-room, they could not tolerate a 7-hour exposure if the temperature exceeded 38° C. The rectal temperature went up to 42° C in 2 to 5 hours and they had to be removed from the hot-room. For these rabbits the maximum air temperature that could be tolerated continuously was somewhere between 33° and 35° C (195).

A shorter-haired breed (New Zealand) was studied by Brody's group (167). In this case the animals were exposed to gradually increasing

PLATE 3

JACK RABBIT (*LEPUS ALLENI*) FROM SOUTHERN ARIZONA

This animal is actually a hare. It has no burrow, but on a hot day it will take advantage of even the smallest patch of shade. The possible role of the large ears in heat dissipation is discussed in the text (see p. 136)

(see p. 136)

(Courtesy, U.S. Department of the Interior, Fish and Wildlife Service)

temperatures over a period of 3 months, giving them an opportunity to make physiological adjustments to the extreme conditions. This should reveal the maximal tolerance better than acute exposures over a few hours. The rectal temperature at various ambient conditions is shown in Fig. 26. At an air temperature of 38° C, the rectal temperature was about 41° C, and at 40° C ambient it rose to 42° C. The lethal rectal temperature for a rabbit is probably between 42° C and 43° C, as for mammals in general (167, 195).

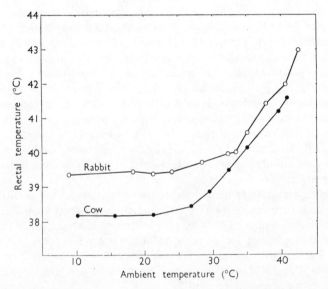

Fig. 26. Rectal temperature of rabbits in relation to environmental temperature. The response of cows is included for comparison. (Reproduced with permission from Johnson et al (167).)

One of the conspicuous reactions of a rabbit to hot atmospheres is an increase in respiration rate. Normal respiration rates are between 50 and 100 per minute, and with increasing temperature the rate gradually rises. In Angoras rates have reached as high as 700 per minute at air temperatures of 43° C (195). The increase in respiration rate is gradual, not sudden and well defined as in the dog. The very high rates in Angoras are perhaps not characteristic for rabbits in general, because other investigators have usually reported increases to between 200 and 300 respirations per minute. In the excellent report by the Missouri group (167) the respiration rate in a number of animals went up from about 90 at low temperatures to close to 300 per minute when ambient temperature exceeded 40° C. Between 10° and 20° C there was no appreciable change, at 20° C there was a sharp inflection of the curve and from this point the respiratory rates rose gradually and uniformly.

As the respiration rate increases, the rabbit will change to open-mouthed breathing, but since the breathing does not become correspondingly shallow, the respiratory volume is greatly increased. It would therefore be more correct to say that the rabbit displays hyperthermic polypnea, rather than panting. At high rectal temperatures there is dripping of saliva from the mouth, but the rabbit does not spread it over its fur as the cat and other animals do (277).

Evaporation. According to Lee the evaporation from the lungs accounts for only about one-quarter of the total evaporation at high temperature (195). The same conclusion has also been reached by others (173). This indicates that evaporation from the skin must also increase with temperature, and there are in fact many suggestions to this effect in older investigations. Although it has been stated that the domestic rabbit has no sweat glands (116), there seems to be a considerable increase in cutaneous water loss at high temperature (173, 233). The diffusion loss of water through the skin appears to be augmented by increased circulation. This view gains support from the finding that when skin circulation is stimulated with drugs, cutaneous water loss increases conspicuously (116).

The determinations made by the Missouri group of the partition in water loss between respiratory and surface evaporation shows that, at moderate ambient temperature, skin evaporation accounts for 60 per cent and respiratory for 40 per cent of the water loss (167). Although both increase with increasing temperature, cutaneous evaporation rises faster so that the proportion changes to about 80 per cent for skin and 20 per cent for respiration at 42° C.

Other heat loss. The most intriguing finding of the Missouri group is that evaporative cooling accounted for only a small fraction of the heat production (see Fig. 27). It is not surprising that at low temperatures evaporation absorbs only 10 per cent of the produced heat. Under these circumstances the major part can easily be dissipated by conduction and radiation. At the high temperature (40° C), however, the total evaporation accounted for only 30 per cent of the heat production. Since the rabbits could tolerate this temperature for extended periods of time, the remaining part of the heat must have been dissipated somehow, and there is no other possibility than conduction and radiation. For comparison it can be mentioned that at this temperature both man and cow dissipate the entire heat production by evaporative cooling, and the rabbit is therefore quite different. Since the rabbit maintained a rectal temperature of 42° C at 40° C ambient, the gradient would permit a net heat flow to the environment. The surprising thing is that the small gradient should be enough to take care of the major part of the heat production, with only a small part accounted for by evaporation. Until detailed investigations have been made we must assume that this gradient, aided by the large surface and thin fur of the ears, is sufficient to dissipate two-thirds of the heat production. This situation is indeed a challenge to an imaginative investigator to obtain a more precise account of the various avenues for heat exchange in the rabbit at high temperature.

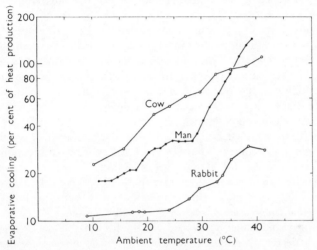

FIG. 27. The fraction of the metabolic heat of a rabbit which is dissipated by evaporation is about 30 per cent at high ambient temperatures. The remainder of the metabolic heat is dissipated by convection and radiation to the hot environment. In cows and in man evaporation has a much more important role in heat dissipation. (Reproduced with permission from (167).)

THE DILEMMA OF THE JACK RABBIT

What implication do the findings on the domestic rabbit have for the solution to the puzzling conflict between apparent heat load and lack of water for the jack rabbit? They give, at least, some important suggestions.

First of all they point out that evaporation is responsible for only a small part of total heat dissipation at high temperature. Conduction and radiation can take care of the main part of the heat dissipation if the surroundings are only slightly cooler than the body. The jack rabbit has very much larger ears than its domestic relative and it should be able to use these surfaces to at least as great advantage.

Microclimate. Descriptions of the behaviour of jack rabbits in the hot desert indicate that they utilize every small advantage offered by the environment (347). During the hot season jack rabbits are invariably found in the shade during the day-time, frequently in a depression near a mesquite bush. If they are chased from their resting place they will rapidly run for a short distance and seek out a new place under a bush, behind a rock, or in a depression in the ground. If they are continually chased over the desert they become increasingly reluctant to leave the shade, and apparently soon suffer from overheating. Dill found that on a very hot day two men could easily run down a jack rabbit if they used some persistence as the animal seemed to become the victim of heat prostration (106).

One advantage of sitting in shade is that the ground temperature is not as high as in the open sun; in well-shaded areas it is even below the air temperature (347). Unfortunately, careful measurements of microclimate and soil surface temperature have not been made where the jack rabbits hide out, but measurements of soil as well as air temperatures indicate that both are lower in and near desert shrub vegetation (mesquite) than in the open desert (347).

Since we have no accurate description of the microclimate where the jack rabbit prefers to rest, I have put together a suggested situation from the information at hand. The picture is based on considerations of heat exchange by radiation and, although hypothetical, is consistent with current knowledge and can be considered a suitable working hypothesis.

Radiation temperature of the sky. In our discussions of large animals, such as man and camel, we considered the heat load on an organism in the open desert. In these circumstances all usual avenues for heat exchange showed a net movement of heat towards the surface of the animal, conduction from the hot air, radiation from the sun, and radiation from the hot ground. The radiation exchange between the animal and the open sky was not discussed because the integrated environmental radiation temperature gives a flow towards the organism, and it was not necessary to consider the sky separately. This is different, however, if we consider the microclimate of a smaller animal, where the radiation temperature of the sky becomes important as a separate factor in the total radiation picture.

During the day the radiation temperature of the blue sky, integrated over the entire visible and infra-red range, is much below air-temperature. By directing a dermal radiometer towards the sky in the Sahara I found radiation temperatures below 20° C in the day-time and approaching freezing at night, but since the instrument was not designed for such measurements, and I had no means of calibrating the low range, I made no attempts at further study. It is known, however, that sky radiation temperatures are low, except on cloudy days. The lowest mean sky temperature observed in the United States deserts by Lee was 13° C on clear summer days with low vapour-pressure. At night the radiation temperature was lower, with a mean sky temperature as low as 7·5° C. With increasing haziness and cloud cover, the radiation temperatures increased and approached air temperatures (Lee, personal communication).

Any object on the ground is in radiation exchange with the visible sky, and since the surface of an animal is about 35° to 40° C, an appreciable amount of heat is lost to the sky on a clear day, and even more at night. The radiation loss also accounts for the fact that the ground surface at night becomes much colder than the air, especially on very still nights when air movement does not disturb the thin layer of cold air which accumulates at the ground surface. In particular, objects of low heat capacity without direct contact with the ground, such as grass and leaves, can become very cold and reach freezing temperatures when the air is 10 or 15 degrees above freezing.

Ice-making. A convincing example of how efficient the night sky may be as a heat sink is found in a primitive method for ice-making in tropical countries where air temperatures never reach freezing. A delightful description of this process was written in the year 1775 in a letter from Sir Robert Barker to the Royal Society (23):

The process of making ice in the East Indies having become a subject of speculation, I beg permission to present you with the method by which it was performed at Allahabad, Mootegil, and Calcutta, in the East Indies, lying between 25½ and 23½ degrees of North latitude. At the latter place I have never heard of any persons having discovered natural ice in the pools or cisterns, or in any waters collected in the roads; nor has the thermometer been remarked to descend to the freezing point.

The ice-maker belonging to me at Allahabad (at which place I principally attended to this enquiry) made a sufficient quantity in the winter for the supply of the table during the summer season. The methods he pursued were as follows: on a large open plain, three or four excavations were made, each about thirty feet square and two deep: the bottoms of which were strewed about eight inches or a foot thick with sugar-cane or the stems of the large Indian corn dried. Upon this bed were placed in rows, near to each other, a number of small, shallow, earthen pans, for containing the water intended to be frozen. These are unglazed, scarce a quarter of an inch thick, about an inch and a quarter in depth, and made of an earth so porous, that it was visible, from the exterior part of the pan, the water had penetrated the whole substance. Towards the dark of the evening, they were filled with soft water, which had been boiled, and then left in the afore related situation. The ice-makers attended the pits usually before the sun was above the horizon, and collected in baskets what was frozen, by pouring the whole contents of the pans into them, and thereby retaining the ice.

It is here necessary to remark, that the quantity of ice depends materially on the weather; and consequently, it has sometimes happened, that no congelation took place. At others, perhaps, half the quantity will be frozen; and I have often seen the whole contents formed into a perfect cake of ice: the lighter the atmosphere, and the more clear and serene the weather, the more favourable for congelation, as a frequent change of winds and clouds are certain preventives. For I have frequently remarked, that after a very sharp cold night, to the feel of the human body, scarce any ice has been formed; when at other times the night has been calm and serene, and sensibly warmer, the contents of the pans will be frozen through.

This primitive method shows in striking fashion how an empirical approach can lead to the utmost utilization of those laws of physics that govern a process, and how the artisan without any actual knowledge of these can take full advantage of the characteristic properties of the simple materials available. The freezing receptacles are well insulated from the warm ground, placed in a depression where accumulated cold air will remain, on top of corn stems or cane which permit the circulation of air underneath. The containers are made of porous clay so that the water is precooled by evaporation, the clay is thin so the heat conduction is good and heat capacity low, they are flat and shallow, exposing a large surface to radiation loss, and only a thin layer of water is poured in them so that no excess water has to be cooled before freezing can begin.

The value of long ears. If we now consider the jack rabbit in view of this convincing demonstration, we might have the following situation. The animal sits in a depression in the shade on the north side of a bush (see Fig. 28). The ground surface is never exposed to the sun, and is therefore appreciably cooler than the surface in the open, and even cooler than the day-time air temperature. Its temperature instead approaches the mean air temperature which in the summer is about $30°$ C (347). The radiation from the sun is screened out by the bush, and the re-radiation from the hot desert surface does not reach the animal in the depression. The big ears will be in radiation exchange with the visible surroundings. In the bush the surface temperatures on the shade side are close to air temperatures, or perhaps a little lower due to evaporation, and in the sky the temperature is assumed to be 25 degrees lower than the ears.

The radiation loss from the ears can be calculated from Stefan-Boltzmann's law for radiation,[1] and at the temperatures indicated in Fig. 28 the loss from the ears will be 13 cal per hour per cm^2. If the two ears are 400 cm^2, they can radiate about 5 kcal per hour, which is of the magnitude of one-third the metabolic heat production in a 3 kg rabbit.

[1] The net radiation exchange (H_R) between two objects is $H_R = S_0 e_1 e_2 (T_1{}^4 - T_2{}^4)A$, where S_0 is Stefan-Boltzmann's constant, 1.37×10^{-12} cal $sec^{-1} cm^{-2}$, e_1 and e_2 the emissivities, T_1 and T_2 the absolute temperature of the two objects, and A the area in cm^2. In the temperature range under consideration the emissivities are very close to 1 and need not be considered.

Obviously, actual measurements are needed to establish the exact level of radiation from the ears. If we assume that the jack rabbit is in a sufficiently favourable position for radiation heat loss, it should be able to remain in heat balance, even when air temperatures are fairly high. The air temperature in the depression might even be lower than in the neighbouring atmosphere because of the low temperature of the soil, and

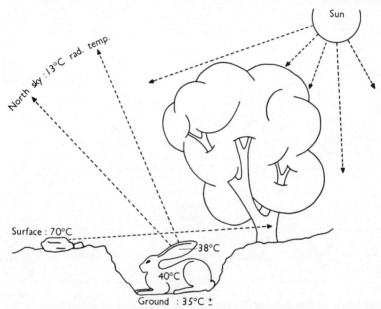

FIG. 28. A hypothetical thermal situation for a jack rabbit. When the animal sits quietly in a shaded depression, radiation to the sky is probably an important factor in reducing the use of water in dissipation of heat.

on a still day any coolness in the micro-atmosphere tends to remain in the depression. On a windy day, however, the situation would be more disadvantageous, removing any local atmospheric advantage and increasing the conductive heat flow to the large exposed surfaces of the ears. Wind in the hot desert always constitutes an increased heat load, both for man and animal.

If this general picture of the role of the large ears of the jack rabbit should prove correct, we have an 'explanation' for the advantage of large ears in desert animals. These have always seemed enigmatic, for in an environment warmer than the body large surfaces merely increase the heat gain. However, the radiation exchange with the sky has heretofore not been taken into consideration in the evaluation of the possible role of the ears. Microclimatic studies, including radiation measurements, are much needed for a realistic evaluation of the suggestions outlined above, and standard meteorological reports are next to useless. The meteorological shelter gives excellent information about the microclimate in a well-ventilated, square, white box, 2 metres above the ground, but little about what the jack rabbit sees as it sits in the shade of a bush. The large animals, on the other hand, are more exposed to standard meteorological conditions, and, incidentally, camels have small ears. Large ears are found in small animals, some rodents, the desert hedgehog, and in particular in medium-sized animals such as desert hares, the kit fox, and the fennec.

SUMMARY

Jack rabbits (actually hares) are common in the south-western United States deserts. They live in areas where no free water is available and depend on a mixture of dry and green food for subsistence. Their physiology has not been investigated, and the domestic rabbit is the closest relative about which physiological information is available.

The rabbit has a poor ability to prevent a rise in rectal temperatures at high ambient temperature. At an air temperature of $40°$ C the rectal temperature is $42°$ C. Under heat stress the respiration is increased from less than 100 to above 300 respirations per minute, but this increase is not a typical panting such as found in the dog. The increased respiratory evaporation accounts for only about one-third of the total water loss, the remainder being due to increased evaporation from the surface of the animal. It has been reported that rabbits have no sweat glands, and the cutaneous evaporation should therefore be due to an increase in the diffusion water loss ('insensible perspiration').

At $40°$ C evaporation can account for only one-third of the total heat loss. The remaining two-thirds must therefore be dissipated in other ways, presumably by conduction and radiation. The temperature gradient between the body ($42°$ C) and environment ($40°$ C) is small, and the large surface of the ears presumably aids in heat transfer over this modest gradient.

It is suggested that the very large ears of the jack rabbit can serve as efficient radiators to the cool sky, which, on clear days, may have a radiation temperature about $25°$ C below that of the animal. By seeking shade, where ground temperatures are low and solar radiation is screened out, and by sitting in a depression where radiation from the hot ground surface is obstructed, the net radiation loss to the surroundings may be sufficient to account for the necessary heat loss, without much loss of water. This seems to be the only way that a non-burrowing medium-sized animal could survive without large amounts of drinking-water in a hot desert.

9

THE GROUND SQUIRREL
A DIURNAL DESERT RODENT

GROUND squirrels are characteristically diurnal animals. The various desert species (*Citellus, Ammospermophilus*) are relatively small, the adults weighing from less than 100 to a few hundred grammes. These attractive animals are often seen outside their burrows, and it is a pleasure to watch them as they move around quickly, dashing from one place to another. They frequently disappear in a hole and come up again, perhaps moments later. In midsummer they remain in their burrows during the hottest hours, and their activity is mostly restricted to the morning and late afternoon. When they are outside they move around a great deal, nibbling some green leaves here, scratching or digging in the ground there, perhaps catching an insect, but much of the activity takes place in shade. They do not remain exposed to the hottest part of the environment for long, and since they frequently disappear in the burrows for shorter or longer periods, they are subjected to a mean environmental temperature which represents some average between the outside heat and the cool depth of the burrow.

Heat evasion

The temperature in burrows of the round-tailed ground squirrel (*Citellus tereticaudus*) was recorded for an entire year in southern Arizona by Vorhies (347). In June, when the maximum air temperature gradually increased to over 40° C and the soil surface temperature was 70° C, the deep burrow temperature remained below 27° C. Even during the very hottest summer when maximum soil surface temperatures reached 75° C, the deep burrow temperatures did not exceed 29° C. There is usually some shade from vegetation and shrubs near the burrows so that the microclimate is less severe than in the open sun, but even so the animals avoid the highest ground surface temperatures by being inactive during the hottest part of the day. It is therefore possible that the ground squirrels, in spite of their predominantly diurnal activity, are sufficiently clever to avoid any serious heat load and thus are spared the necessity of using water for heat regulation.

When ground squirrels are exposed to high ambient temperatures in the laboratory, their body temperature becomes elevated. Apparently there is no physiological mechanism which effectively counteracts the rise in body temperature, and this is what could be expected. As was discussed in Chapter 2, the small animal has such a large relative surface that heat dissipation by evaporation of water is too costly. Body temperatures up to 42·4° C induced no apparent ill effect in antelope ground squirrels (*Citellus leucurus*), but one individual when exposed for 3½ hours to an ambient temperature of 39° C became heated to 43·1° C and died shortly afterwards (97). The animal had salivated profusely during the terminal stage of its exposure, but this reaction did not seem to be sufficient to save it from heat death. While the majority of animals exposed for a few hours to 39° C died, most of those at 38° C survived. From these experiments it seems probable that animals in nature cannot stand prolonged exposure to heat, but that they should be able to tolerate a certain degree of hyperthermia. (At 23° C the mean body temperature was 37·2° C with a range from 35·6 to 38·1° C.)

Although it appears that ground squirrels may avoid expenditure of water for heat regulation, they do need some water in their food. When we tried to keep round-tailed ground squirrels (*Citellus tereticaudus*) on a dry grain diet in Arizona they lost weight and died with hemoconcentration, apparently from lack of water.

In nature the ground squirrels have a great preference for green plant material—fresh shoots of grass, the leaves of the mesquite, leaf buds— and they have no special liking for dry plant material and seeds. Vorhies (347) stated that the roundtailed ground squirrel does not depend on cactus as a water source, but the average water content of its food may still be some 60 to 80 per cent.

Another species, the Nelson antelope ground squirrel (*Citellus nelsoni*) has a great preference for insects (147). During the winter months, when few insects are available, green plant material dominates the diet, but as insects become common in May, they make up over 90 per cent of the diet until they disappear again around November or December (see Fig. 29). Occasionally these ground squirrels will also eat vertebrates such as lizards, if they succeed in catching them. Apparently they have a liking for flesh, for they have been successfully trapped by using dried kangaroo rat meat as bait. They are very adept at catching insects, not only slow-moving beetles, but also faster prey, for great numbers of crickets and grasshoppers are found in their stomachs. Hawbecker has seen them catch grasshoppers by leaping with the insect until both came down at the same place at the same time. A June beetle was caught by a squirrel which ran along on its hind legs and pawed the air until it hit the low-flying insect (147).

Utilization of salt solutions. Experiments on antelope ground squirrels (*Citellus leucurus*) show that they can profitably drink solutions of sodium chloride more concentrated than sea water (33). If the animals are given dry food to eat, they can maintain weight and water balance

PLATE 4

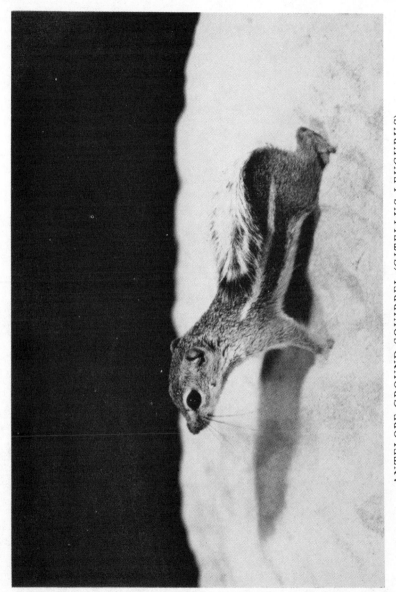

ANTELOPE GROUND SQUIRREL (*CITELLUS LEUCURUS*)

This diurnal rodent spends much of the day moving swiftly around in search of food. On summer days it passes the hottest hours in its burrow

(*Courtesy, Dr. Jack W. Hudson, Rice University*)

indefinitely with water rations equal to 2 per cent of their body weight per day, but if they are given free access to water, they will drink 13 per cent of the body weight per day (159, 160). If the water is replaced by increasing concentrations of sodium chloride solution they are able to utilize concentrations as high as 800 mM, 1·4 times as saline as sea water. On 1000 mM solutions (5·8 per cent NaCl) they lose weight. It

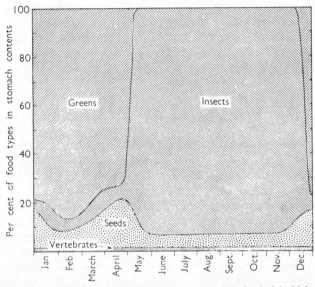

FIG. 29. Stomach analyses show that a major part of the food of the Nelson antelope ground squirrel has a high water content. Insects make up over 90 per cent of the diet during the warm months, but are mostly replaced by greens in winter. The figure represents records over a 4-year period. (Reproduced with permission from Hawbecker (147).)

was found, however, that even this concentration is better than no water at all, for groups of animals lost less than one-half as much weight as those that got no water whatsoever, and they also survived longer.

Obviously, the kidney of an animal that can drink such concentrated salt solutions must be a very efficient organ, capable of producing a highly concentrated urine. The kidney function has not been studied in detail, but it is known that antelope ground squirrels during dehydration can produce urine with an osmotic pressure in excess of 3500 mOsm, 1200 of which are due to electrolytes (33). The urine concentration may be 9·4 times as high as the plasma concentration (159, 160), and a U/P ratio of 9·4 is higher than that reported for any of the animals discussed previously in this book. There are, however, other desert rodents which by far exceed the ground squirrels in concentrating ability, although others again have a much less powerful kidney. One such animal, which is still able to lead a successful life in the desert, is the American pack rat, which will be discussed in the next chapter.

Aestivation and hibernation

Many ground squirrels have been reported to remain in the burrows in a state of dormancy or aestivation which begins in the late summer and gradually merges into the winter hibernation. In the early spring the animals reappear, taking advantage of the green vegetation which has come out after the winter rains. They reproduce rapidly in the spring, and the half-grown young animals are seen among the adults in the early summer. Late in the summer all activity ceases again, and the animals remain invisible until next spring.

Apparently species differ widely in their aestivation and hibernation habits, and it is also possible that there may be geographical variations due to local climate or other differences. The round-tailed ground squirrel (*Citellus tereticaudus*) disappears in late August and early September and thus avoids the dry, hot autumn period in southern Arizona (347).

Aestivation and hibernation have been studied in the laboratory by Bartholomew and Hudson (35), and these authors point out that while their experimental subject, the Mohave ground squirrel (*Citellus mohavensis*) goes through prolonged periods of inactivity and dormancy, the closely related antelope ground squirrel (*Citellus leucurus*) neither hibernates nor aestivates.

The question of aestivation and its influence on water balance will be discussed in greater detail in a separate chapter (page 187), and no further particulars will be given here.

SUMMARY

Ground squirrels are diurnal rodents of relatively small size, weighing from less than a hundred to a few hundred grammes. Although they are typically diurnal, they remain in their burrows during the hottest hours of the day and are fully active only in the relatively cool morning and late afternoon. When they are outside they move around rapidly with frequent returns to the cool burrows and the mean temperature to which they are exposed is therefore lower than the hot desert day.

Ground squirrels include in their diet, fresh grass, green leaves, buds, &c., as well as insects, but cactus is not utilized. In the laboratory they are unable to survive on dry food and need water or moist food. They can be sustained on salt solutions as concentrated as 800 mM and have a powerful kidney which can concentrate the urine to almost ten times the plasma osmotic concentration.

Some species of ground squirrels enter a state of dormancy or aestivation during the late summer, and remain inactive in a state of hibernation during the winter. Other species neither aestivate nor hibernate. Therefore aestivation, which to all appearances is a means to avoid the driest period of the year, is not an essential adaptation for these diurnal desert rodents.

10

THE PACK RAT
A DESERT RODENT IN NEED OF WATER

THE native American 'rat' is the wood rat, which in the arid West is better known as the pack rat or trade rat. Wood rats of the genus *Neotoma* are reminiscent of the common or Norway rat, both in shape and size, but they are much more beautiful animals with large black eyes, soft grey colour, and white underside. In the desert and arid plains of the West the pack rats build their nests in large conspicuous heaps of dead twigs and other debris which they drag together. In regions where cactus grows their spiny joints seem to be preferred for the protection they give.

The animals have a mania for collecting and seem particularly attracted by metal objects. Perhaps it is because they are readily missed that coins, belt buckles, keys, and other essential small things seem to be preferred when the pack rat rustles around in a camp at night, frequently leaving a pebble or other valueless object in place of what it takes away. The habit of making an exchange when amassing property earned the animal the name of trade rat or pack rat among the old prospectors in the West. Of course, there are fabulous legends about trade rats carrying off a cake of soap or some other insignificant item leaving a solid nugget of gold in payment!

The large pile of debris collected by the pack rat shelters and protects its nest underneath. This is usually found at the trunk of a mesquite bush or a cactus, and the partial shade reduces the temperature. Measurements at a nest showed soil temperatures up to $46°$ C while they were $75°$ C on the open desert surface (347). Although the nest of the pack rat is rather shallow the maximum temperature in the nest did not exceed $31°$ C. Since the pack rat is crepuscular and nocturnal, it is a typical avoider, living in a microclimate that never attains the high temperatures we consider typical of the desert.

Water. Like other desert rodents the pack rat has no need for a supply of drinking-water. Its adaptation to the aridity of the environment is not as difficult to explain as that of kangaroo rats and pocket mice which subsist entirely on air-dried food. The pack rat needs more water, and it is obvious that the source is its food.

The principal foods of pack rats are green and succulent and furnish an abundant supply of water. The animals are found in greatest abundance where cactus is common, and these plants make up nearly one-half of the food for the year (346). Cactus contains nearly 90 per cent water, and the consumption of this item increases during the driest time of the year so that in May it comprises more than 90 per cent of the diet. During part of the year the green leaves and pods of the mesquite (*Prosopis*) are important, though at other times, when there is an abundance of fresh green grass, this is preferred.

Apparently the pack rat is seldom, if ever, hard pressed for moisture. It is well adapted to arid conditions, not by any special tolerance, but by

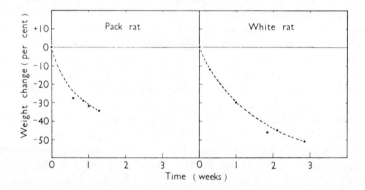

FIG. 30. Weight loss in pack rats and white laboratory rats when fed on dry grain without drinking-water. (Reproduced with permission from (290).)

living where the juiciest food is available, preferring this to dry seeds and other material that might seem more nutritious (346).

Dry food. If the pack rat is given only dry food its ability to survive is low, in fact lower than in the white rat. Pack rats fed on dry grain died after 4 to 9 days, while white rats survived for 15 to 21 days under otherwise identical circumstances (290). The rate of weight loss was similar in the two animals, but the pack rats died when they had lost about 30 per cent while the white rats tolerated 50 per cent loss (see Fig. 30). This reveals the paradoxical situation that a desert animal is less tolerant to water deprivation than a relative of similar size which has no special adaptations to life in the desert.

The pack rat also has a less efficient kidney than the white rat. It can attain as high concentrations of electrolytes, almost 700 mEq per litre, but its ability to concentrate urea seems to be definitely less. When kept on a high-protein diet in order to increase the load of urea, the highest urea concentration in the pack rat was about 1800 mM per litre, against 2500 mM per litre in the white rat. This difference probably is not of

PLATE 5

PACK RAT (*NEOTOMA* sp.)

The American pack rat moves with ease and grace over the sharp spines of cactus which constitute its most important source of water. While a white rat gets helplessly caught on the barbed spines the pack rat bites carefully between them to get at the juicy flesh

(*Courtesy, Life Magazine. (c) 1961 Time, Inc.*)

major significance to survival, as the animals lost weight at about the same rate when deprived of water, and other factors must account for the unequal survival times.

The pack rat has, however, an advantage above the white rat in its ability to utilize food which the latter cannot. When we first made this observation it was a surprise that the omnivorous and hardy white rat should be unable to utilize food sufficient for the native American rat.

The original intent of the experiment was to see if the pack rat could live on cactus as its sole food. Normally pack rats eat large amounts of the fleshy joints of the cholla (*Opuntia* spp.) which they handle with great skill and deftness. The extremely sharp barbed spines of this cactus penetrate the human skin easily and may even go through a leather boot if one carelessly kicks a joint lying on the ground. The joints of *Opuntia fulgida* come loose from the stem very easily, and the slightest brush against the cactus as one walks by will cause a joint to come off and stick painfully to the skin. This characteristic has earned the cactus the name 'jumping cholla' because the joints seem to jump at the passer-by. The pack rat moves with agility in and around this cactus, climbs the stems, runs unharmed over the joints lying on the ground, and drags the spiny pieces home to its nest. It bites into the flesh between the spines without getting hurt, seemingly protected by an invisible armour.

When pieces of the same cactus are given to a white rat, it will get stuck on its first approach, give a sharp cry and make a sudden jump which only lodges the spines more deeply. The animal becomes frenzied with pain as it unsuccessfully tries to free itself. To see if the spines can penetrate the skin of a pack rat, I once dropped a piece on an animal and the spines went into the leg muscles. Instead of jumping with pain the animal turned its head back and easily freed itself by biting off the spines in a most casual way. Thus, a difference in behaviour makes this important water source accessible to one animal while it cannot be approached by the other.

In order to make the cactus available to the white rat, the spines can be removed by burning. It suffices to take the pieces with a pair of tongs and pass them through a gas flame. They can now be approached also by the white rat, which will eat some, but only reluctantly. In our experiments the white rats rapidly lost weight on this diet, and died sooner than they would have without any food. Apparently the cactus contains some harmful component, although we do not know its nature. There are two main possibilities. In addition to the long spines the *Opuntia* cacti have small bundles or clusters of hundreds of fine silica needles (glochids), nearly invisible to the eye, which penetrate the skin and cause intense irritation. These glochids are located so deeply that they are not removed by the burning, and if eaten by the rat they might cause extensive damage to the walls of the gastro-intestinal tract. The other possibility is that the cactus contains some noxious chemical substance, tolerated by the pack rat but not by the white rat. One toxic substance found in some cacti is oxalic acid. To mammals oxalic acid is highly poisonous because it binds calcium ions as insoluble calcium oxalate, and as blood-calcium level is lowered, normal nerve function is impaired, the muscles develop tetanic cramps, and the blood will not clot because thrombin is not formed in the absence of calcium. Long-term effects involve the kidney, where calcium oxalate crystals damage the kidney tubules. Is it possible that the oxalic acid found in cactus can be tolerated by the pack rat while it is harmful to the white rat? Although this question was never completely answered with the identification of the factor noxious to white rats, it led to an absorbing study of an unusual type of calcium metabolism.

Calcium metabolism in the pack rat. The interest in calcium excretion in the pack rat began with the observation that urine samples from recently trapped animals contained such large amounts of a white precipitate that the urine looked like heavy cream. Frequently, the urine was also strongly coloured, orange, or even rust coloured or deep red. If pack rats were given cactus and grain to eat in the laboratory their urine contained the white precipitate, but white rats on the same diet had a clear yellow urine. Obviously, there was a difference in the mineral metabolism and excretion of the two animals.

The precipitate could be dissolved in dilute hydrochloric acid, and the formation of bubbles suggested that it could be calcium carbonate. A determination of the amount of calcium in the precipitate and of the carbon dioxide evolved showed that it was mostly calcium carbonate. X-ray crystallography confirmed this conclusion and showed the crystal form to be that of calcite. The finding of this common substance in such unusual quantities in the urine of a mammal brings up two problems, the first concerned with the fact that pack rats absorb from the intestine much greater quantities of calcium than other mammals can, the second with the renal mechanism involved in such a very unusual ability to excrete calcium.

Calcium oxalate is a highly insoluble compound, which if added to the diet of white rats passes through the gastro-intestinal tract without being absorbed (120). Although soluble oxalic acid and oxalates are highly toxic, calcium oxalate is completely innocuous and has no effect beyond its mere presence as any other insoluble compound.

If calcium oxalate is added to the diet of pack rats, there is a striking difference in the appearance of the urine as well as its calcium content (see Table XVIII). While the white rats excrete a completely clear, light yellow urine when calcium oxalate is in the diet, the pack rats produce a creamy urine containing large amounts of calcium carbonate.

These results can be interpreted in several ways. First of all, the pack rat is able to absorb calcium from a virtually insoluble compound, calcium oxalate, while this compound just passes out with the faeces in white rats. If only the calcium were absorbed, leaving the oxalate ion behind, one would expect to find water-soluble oxalate or oxalic acid in the faeces, but this was not the case. (There was, however, also in

TABLE XVIII

Urinary excretion of calcium in white rats and pack rats fed a diet containing calcium oxalate

	Control, whole wheat flour		Whole wheat flour plus 10 per cent calcium oxalate	
	Ca, mEq/l	pH	Ca, mEq/l	pH
White rats	7·4	6·0	6·2	5·9
Pack rats	8·1	5·1	371·5	8·2

the pack rat much calcium oxalate that passed unabsorbed through the intestine and out with the faeces.) Since no oxalic acid was found in the urine, it must have been destroyed, either in the intestine before absorption could take place, or by metabolic processes in the body after its absorption. Since no mammals are known to metabolize oxalic acid, which is a highly toxic compound, it seems more likely that it was destroyed in the intestine, probably by the bacterial flora. This problem is, however, not in any way settled.

The metabolism of oxalic acid in the mammal, whether bacterial or not, is important. One of the major problems for livestock in the western United States is the content of oxalic acid in a number of plants, in particular of the family *Chenopodiaceae*. One of these, *Halogeton* (*Halogeton glomeratus*), can destroy a flock of sheep overnight if they graze on it. This weed, which was introduced into the United States as late as 1935 and now covers millions of acres, may contain as much as 20 per cent of oxalic acid per dry matter, and a few hundred grammes of it are enough to kill a sheep (324). A study of how oxalic acid is metabolized in the pack rat might give important clues as to how the problem can be handled in livestock.

What is the renal mechanism for excretion of the large quantities of calcium carbonate? This question was examined by D. L. Trout in my laboratory. Two per cent calcium carbonate was added to whole wheat flour, which was baked into bread and dried. Calcium carbonate is rather inaccessible to absorption in mammals in general, and white rats on the test diet absorbed only 2·5 per cent of the calcium taken in with the food. The pack rats, on the other hand, absorbed most of the calcium, for 70 to 79 per cent of that ingested was recovered in the urine. The urine was thick with the precipitate and the calcium concentration went up to values as high as 1150 mEq per litre, virtually all of it in the form of calcium carbonate.

Is this renal secretion of calcium so high that it is necessary to postulate a secretion of calcium in the renal tubule, or is the amount entering the renal tubules by filtration in the glomerulus sufficient to account for the large amounts in the urine? A number of complications arise as one tries to answer this question. To begin with, only about one-half of the calcium in the blood-plasma is present as free calcium ions; the remainder is partly bound to proteins, partly in other un-ionized form. It is therefore difficult to determine accurately the concentration of filterable calcium in the plasma, which differs from the total amount, and it is necessary to know this in order to establish how much calcium is filtered in the glomerulus. The volume of glomerular filtrate can be determined in the usual way by use of the inulin clearance, but since pack rats are difficult to handle we preferred to use as an approximation the creatinine clearance. Some technical difficulties also arise in determining the exact concentration of calcium in the urine, for most of it is present as precipitated calcium carbonate and tends to settle out at the neck of the bladder. It is therefore discharged irregularly, one urine sample having a very high, another a relatively low calcium content. It is therefore necessary to make complete collections of all urine over a long period of time, including a series of evacuations. When the amount of calcium in the urine was now compared with the amount that had been filtered in the glomerulus in the same period, it was found that all of it could have been derived from the glomerular filtrate. It is therefore not necessary to postulate a tubular secretion of calcium as responsible for the tremendous amounts of this substance in pack rat urine.[1]

Many persons who have handled laboratory hamsters have noticed that their urine is thick and creamy, and it is interesting that hamsters belong to the same family of rodents as the pack rat (*Cricetidae*). It is

---

[1] In forty-eight clearance periods the mean calcium : creatinine clearance ratio was 0·34. The standard deviation ($\pm$ 0·1) was high due to the irregularity in the evacuation of the precipitated calcium carbonate from the bladder. A careful evaluation of all samples with particularly high calcium content showed that these were usually obtained in very short collection periods, indicating that excess precipitate was eliminated from the bladder. There was no valid evidence that the clearance ratio exceeded 0·5 in any of our experiments. A clearance ratio exceeding 1·0 would be considered evidence of tubular secretion of calcium.

possible that further studies on calcium and oxalate metabolism could be done on hamsters rather than pack rats, since they are more easily obtained as well as handled.

SUMMARY

The pack rats, or wood rats (*Neotoma*), are desert rodents which need much water. They are independent of drinking-water but must have quantities of succulent vegetation. On a year-round basis almost half the food of the white-throated wood rat, a southern Arizona species, is made up of cactus which has a water content of almost 90 per cent. During the driest months the proportion of cactus in the diet increases to nine-tenths of the food bulk.

The microclimate of the pack rat's nest indicates that this nocturnal animal is never exposed to serious heat stress.

The pack rat has little tolerance to water deprivation. It cannot live on dry food and requires large quantities of water or juicy plant material. If given only dry food it survives for about a week while white rats on the same regimen live for 2 to 3 weeks. This reveals the paradoxical situation that a typical desert rodent has much less tolerance to water deprivation than the ordinary laboratory rat, a domesticated descendant of the Norway rat (*Rattus norvegicus*).

In captivity the pack rat can use cactus as a water-supply, but white rats cannot. The component of cactus noxious to white rats has not been identified, but a search for the cause revealed that the pack rat metabolizes oxalic acid, a highly toxic substance which remains unmetabolized in other mammals. The pack rat also has an unusual type of calcium excretion. While other animals absorb and excrete in the urine only a few per cent of ingested calcium, the pack rat absorbs calcium from the intestine in large amounts and excretes it in the urine as a precipitate of calcium carbonate. How this can take place without formation of kidney stones or concretions in the urinary tract is unknown.

11

THE KANGAROO RAT
A RAT THAT NEVER DRINKS

T HERE is hardly a more intriguing problem in the physiology of desert animals than the water balance of the many small rodents that live on air-dried food and never drink water. The best known of these are the kangaroo rats (*Dipodomys*) which live in the deserts of the south-western United States, but all the major deserts of the world have a variety of small rodents that fill the same ecological niche and have the same striking ability to live without water.

Of the two major problems of the desert, heat and water, the first can be actively dealt with only at the expense of the second and unavailable commodity. We will therefore first discuss the problems of heat and show that the small rodent is not particularly tolerant to high temperature, it is an escaper which avoids use of water for heat regulation. We can then proceed to the discussion of how these animals, in the absence of heat stress, manage their precarious water balance.

TEMPERATURE

Burrow temperatures

The nocturnal desert rodents avoid the high air temperatures of the day and the intense radiation from the sun. They remain in their underground burrows until late in the day and come out at night to seek their food when the temperature is more moderate. Are they free from heat stress as they spend the day in their underground retreats?

The temperature of the ground surface shows extreme variations. During the day the air temperatures may be $45°$ C and the ground surface, heated by the sun, may attain a surface temperature of $70°$ C or more. At night, if radiation to the sky is unimpeded, the surface temperature may fall far below that of the cool night air. Thus, the diurnal variations in the temperature of the soil surface may be two or three times as great as the variation in air temperature.

The tremendous temperature variations at the soil surface diminish rapidly with increasing depth. The extent of the damping depends on the nature of the soil and its water content. Fluctuations of $3°$ C at 20 cm depth could be a representative example with diurnal variations virtually lacking at 80 cm (128).

PLATE 6

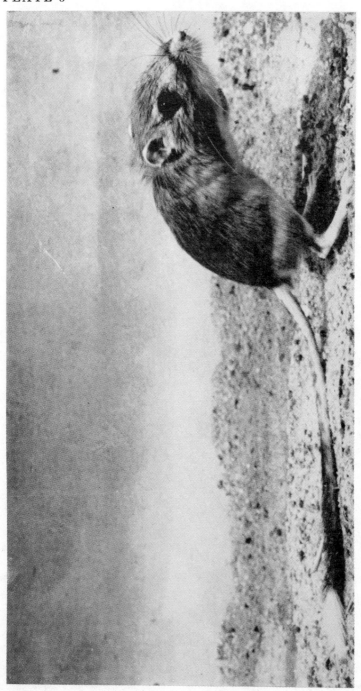

BANNER-TAILED KANGAROO RAT (*DIPODOMYS SPECTABILIS*)

Kangaroo rats, the commonest rodents in the Arizona and California deserts, have become known as the rats that never drink. By preference they live on seeds and other dry plant material and only rarely do they include any green food in the diet

Desert subsoil temperatures measured in Arizona show that the surface temperature varies by more than 80° C during the year, but the annual fluctuations at 1 metre depth are reduced to about 12° C (338). These data have been used by Misonne for a very instructive diagram (Fig. 31) (226). In the Sahara, Pierre found a similar range, in sand the annual variation at 1 metre was 11·2° C (258). This is a common depth of many animal burrows, and the highest temperature hardly ever exceeds 30° C, in other words, it imposes no heat stress at all.[1]

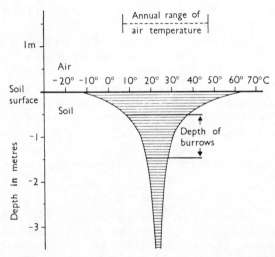

FIG. 31. The annual range of soil temperatures decreases rapidly with increasing distance from the surface. Most burrows are at a depth where the maximum temperature never reaches a level which necessitates active heat regulation by evaporation of water. (Reproduced with permission from Misonne (226).)

The temperature in the burrows of a number of desert rodents was measured by Vorhies throughout a whole year near Tucson, Arizona (347). In a burrow of a bannertailed kangaroo rat (*Dipodomys spectabilis*) the lowest temperature, 9° C, was observed in January, and the highest, 31° C, in July. These valuable records have been widely quoted and form the basis for the statement that burrow temperatures never reach levels that require active defences against an undue rise in body temperature. This conclusion has many times been corroborated by similar

---

[1] Interestingly, the mean annual soil temperature in Arizona is the same at all depths, 22·5° C, and it is only the amplitude of the variations which changes, diminishing with increasing depth (338). The increase in temperature with depth in the outermost crust of the earth is about 1° to 3° C per 100 metres, i.e. of a magnitude without any significance whatsoever for considerations of burrow temperatures.

measurements made by other investigators, but Vorhies's work remains classical because it includes continuous recordings for a full year.

A serious objection could be raised against most measurements of temperature or humidity in an animal burrow; the undisturbed conditions are altered as the structure is opened in order to place the sensing apparatus or element. The deepest parts cannot be reached through the tortuous runways, and however carefully an excavation is made, the animal is not likely to return and the records cannot show conditions as they are in the occupied and intact nest chamber.

This difficulty has been circumvented in studies where a microclimate recorder was tied to the tail of an animal trapped in front of its own burrow (294). As the animal was released, it usually ran to its nest chamber, and the record indicated the actual temperature and humidity in the burrow in the presence of the animal. A series of such records made in the same area where Vorhies worked showed maximum temperatures usually around 30° C and never exceeding 34·0° C. The device of letting the animal carry the recorder into the burrow and stay with it throughout the day has thus enabled us to confirm the accepted opinion that temperatures in the burrow never attain a level where active heat regulation is required.

Temperature tolerance

Normally a kangaroo rat finds protection against high temperatures, but what would happen if, for some reason, it were unable to return to its deep burrow after a night's foraging. If pursued by a predator a kangaroo rat will seek to dash into one of the several small escape burrows it usually has here and there in its territory. While the main burrow has a number of entrances and a complicated network of tunnels, the escape burrows are shallow and uncomplicated. If the animal is forced to take refuge in one of these the temperature may reach levels that become critical to survival. It is therefore of interest to know whether they have any unusual tolerance to high temperature.

The observations on lethal body temperatures and tolerance to heat discussed in the following refer to previously unpublished studies of Merriam's kangaroo rat (*Dipodomys merriami*), a relatively small species with a body weight of about 35 to 40 grammes. In captive animals kept at about 20° to 25° C, the body temperature is usually around 36° to 38° C.[1] Exposures to different temperatures show that they are able to maintain their body temperature within reasonable limits at air temperatures ranging from freezing to 37° C (see Fig. 32).

[1] Rectal temperatures measured with deeply inserted iron-constantan thermocouples.

Animals exposed to 0° C showed a slight initial drop in body temperature which stabilized after some hours and remained constant over the next 20 hours. Kangaroo rats therefore can resist freezing temperatures, although their burrows never get this cold. At air temperatures between 22° and 33·5° C, the animals always tended to show a drop in rectal temperature after they were taken from their cages in the morning and then stabilize at a level below the initial temperature. It is difficult to say whether this is part of a diurnal rhythm or a response to the repeated handling of the animals as the thermocouples were inserted. It should be possible to separate these two possibilities by making continuous temperature recordings in undisturbed animals.

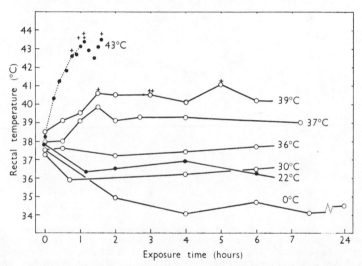

Fig. 32. Rectal temperatures in kangaroo rats exposed to various environmental temperatures. Each point on the curves represents the average of a group of five or six individuals. (The unconnected vertical crosses designate individual fatalities at the highest temperatures.)

At an air temperature of 36° C the animals maintained a rectal temperature slightly below 38° C. Further increases in the air temperature caused the rectal temperature to rise above the initial level, and after 8 hours' exposure to 37° C the rectal temperature stabilized at 39° C. At an air temperature of 39° C, the first fatalities occurred. Out of a group of five animals, one died after 1½ hours, two at 3 hours, one at 5 hours, while the fifth was still alive at 6 hours, but evidently much distressed.

The rectal temperatures measured in these animals were between 40·5° and 41·1° C, and this body temperature seems to be lethal to

kangaroo rats if the exposure lasts for several hours. At an air temperature of 43° C, their body temperatures increased rapidly, and they all
died in 45 minutes to 1½ hours. In order to obtain a more detailed record
of the response to the 43° C air temperature, five more animals were
exposed and their rectal temperatures recorded at more frequent intervals (see Fig. 33). During the first 15 minutes of exposure, the temperature of all five animals increased by about 3° C. In one of the animals the
temperature continued to rise at a slowly diminishing rate until it died
when the rectal temperature had reached 44·5° C after 45 minutes. The

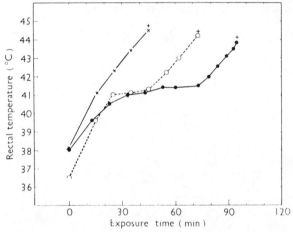

FIG. 33. When kangaroo rats were exposed to an air temperature of 43° C their rectal
temperature increased rapidly and the animals died at points designated by crosses (+).
The curve to the left represents an animal that reached a lethal rectal temperature
(44·5° C) in 45 minutes. The curve to the right represents the individual that showed
the greatest ability to resist the temperature rise, indicated by the almost horizontal
course of its temperature curve for a period of about 40 minutes. Three more animals
displayed intermediate responses, but for clarity only one of these curves is given in
the graph.

other four animals of the group showed, to a variable degree, a deviation
from this pattern. When the body temperature reached 41° C there was
a break in the curve indicating an active resistance to the rising temperature. In one of the animals (to the right in Fig. 33) the curve formed
a plateau, and for 40 minutes the rectal temperature increased no more
than 0·5° C. After this the ability to resist was apparently exhausted, and
the lethal temperature was rapidly attained as the temperature rose at
the same rate of heating characteristic for the less-resistant animals.

A curious phenomenon occurred in the animals exposed to lethal and
near-lethal temperatures. The fur under the chin and throat became wet,
completely soaked with moisture, apparently from a copious flow of

saliva. In the animal that showed the characteristic resistance to heating
in Fig. 33, the plateau in the curve coincided with the wetness of the
throat. Salivation reactions in response to heat are known from other
animals (cats, rabbits). In the kangaroo rat it seems that salivation is an
emergency reaction which occurs when the body temperature approaches
the lethal limit. A similar response occurs in ground squirrels (160) and
in the Egyptian rodent *Jaculus* (182). It can only give a temporary defence
against the temperature rise, but its biological significance seems evident.
If an animal temporarily is unable to retreat to its deep burrow, it may

TABLE XIX

Water evaporated during heat stress in kangaroo rats

Air temp.	Exposure time, hr	Water evaporated, g	Evaporation	
			g/hr	g/hr/100g body weight
25°			0·048	0·12*
36°	6	0·68	0·11	0·29
37°	7½	1·8	0·24	0·61
39°	4	3·0	0·75	1·82
43°	0·67	2·8†	4·2	10·3

* The value at 25° C quoted from (293). The other values estimated from the
weight loss.
† For the one individual whose temperature record showed the pronounced
plateau in Fig. 33. Four other animals evaporated 0·3, 1·3, 1·5, and 2·1 grammes,
respectively, but for these the time was too short for a reasonably accurate
estimation of the rate of evaporation.

be essential to survival that it has some means of resisting a temperature
rise. Its water resources are not sufficient to carry on active heat regulation by evaporation for any length of time, but an emergency reaction
of this type may still be the difference between life and death.

The amount of water evaporated at various temperatures has been
compiled in Table XIX. The water loss was greatly increased at high
temperature, and at 43° C it was about 10 per cent of the body weight
per hour. The air temperature in the desert during the day is of this
magnitude, and such conditions can be tolerated for a very short time
only. Since in the desert the heat load includes radiation as well, it is
obvious that the use of water for temperature regulation is not a physiological mechanism open to further exploration by the small mammal;
the only satisfactory way is to avoid completely the hot conditions of the
desert day.

WATER

Can kangaroo rats live without water?

There have been many reports over the years that kangaroo rats and other small desert rodents can live on air-dried food without drinking-water. Although the observations were reported carefully, they seemed unbelievable to many investigators. Instead, the fact that many desert rodents live miles away from any visible source of water, and that months or even years may elapse between rains, has been explained by the nature of their food, supposedly juicy plants and bulbs. This subject was carefully reviewed by Vorhies (347) who eliminated one after another of the 'explanations', the digging down to ground water, the eating of succulent food, the availability of dew, &c. When I first met this experienced field investigator at the University of Arizona in 1947, he expressed complete confidence in the ability of kangaroo rats to live without any moist food. Since this came from a man who knew the desert and its animals as well as anybody, it was evident that kangaroo rats deserved more attention from the physiologist than they had received so far.

Since Vorhies's review, ample documentation has established as an accepted fact that kangaroo rats can live on air-dried food. The question of how these delightful small animals manage to do so requires a discussion of all avenues of water loss as well as a careful scrutiny of the modest sources of water available to them. The solution can perhaps best be presented by raising a series of questions where the answers will provide a composite picture of how it is possible to live without drinking.

Do kangaroo rats store water?

Almost all deserts have occasional rainfalls, and the North American deserts have almost certain precipitation in the rainy seasons which occur each winter and in some places in the summer as well. Dew is another possible source of free water, but during the hottest part of the year it is a rare phenomenon. Could the kangaroo rats somehow store water in their bodies and slowly utilize these resources in the long periods when no free water is available from dew or rain? The simplest way to settle this question is to determine the total water content in the animals to see if it decreases as they are kept for long periods on a dry diet. If they slowly use up their water the body should become increasingly dehydrated, and if they begin with a store of water, this should be evident from an initial high water content.

When we kept kangaroo rats[1] on dried rolled oats or barley they

---

[1] In the following the term 'kangaroo rat' refers to Merriam's kangaroo rat (*Dipodomys merriami*) unless another species is specifically mentioned. This species is exceedingly abundant on the Santa Rita Range, south of Tucson, Arizona, where our

maintained their body weight for week after week, or even gained slightly. After more than 7 weeks on the dry food the water content of their bodies was still of the same magnitude as in mammals in general, and as high as it had been early in the experiment (see Fig. 34). There was no trend towards a decrease in water content during the long period of water deprivation. In fact, the animals had gained about 4 per cent in weight, and since the water percentage was unchanged the total amount of water in their bodies had been slightly increased (290).

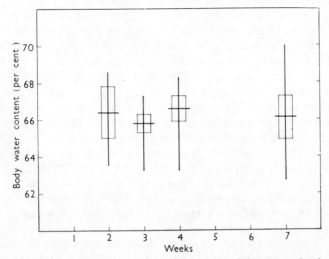

FIG. 34. Total body water remained unchanged when kangaroo rats lived on dry rolled oats without any drinking-water for periods up to 7 weeks. Horizontal lines, mean; white boxes, mean error; vertical lines, range. (Reproduced with permission from (270).)

Would free access to water increase the water content of their bodies? Usually, kangaroo rats do not drink even if water is offered to them. However, when they were given small pieces of watermelon, they would occasionally nibble a little, showing that they would be able to take advantage of this source of water, should they choose to do so. When watermelon was available at all times, the percentage of water in their bodies after 2 weeks was 66·3±0·2 per cent and after 54 days 67·2±0·6 per cent. This is very close to the water content of dry-fed animals (66·5 per cent), and the availability of free water therefore did not lead to any 'storage' that could be meaningful as a water reserve.

Is the situation the same in wild animals when they live in their

field work was conducted and laboratory animals were trapped. Those other kangaroo rats which have been investigated show only insignificant differences, and in principle the findings described here should apply to all species of this genus.

natural habitat and eat their normal food? Southern Arizona has two rainy seasons, one in winter and one in the late summer. In the early summer the desert is extremely dry, air humidity is low, and temperatures are high. In June, when no rain has fallen for months, the environment is as dry as the animals will ever experience. Animals trapped at this time should show the maximum difference from those trapped after the summer rains when they have had an opportunity to replenish their water content, if this is what they do. However, the difference in water content between the groups was only 0·1 per cent. Evidently, they had not taken advantage of the availability of water to replenish stores that could tide them over the long drought in the fall before the winter would bring new rains. This makes it reasonable to conclude that physiological storage of water is not a factor in the kangaroo rat's ability to live on dry food.

Do kangaroo rats tolerate dehydration of the body? It has been assumed that kangaroo rats are able to withstand a greater degree of desiccation than other mammals (156, 347). Since the animals do not become dehydrated when water is withheld, other means must be found to dehydrate them. The simplest method to bring them into negative water balance is to feed them a dry diet which is especially high in protein, such as soybeans, which contain about 40 per cent protein. The large amount of urea formed on this diet requires extra water for urine formation, and on this régime kangaroo rats lose weight and die after about 2 to 3 weeks.

In kangaroo rats kept on soybeans the weight loss at the time of death was about 34 per cent, but the average water content of the bodies was still 67·2 per cent (291). This is not a reduction from the normal water percentage in kangaroo rats, and the conclusion must be that although the animals were in negative water balance, the proportion of water in the body remained the same while they gradually lost weight. Thus, although a considerable amount of water had been lost the body was not really desiccated. Other small rodents, when dying from water restriction, also contained about 66 per cent water (79). In this respect there is no difference between kangaroo rats and other rodents which lack the special ability to survive without water.

This adds further evidence to the conclusion that the survival of kangaroo rats without drinking-water is in no way related to an exceptional ability to tolerate dehydration of the body. When fed on a dry diet they remain in water balance, and the physiological mechanisms responsible for this performance do not include any deviation in water content of the body from the usual mammalian pattern.

Can kangaroo rats absorb atmospheric water?

It is quite unconventional to raise this question, but it is necessary that it be examined before we can discuss how water intake and water expenditure can be balanced. The reason for asking this question to begin with is that some arthropods can absorb water from the atmosphere. This was demonstrated by Lees, who showed that ticks previously dehydrated in very dry air will take up water if kept at 90 per cent relative humidity. This gain continues until normal composition of the tissue fluids is restored (198). Similar findings in a number of insects testify to the wide occurrence of the phenomenon, but the nature of the mechanism for 'hygroscopic' absorption of atmospheric water vapour remains obscure.

The existence of a hygroscopic function in arthropods makes it necessary to consider whether a similar phenomenon could occur in mammals. This is, however, extremely unlikely.

It has not been demonstrated where the hygroscopic function in insects is located, but it is probably associated with the tracheal system. The hard outer cuticle of the insect, which is virtually impermeable to water because of a waxy coating, does not seem a likely possibility. In mammals the only parts in contact with the air are the skin and the mucous membranes of the respiratory passages and lungs, structures which are extremely different from insect tissues. The cornified epithelium of the mammalian skin seems unsuited for any active transport of water inwards, and where it has been examined there is a slow diffusion loss of water from the underlying fluids through the skin to the atmosphere. The mucous membranes of the respiratory passages have a moist surface from which evaporation takes place whenever the vapour pressure of the atmosphere is lower than that at the surface.

In those mammals that have been examined there is always a loss of water vapour from the skin as well as the lungs, although the amount varies with the humidity of the air. No evidence whatsoever points to the possibility of a hygroscopic function similar to that in insects. Finally, an important argument against a hygroscopic function is that the water balance of kangaroo rats and other desert mammals can be fully explained by known physiological processes.

Can kangaroo rats conserve water by storage of waste products?

The most obvious source of water loss in mammals is the formation of urine. Could the animals avoid this use of water by withholding the excretory products in time of shortage and eliminate them when water is more freely available? 'Storage excretion' is known to occur in insects, where the uric acid formed in protein metabolism may be deposited within the organism, frequently in the fat body, instead of being eliminated (352). In insects this storage may even be a lifetime proposition so that the waste products remain in the body and are never excreted.

Before we settle the question of a retention of excretory products, we must know whether kangaroo rats excrete urea such as other mammals do. In birds and reptiles protein metabolism leads to the formation of uric acid, which, due to its low solubility, can be excreted as a semi-solid paste with very little expenditure of water. This well-known scheme suggests that uric acid might be a means for water conservation in desert mammals as well. We have found, however, that urea is always formed as the end product of protein metabolism in kangaroo rats. Even when they are on a high-protein diet and in negative water balance, urea is excreted in the urine in amounts corresponding to the quantities of protein metabolized.

TABLE XX

Plasma concentrations in kangaroo rats kept on a dry diet did not increase significantly and were similar to those in animals with access to water ('Wet' diet). From (290)

	No. of animals	Days on diet	Plasma urea, mM	Plasma electrolytes, mEq/l
Dry diet	6	14	12·5	161
	6	21	11·0	149
	7	28	10·9	150
	3	32	13·6	152
'Wet' diet	6	14	10·2	158

If any part of the urea were to be retained in the body, its concentration in the blood-plasma should increase. Urea is a substance which diffuses freely throughout body fluids and cells, and the plasma concentration represents its concentration in all body water. If it were withheld from excretion, this should be reflected in a rising plasma concentration.

When we kept kangaroo rats for increasing lengths of time on the dry laboratory diet, there was no significant change in the plasma concentration of urea (see Table XX), and animals that were given pieces of watermelon so that water was available had urea concentrations in the same range as those that lived on only dry food. The plasma electrolytes, which for the greater part are sodium and chloride, showed this same similarity between dry-fed and wet-fed animals, and there was no significant change in the concentration during several weeks of water deprivation (290). It is therefore justifiable to conclude that neither urea, sodium, or chloride are withheld from excretion as a means to reduce the amount of water used for urine production.

WATER BALANCE—LOSS

For an animal to remain in water balance the water intake must equal or exceed the loss. The intake consists of (*a*) drinking-water, (*b*) free water in the food, and (*c*) water formed by oxidation (oxidation water or 'metabolic' water). While most animals consume considerable amounts of drinking-water, kangaroo rats must manage their water balance on the two last components. Their dry food contains only small amounts of absorbed water, and oxidation water is their main source. This meagre supply must suffice to cover all losses, which take place via three main routes, (*a*) by evaporation, (*b*) in the faeces, and (*c*) in the urine. In the following, we shall discuss in detail these three avenues of water loss and the physiological peculiarities that enable kangaroo rats to manage their precarious water balance.

Evaporation

Evaporation of water takes place both from the skin and from the respiratory tract. Even if there is no detectable sweat, and also in the absence of sweat glands (abnormal in man, normal in many other mammals), there is a loss of water vapour from the surface of the skin. This water loss is called insensible perspiration, but a more descriptive term is diffusion water loss (72, 351). In the non-sweating animal the water loss from the moist surfaces of the respiratory passages is relatively more important than evaporation from the skin. Its magnitude depends on the difference in water content between inspired and expired air and on the volume of air passing over the moist surfaces.

It has not been possible to devise an experimental procedure which separates the pulmonary and cutaneous evaporation in an undisturbed kangaroo rat. The application of masks, diaphragms, and valves has proven unsuccessful, and attempts at immobilization of the animal with anaesthesia has caused an immediate increase in the evaporation to at least twice the usual values (293). However, for the computation of the water balance it is sufficient to know the combined evaporation from lungs and skin, and such determinations have been carried out successfully.

It is not feasible to express the water loss per unit body weight because the metabolic rate and ventilation may be entirely different in two animals of the same body size. If, however, the water loss is expressed relative to oxygen consumption, the computation of water balance can be made in terms that can be compared directly from one animal to another. Such determinations gave the results listed in Table XXI.

The total evaporation is significantly lower in all the wild rodents than in laboratory rats and mice or in man (where the figure represents

evaporation from the lungs alone). What are the reasons for the seemingly low evaporation in the desert rodents? Or is the evaporation in
the laboratory rodents abnormally high?

There are two ways in which a reduction in evaporation from the
lungs could be accomplished: (1) the volume of air passing over the
respiratory surfaces for a given oxygen consumption could be reduced,
or (2) each volume of respiratory air could contain a smaller amount of
water. The first possibility would be realized if more than the usual
amount of oxygen could be extracted from the alveolar air. Atmospheric
air contains 21 per cent oxygen, and this is reduced to 16 per cent in the

TABLE XXI

Evaporation of water in various animals breathing dry air. From (293)

	Aver. weight g	Evaporation, mg H_2O/mlO_2
Merriam's kangaroo rat, *D. merriami*	36·1	0·54±0·04
Bannertailed kangaroo rat, *D. spectabilis*	100·1	0·57±0·07
Pocket mouse, *Perognathus sp.*	25·2	0·50±0·07
House mouse, *Mus musculus*	27·3	0·59
Golden hamster, *Cricetus aureus*	95·1	0·59±0·05
Albino rat, *Rattus norvegicus, var. alb.*	102·0	0·94±0·09
Albino mouse, *Mus musculus, var. alb.*	29·2	0·85±0·07
Man (evaporation from lungs only)	70 000	0·84

expired air of man. If it could instead be reduced to 11 per cent, the
volume of air respired would be reduced to half the usual volume and
the evaporation reduced accordingly. This hypothesis would require
lower than usual oxygen tensions in the alveolar air, and for the blood
to become fully saturated the oxygen dissociation curve should be shifted
to the left as compared with the usual curves. Such a shift is found in the
llama which normally breathes at the low oxygen pressure of high altitudes (140), but no shift was found in kangaroo rat blood (130). The
second hypothesis, that the expired air contains a reduced amount of
water by being saturated at a relatively low temperature, was found to
be sufficient to explain the low evaporation.

The direct measurement of the temperature of the expired air is
difficult because it would be necessary to have a sensing element with
such low heat capacity that it would not appreciably change the temperature of the air, and the recording instrument should be able to record
the changes at rates of respiration up to several hundred per minute.
However, in kangaroo rats as well as in white rats breathing in dry air
the surface temperature of the nasal mucosa near the tip of the nose was

around 24° C. Calculations, based on the dimensions of the air passages, the speed of the air, and the rate of heat transfer, show that temperature equilibrium exists between the expired air and the mucosal surface, so that the temperature of the expired air is also 24° C as it leaves the tip of the nose (296). A calculation of the temperature at which the expired air should be saturated in order to give the rate of evaporation actually found in kangaroo rats (0·54 mg water per ml oxygen) gives 25° C. This is amazingly close to the observed nasal temperature and supports the hypothesis of a low temperature of the expired air.

The mechanism that permits the establishment of a low nasal temperature can be understood if the nasal passage is regarded as a counter-current heat exchanger with intermittent flow in a single tube instead of the usual continuous flow in two tubes. During inspiration water evaporates from the moist nasal mucosa, removing heat and decreasing the surface temperature. When during expiration the warm, moist air from the lungs passes over this cool surface, the air is cooled and part of the water condenses again. During the next cycle this water evaporates during inspiration and is redeposited during expiration, and so on. The net result is that the expired air leaves the nose with a temperature below that of the body and, although saturated, contains less water than the pulmonary air.

The white rat, which also has a low nose temperature, evaporates more water than the kangaroo rat. How is this explained? It has been found that the white rat in addition to the evaporation from the lungs evaporates about an equal amount from the skin (332). The difference between the white rat and the kangaroo rat therefore seems to be due to an almost complete absence of cutaneous evaporation in the kangaroo rat. The high pulmonary evaporation in man is due to the much higher temperature of the expired air, which under normal circumstances is about 33° to 35° C.

The rates of evaporation listed in Table XXI refer to the water loss when the inspired air is completely dry. If the air contains some water, it is obvious that it takes less water to bring the expired air to saturation. Consequently, the evaporation from the animal depends on the humidity of the atmosphere, for every milligramme of water in the inspired air means a corresponding reduction in water loss. Since warm air at a certain relative humidity contains more water than cold air at the same relative humidity the respiratory evaporation will be lower in the warm air. It is the absolute humidity of the air that is most meaningful because it determines how much additional water must be added by the animal to bring the air to saturation.

It is important to emphasize the relevance of the absolute humidity because it is frequently believed that a cool and moist burrow is a great advantage to the desert animal. Once the burrow temperature is so low that evaporation is not needed for heat regulation (and we have seen that this normally is the case), a further decrease in temperature should be of no benefit, on the contrary, it can be expected to increase evaporation. For example, at 30° C saturated air contains 30 mg H_2O per litre air, and at 20° C only 17 mg H_2O per litre. A warm, moist burrow therefore has a much higher absolute humidity than a cool, equally moist burrow. It is, however, not a simple matter to state the effect of the various temperatures and humidities on evaporation because it is not known to what extent these influence nasal temperatures and thus the temperature of the expired air.

Water used for urine

The more concentrated urine an animal produces, the less water is used for the elimination of excretory products. A highly concentrated urine therefore becomes an exceedingly important factor in the water balance of the small desert rodent.

The urine concentrations found in kangaroo rats are indeed very high. They are a great deal higher than concentrations observed in such desert veterans as the camel and are only matched by the urine of other desert rodents from various parts of the world (see Table XXVI, page 181). The most concentrated urine we found in a kangaroo rat contained 3840 mM urea per litre, or 23 per cent of urea. This is almost five times as high as the most concentrated urine produced by man—in other words, the same amount of urea requires only one-fifth as much water in the kangaroo rat.

In order to produce such a concentrated solution the kidney performs osmotic work which mostly consists in the withdrawal of water from the initial fluid formed by ultrafiltration in the glomerulus. It could perhaps be expected that some of the solutes of the urine would be precipitated as the water is withdrawn, but this did not happen in our laboratory animals that were kept on a high-protein diet. Urea is easily soluble in water and does not crystallize from a 23 per cent solution.

On a different diet other urine components, not so easily soluble, may be predominant. This sometimes occurred in animals that were trapped in the field during the dry season. We were interested in knowing the urine concentrations in these animals that came directly from their natural habitat. To be certain that evaporation would not introduce any errors in our sampling techniques, a droplet of urine was taken directly into a micropipette as it appeared at the external opening of the urethra. Occasionally we found that the sample almost instantaneously solidified in the pipette and could not be expelled, and both the sample and the pipette were lost. Apparently, there is some protective mechanism against crystallization in the super-saturated solutions while they are still in the bladder, for we never found kangaroo rats with concretions in the urinary passages.

Drinking sea water. Since the maximum electrolyte concentration in the urine of the kangaroo rat, about 1200 mEq per litre, is about twice as concentrated as sea water, it should be perfectly feasible for this animal to drink sea water with impunity.

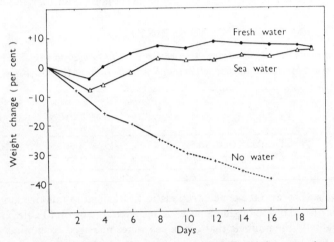

FIG. 35. Weight changes in adult kangaroo rats kept for 16 days on soybeans, with fresh water, sea water, or no water to drink. As shown by their ability to maintain body weight kangaroo rats can drink sea water with impunity. The animals without water died in 8 to 16 days. (Reproduced with permission from (292).)

Since kangaroo rats normally do not drink, it could not be expected that they would be enthusiastic about sea water if this were offered to them. To make them drink it would be necessary to induce a negative water balance so that drinking becomes the only way in which they can replenish their water content. This can easily be attained by feeding the animals dry soybeans. Due to the high protein content, larger than usual amounts of urea have to be excreted, and at the same time protein yields less oxidation water than the other common food components, fats and carbohydrates.

When put on a soybean diet with sea water to drink, kangaroo rats lost weight for the first 2 or 3 days. Afterwards they recovered equally as well as control animals which drank fresh water, and the weight after 16 days was even somewhat higher than the initial weight. The animals kept on the dry soybeans were not able to survive, they lost weight and died in 8 to 16 days (see Fig. 35).

Sea water contains appreciable amounts of magnesium and sulphate, which in man causes diarrhoea due to the laxative effects of these salts. The kangaroo rats that drank sea water suffered the same effect, they got diarrhoea, but in spite of this extra drain on their water resources, they were perfectly able to maintain their water balance.

To demonstrate that the animals really were in water balance and excreted the surplus of urea and salt, it was necessary to show that their body concentrations of these substances were not higher than in normal

TABLE XXII

Plasma concentrations of urea and electrolytes in kangaroo rats induced to drink by feeding a diet with a high protein content (dry soybeans)

	Plasma urea mM/l	Plasma electrolytes mEq/l
Drinking fresh water	12·5	156
Drinking sea water	12·3	157

animals. The average concentrations in five kangaroo rats drinking sea water turned out to be the same as in fresh-water controls (Table XXII). Evidently the animals that drank sea water managed to eliminate the excretory products in spite of high salt intake and the extra drain of the diarrhoea (292).

The question of whether the drinking of sea water can be tolerated has been the subject of considerable attention. Tradition has it that the castaway at sea must not drink sea water, which will only increase his thirst and hasten the arrival of death. Another question which the biologist has often discussed is whether seals and whales drink sea water.

If a man without other water resources drinks sea water the physiological results are inevitable. The extra salt increases the osmotic concentrations of his body fluids, thus aggravating his thirst which to begin with was caused by an increased osmotic concentration. More sea water will, of course, merely accelerate the physiological deterioration. As the kidneys work to eliminate the excess salts they will produce a urine as concentrated as possible. In man the maximum urine concentration is only about two-thirds of the salt concentration in sea water. Therefore, if, for example, 1 litre of sea water is ingested, $1\frac{1}{2}$ litres of urine must be formed to eliminate the salts. The result is that the extra $\frac{1}{2}$ litre of water is taken from the body fluids, thus increasing the water deficiency and raising the osmotic concentration in the body. Therefore, whether the salts are excreted or not, the inevitable result when a man drinks sea water is increasing osmotic concentrations and a faster physiological deterioration than if no water at all is taken.

Since the maximum urine concentration in the white rat is a great deal higher than in man, and actually somewhat exceeds that in sea water, it is reasonable to ask whether rats can utilize sea water for drinking. The results of such experiments show that no appreciable benefit is gained, the magnesium and sulphate cause intestinal difficulties with diarrhoea and increased water loss, and the urine does not become sufficiently more concentrated than the sea water to make any net water available (4, 22).

The question of whether seals, and particularly whales, drink sea water is not adequately settled. It is therefore important that an animal such as the kangaroo rat can utilize sea water for drinking, although normally it never sees the sea in its natural desert habitat. It demonstrates the ability of the mammalian kidney to evolve into an extremely powerful organ of excretion, and marine mammals equipped with a similar kidney should have no difficulties in eliminating salts, whether ingested with their food or by drinking sea water. Whether or not these animals actually do drink sea water is another question which is not easily answered.

Antidiuretic hormone. It is well known that the volume of the urine and its concentration is under endocrine control. An increased release of the antidiuretic hormone (ADH) from the neurohypophysis leads to an immediate renal response with increased tubular reabsorption of water, usually yielding a smaller volume of more concentrated urine. It is therefore reasonable to inquire into a possible connexion between ADH and the exceedingly high urine concentrations in the kangaroo rat. Could these high concentrations be caused by unusual amounts of ADH?

When an animal excretes a maximally concentrated urine under the influence of ADH, this concentration cannot be increased further by additional amounts of ADH. The kidney has a characteristic concentrating ability which depends on its structure, which differs from species to species. The amount of ADH produced in the hypophysis and released into the blood-stream determines to what extent the capacity is utilized at a given moment, but when the concentrating mechanism works at its maximal capacity the release of more hormone should have no further effect.

Although a high concentration of antidiuretic hormone cannot explain high urine concentrations, it is of interest to compare the role of this hormone in the kangaroo rat with its function, in, for example, the white rat. Ordinary white rats which have an adequate fluid intake have a small amount of ADH circulating in the blood and none is excreted in the urine. However, if they are deprived of drinking-water for 2 or 3 days, ADH activity can be detected in their urine. In kangaroo rats there is always a detectable amount of ADH in the urine (10). Apparently the excretion of this hormone is a normal event in these animals and explains why they frequently secrete a concentrated urine even when water is available to them. The concentration of ADH in the kangaroo rat urine was much higher than in ordinary rats that had been thirsted for 2 or 3 days, but this is not very meaningful because the total volume of urine is so much smaller in the kangaroo rat, and, furthermore, it is not certain that the concentration of ADH in the urine can be taken as a measure of the rate of secretion. In this respect the amount of hormone circulating in the blood is probably more meaningful. In the serum of twenty kangaroo rats the ADH activity was found to be quite low and in eight of them there was no detectable ADH activity. In animals that were disturbed by blood sampling (by heart puncture), with or without anaesthesia, there was an increase in the ADH activity (11). This increase was much greater in kangaroo rats than in white rats treated the same way, but it is difficult to suggest a meaningful interpretation for this difference.

In a study of the adrenal cortex of the kangaroo rat it was brought out that this animal not only tolerates more salt than the white rat, but it can also thrive on a diet with a sodium content far below the minimum required by the white rat. The damage incurred to the adrenal gland and the kidney on a high sodium diet is less in kangaroo rats than in white rats (236). Further studies of the endocrinology of the kangaroo rat are needed.

Kidney structure and its significance. In view of its unusual concentrating ability it is of interest to know the structure of the kangaroo rat kidney. Basically, it is similar to the kidney of other rodents; its size is not unusual, and the number of glomeruli and their size are normal for this size animal (287). A conspicuous feature is the long papilla (319), which, as we shall see, is of importance to the concentration process.

The ability to form a concentrated urine is correlated with the characteristic loop of the kidney tubule, known as Henle's loop. Only mammals and birds can produce a urine which is more concentrated than the blood, and it has been pointed out that only these two groups possess kidneys that have Henle's loops (217). Furthermore, there is a close correlation between the development of this loop and the concentrating ability of the kidney (307). In most birds, which can produce a urine only about twice as concentrated as their plasma (U/P ratio = 2), the loops are fewer and not as well developed as in mammals.

Among mammals there is a remarkable correlation between the length of the loop structure (expressed as the relative thickness of the renal medulla) and the aridity of the habitat in which animals live. Desert rodents, antelopes, camel, giraffe, and lion have the greatest relative development of the renal medulla (which contains the loop structure), and animals that have an aquatic habitat such as beavers, water rats, and platypus have a thin medulla and very short loops. An excellent survey of the structure of mammalian kidneys was made by Sperber, who brought out this correlation with convincing clarity (319). His studies of the kidneys of 139 species of mammals included careful microdissections where single nephrons were isolated and the various parts were measured. Of the thirty-four rodents examined by Sperber, seven have a particularly long renal papilla, in fact so long that it extends beyond the pelvis of the kidney and into the ureter. These seven species are desert animals, and among them are some which later have been found to produce extremely concentrated urine.

The significance of the long Henle's loop is evident in the light of the countercurrent hypothesis for the concentration of urine (145). This hypothesis explains how an active transport which works over a moderate gradient can be built up in a loop structure into a considerable concentration difference. The principle of the mechanism is the ability of the ascending leg of the loop to transport material to the descending leg. The result is an accumulation of the transported substance in the loop and an increase in its concentration. This gives a multiplier system where the effect of the basic transport process increases in magnitude as the length of the loop increases. Thus, the longer the loops in the kidney, the more concentrated urine can be formed, precisely as we find it in desert rodents.

There is an overwhelming amount of evidence in favour of this hypothesis which is now generally accepted. Micropuncture studies, in which micropipettes with tips of a few micra are inserted into the lumen of a single renal tubule for the removal of minute samples, have shown that the filtrate formed in the glomerulus is isotonic with the plasma. As the fluid passes into Henle's loop, it becomes increasingly concentrated, but becomes dilute again as it leaves the loop. As the fluid passes through the collecting ducts, which run parallel to and interspersed with the loops, the high osmotic concentration in the surrounding tissue causes withdrawal of water. Thus the final concentration of the urine as it is discharged at the tip of the renal papilla corresponds closely to the concentration established by the multiplier system of the loop structure (132, 133).

It is very interesting that essentially this sequence was suggested as early as 1935 in a paper by Howell and Gersh (156). These authors injected in kangaroo rats (*Dipodomys agilis*) a solution of sodium ferrocyanide, and the concentration of this substance in the renal tubule was afterwards demonstrated by the formation of Prussian blue. The microscopic picture which resulted suggested that concentration of the tubular fluid took place in the loop of Henle and in the collecting ducts. Undoubtedly, this finding was a result of the fact that Howell and Gersh examined the kidney of an animal where the renal concentrating mechanism is more highly developed than in most other mammals.

Water loss in the faeces

Kangaroo rats eliminate small, firm, almost black pellets of faeces. The water content is quite low; when the animals ate a uniform diet of pearled barley it was on the average about 83 grammes of water per 100 grammes dry faecal matter. White rats on the same diet eliminated

TABLE XXIII

The amount of water eliminated with the faeces in the kangaroo rat and in the white rat

	Faeces, grammes dry matter/ 100 g food	Water, mg/g dry faecal matter	Water lost with faeces for 100 g barley eaten
Kangaroo rat	3·04	834	2·53 grammes
White rat	6·04	2246	13·6 grammes

faeces which contained 225 grammes of water per 100 grammes dry matter (295). In addition to the much lower water content of the faeces in the kangaroo rats, the food was better utilized so that a smaller amount of dry matter was eliminated (see Table XXIII). The net result was that white rats used five times as much water for formation of faeces as the kangaroo rats did when they ate the same amount of food.

The reason for the low water content of the faeces and the physiological mechanism involved in the withdrawal of water from intestinal contents has not been investigated, and, as mentioned under the discussion of the camel, investigations of this subject could prove most interesting.

The reason for the higher utilization of the feed in the kangaroo rat may be connected with its habit of eating its own faeces (coprophagy). When a kangaroo rat is observed in the laboratory, it may appear that it is licking or cleaning itself, but a careful observer may note that it takes expelled faecal pellets directly into the mouth and reingests them. Such coprophagy in *Dipodomys* was first noted in animals fed on an air-dried diet (156).

Coprophagy is not unusual in small herbivores, and it has been demonstrated that it is essential to normal digestion in rats and rabbits (129, 333). The advantage of coprophagy is not merely that the feed is better digested during the second passage through the digestive tract, but primarily that a number of vitamins synthesized by bacterial action in the large caecum can be utilized by the animal. While the ruminant has bacterial fermentation at the beginning of the digestive tract and there-fore can utilize synthesized products on the first passage, the fermenta-tion in other herbivores takes place in the caecum, which is located towards the end of the digestive tract. Reingestion permits a second passage and gives many of the nutritional and synthetic advantages that the ruminant enjoys without resorting to coprophagy.

The kangaroo rat is likely to benefit nutritionally from the reingestion, but a further advantage is gained through a reduction in the amount of undigested material and the consequent reduction in water loss. The kangaroo rat is in such a precarious water balance that any small step towards a greater economy in water expenditure is an essential part in the total picture.

TABLE XXIV

The amounts of oxidation water formed in the metabolism of 100 grammes of dry pearled barley

	Composition g	Oxidation water, g	Oxygen used, litre
Starch	88·00	48·8	70·40
Fat	1·12	1·2	2·28
Protein	9·24	3·7	8·76
Total	98·36	53·7	81·44

WATER BALANCE—GAIN

The total water gain for an animal that does not drink can readily be calculated from the composition of the food. In addition to the free water which is absorbed even in the driest plant material, water is formed in the oxidation of the nutrients, and the amount can be esti-mated from the amounts of carbohydrate, fat, and protein in the food (cf. Table II, page 30).

The estimation of oxidation water is facilitated when the diet has a constant composition, and we chose pearled barley as a suitable uni-form feed. This grain has had the outer parts removed, leaving a rather uniform core. When the animals are fed whole untreated grains they selectively leave some parts of the grain and eat others, thereby making it difficult to ascertain the precise composition of the parts consumed.

The amounts of water available from 100 grammes of dry pearled barley are listed in Table XXIV. One hundred grammes are what a kangaroo rat eats in about a month, but the quantity of water formed is, of course, the same whether it takes longer or shorter to metabolize the grain.

In addition to the water formed in oxidation, water is present in the dry barley as absorbed moisture in an amount that varies with atmospheric humidity. At zero humidity, which never occurs in nature, there is by definition no free water in the grain, for the amount of 'free water' is determined by exposing a sample to zero humidity in a desiccator. However, as atmospheric humidity is increased, more and more moisture becomes absorbed. At a few selected constant humidities the 100 grammes of pearled barley contained the following amounts of water after it had time to reach equilibrium with the atmosphere (Table XXV).

TABLE XXV

The amount of water absorbed in 100 grammes of dry pearled barley when in equilibrium with air of various relative humidities

Relative humidity,	10 per cent	33 per cent	43 per cent	76 per cent
Absorbed water, g	3·72	10·20	11·72	18·12

The amounts of absorbed water are considerable, particularly at the higher humidities. In the dry desert air, often as low as 10 per cent or 15 per cent r.h. during the day, the moisture content of plant material is fairly low, but this is partly offset by the rising relative humidity as the air cools off at night. This is the time when desert rodents are out seeking their food, and material scattered on the ground surface can rapidly absorb moisture from the thin layer of air closest to the ground which cools most rapidly. Even when no visible dew is formed, the moisture content of hygroscopic plant material rises rapidly. The quantities of water made available this way have not been accurately estimated, and carefully executed studies are likely to yield interesting information.

Another factor that may contribute to an increase in absorbed water is the habit of many rodents of storing food in their burrows. A single bannertailed kangaroo rat (*D. spectabilis*) may store several kilogrammes of plant material (343). At the higher humidity in the burrow this food takes up water, adding an appreciable amount to the water gained from oxidation. The small Merriam's kangaroo rat (*D. merriami*) which has been discussed above does not have large stores of food, but it has a knack for sneaking into the den of its larger cousin, the bannertailed kangaroo rat, which apparently hoards more than it can use. Whether the moisture content of stored food really increases above what it was when the food was collected is a question where speculation helps little. This important problem has been examined in Israel by Shkolnik, who found that the seeds of *Zilla spinosum* (a cruciferous desert plant) contained 4–7 per cent water when air dried, but when stored in the burrows of *Meriones crassus* they contained 30 per cent water (personal communication).

More information about the water content of 'dry' plant material is needed, and the improvements in microclimatological methods in recent years should greatly facilitate the collection of the necessary data. This problem is one of the many where the climate observed with standard meteorological instruments 2 metres above the ground gives insufficient information for a consideration of the events in the micro-atmosphere in which the animals live.

CAN WATER LOSS AND GAIN BE BALANCED?

If we assume that a kangaroo rat lives in completely dry air and over a period of time eats and metabolizes 100 grammes of dry pearled barley, the total water gain consists of oxidation water only, which is 53·7 grammes. How far does this water go towards covering the combined losses from evaporation, urine formation, and faeces?

This question can be answered fairly easily from the information which has been discussed earlier in this chapter. In Table XXI, which gives the amount of evaporation per millilitre oxygen used, we find that 0·54 grammes of water is evaporated for each litre of oxygen consumed. Since the metabolism of 100 grammes of barley requires the uptake of 81·4 litres of oxygen, the inevitable evaporation will be 43·9 grammes of water.

The 100 grammes of barley contain 9·24 grammes of protein which, when metabolized, yield 3·17 grammes of urea. If this urea is excreted in a urine containing 20 per cent urea, a reasonable assumption since the maximum concentration is 23 per cent, 13·5 grammes of water go for urine formation. (This calculation involves the specific gravity of a 20 per cent urea solution, which is 1·05, so that 85 grammes of water are excreted for each 20 grammes of urea.)

The amount of faeces formed from 100 grammes of barley is 3·04 grammes dry faecal matter, and this involves a loss of 2·53 grammes of water (see Table XXIII).

Adding all these water expenditures, we find that 59·9 grammes of water is the inevitable minimum loss when 100 grammes of barley are metabolized and yield 53·7 grammes of oxidation water. In other words, if the animals are kept in completely dry air and no free water is absorbed in the grain, they will be in negative water balance and should not be able to survive.

Since the difference between loss and gain is about 6 grammes, balance could be achieved if this much moisture were absorbed in the grain. This occurs at a relative humidity somewhere around 20 per cent. However, at the increased atmospheric humidity the evaporation from the respiratory tract will be less than the amount we have used in the calculation above. Therefore, as the water gain increases with the higher atmospheric humidity, so does evaporation decrease. The dependence on atmospheric humidity in the water balance of the kangaroo rat can

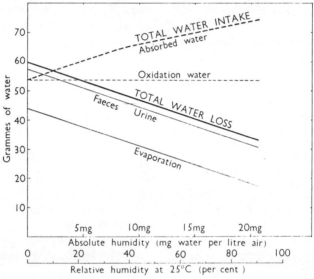

FIG. 36. The water balance of kangaroo rats at various air humidities. The calculation was made for the metabolism of 100 grammes of dry pearled barley, an amount normally consumed in about a month. The water expenditures for evaporation, urine, and faeces are superimposed on each other so that the fully drawn thick line represents total water loss. The water intakes, oxidation water and water absorbed in the grain, are likewise superimposed so that the heavy dashed line represents total water intake. At the intersect of the two top lines the animals should just be able to remain in water balance; at lower humidities they should be in negative water balance and lose weight. (Reproduced with permission from (295).)

most easily be represented in a composite diagram which indicates the expected water balance at various humidities (Fig. 36).

In this diagram the evaporation is related to atmospheric humidity, showing the decrease which results from an increasing amount of water vapour in the inspired air. The calculation of this slope is difficult because the temperature of the nasal mucosa, and consequently also the amount of water in the expired air, changes with changing humidity. For this reason the slope is an approximation and only its order of magnitude is reasonably accurate. Above the curve for evaporation are added the minimum uses of water for formation of urine and for faeces. The top curve (thick fully drawn line) therefore shows the total sum of the minimum water losses as it varies with atmospheric humidity.

The oxidation water, which is independent of atmospheric humidity, is supplemented by an increasing amount of absorbed water at higher humidities, giving a total water gain which likewise increases with humidity (heavy dashed line).

This diagram shows exactly what was said above; at zero humidity the water loss exceeds the gain, but with increasing humidity this changes to a more favourable water balance. The point where the water gain is sufficient to cover the minimum loss is at about 10 per cent relative humidity, which at $25°$ C (the temperature for which these calculations were made) corresponds to 2 mg of water per litre air. Below this humidity limit a kangaroo rat should be in negative water balance and slowly lose water, above it the kangaroo rat should be in positive water balance and thrive on the dry diet.

A humidity appreciably lower than 2 mg per litre air could probably not be found, even in the most extremely dry deserts, and the desert rodent should therefore be able to remain in water balance. For the wild desert rodent, however, many variables enter into the picture in addition to the inevitable inaccuracy of our calculations. Much time is spent in a burrow with higher humidity than the outside air (294); the composition of the food varies; its moisture content is higher when it is picked up at night; and if the food is stored in the burrow it also takes up moisture. On the other hand, the amount of oxidation water depends on the relative proportions of carbohydrate, fat, and protein in the food. If the amount of protein is increased, as it is in the seeds of the pea family, the amount of oxidation water is smaller, and at the same time additional urea is formed which requires more water for urine formation.

Experimental confirmation of the water balance account

The simplest way to check on the validity of all the calculations given above—which form a synopsis of the available information about water balance in kangaroo rats—would be to maintain these animals on pearled barley at various atmospheric humidities. Therefore, a group of kangaroo rats was kept in a room with controlled temperature and humidity and fed pearled barley which had been left in the same atmosphere for several days so that the moisture in the grain was in equilibrium with the air. At 50 per cent relative humidity, the animals had no difficulty in maintaining water balance and actually gained in weight during the 8 days they were observed. In a following period with 15 per cent ʒlative humidity some of the animals lost slightly, but they regained their weight when the humidity was reset to 24 per cent. After 9 days the humidity was decreased to 10 per cent, and as a group the animals almost maintained their weight. However, a decrease to 5 per cent relative humidity brought on a more rapid weight loss, indicating that in this very dry air the animals could not maintain water balance.

On the basis of these results it is appropriate to conclude that the accounts outlined in this chapter have been verified by the ability of kangaroo rats to live under the predicted conditions. It is also justifiable to say that there is nothing mysterious about their ability to live on air-dried food without any drinking-water, the major physiological factors are known, the unique aspect is merely in the unusual degree of economy in all aspects of water expenditure.

Can oxidation water be increased?

It is obvious that there are no metabolic pathways that could produce water in excess of that derived from the hydrogen in the food. On the other hand, one could ask whether the amount of oxidation water could be increased by increasing food intake and metabolism? The answer is an unequivocal 'yes'. Would this be of any advantage to the animal? The answer is 'no'.

At any atmospheric humidity, except the lowest, the animal is already in water balance, whether its metabolic rate is high or low. For the account it makes no difference whether the 100 grammes of barley discussed in the preceding are metabolized in 1 month, 2 weeks, or 1 week. At a given humidity the requirements for low evaporation, concentration of the urine, and dry faeces, would be the same for the given set of conditions.

At the very lowest humidity, where the animal cannot remain in water balance, an increased rate of metabolism means that the water loss is incurred in a shorter time. Under these conditions it is of no help to increase the metabolism, it would merely aggravate the rate of loss. Accordingly, at the very lowest humidities the kangaroo rat would lose by increasing its metabolism; at the higher humidities it is already in water balance and gains nothing. Therefore, the kangaroo rat is not like the camel, which always loses water by increasing its metabolism. The difference is that in the camel the water loss from the lungs exceeds the amount of oxidation water formed, while in the kangaroo rat the respiratory water loss is appreciably less than the oxidation water.

How do these generalizations compare with the behaviour of kangaroo rats? Seemingly, they increase their metabolism when fed entirely dry feed. Animals with access to a running wheel and fed on dry grain ran up to 9000 (av. 4340 ± 1120 S.D.) revolutions in one night, while animals that also received a small piece of watermelon only ran about

400 to 1100 (av. 697±134 S.D.) revolutions (296). Animals with high activity decreased their activity the first night after being fed a few grammes of watermelon. Similar results have been obtained for another species of kangaroo rat, *Dipodomys panamintinus* (237).

These experiments may suggest that there is a mechanism for increased formation of oxidation water. It is, however, not necessary to interpret the increased activity as due to a need for water, for if the atmospheric humidity is anything but the very lowest, the animals are already in positive water balance, whether they run much or not. In extremely dry air it should be useful for them to stop running, but this does not seem to happen. When confined and allowed no exercise they actually lost less water under the driest conditions than when they were allowed to run. Apparently, under these circumstances their urge to run was not adjusted to the water-balance picture.

Responses involving increased activity seem to be of a more general nature. For example, white rats which are deprived of water will increase their running (348). They are already in negative water balance and activity aggravates the situation. Total caloric restriction also increases the running, and it is equally evident that increased running *per se* serves no metabolically useful purpose for a starving animal. Similarly increased activity is found in rats deprived of thiamin or the entire vitamin B complex (60, 136). It therefore seems that increased activity is not directed towards the amelioration of a physiological condition, but it may still have a rational basis as a survival value, for example, rats which are deprived of calories are more likely to find food if they seek it over a larger territory.

SUMMARY

Kangaroo rats can live for indefinite periods of time on air-dried food without access to drinking-water. In their natural habitat their main dietary components are dry seeds and other dry plant material, even when green and succulent plant material is available. They are nocturnal animals that remain in their burrows during the day and thus avoid the use of water for heat regulation.

Kangaroo rats do not depend on storage of water for their survival on dry food. They maintain their body weight and a normal water content in the body, hence there are no water reserves that are gradually consumed. The inevitable losses of water are through evaporation, formation of urine, and with the faeces.

Kangaroo rats have a lower evaporation from the lungs, relative to the oxygen uptake, than found in large mammals such as man. The low evaporation from the respiratory tract is due to a low temperature of the expired air. Apparently, they lose virtually no water by evaporation from the skin, which has no sweat glands. White rats, which likewise lack sweat glands, lose water from the skin by insensible perspiration in an amount of the same magnitude as the evaporation from the lungs.

The urine of kangaroo rats is highly concentrated. It may contain urea in a concentration of almost 4 molar (24 per cent), and salt in twice the concentration of sea water. This means that very little water is used for urine formation.

The high concentrating power of the kidney suggests that kangaroo rats should be able to utilize sea water for drinking. Although they normally do not drink they can be made to do so by feeding soybeans which have a high protein content and therefore yield large amounts of urea to be excreted. On this feed kangaroo rats will die without water, but they thrive if given sea water to drink.

The faeces of the kangaroo rat have a low water content, and the utilization of the feed is very high so that the amount of faeces for a given amount of food is low. In this way the faecal water loss in a kangaroo rat is less than one-fifth of the corresponding water loss in a white rat.

These combined water losses must, if the animal is to maintain water balance, be covered by an equal water intake. The water intake consists of oxidation water (metabolic water) and of preformed water present in the food. The amount of oxidation water is determined by the composition of the food. On a diet of pearled barley, 54 grammes of oxidation water is formed per 100 grammes of food. In addition, a small amount of water is present in the food as absorbed moisture. This amount increases with increasing atmospheric humidity.

It can be calculated that the water gain equals the losses at any atmospheric humidity above about 20 per cent relative humidity at 25° C. Experiments in which kangaroo rats were exposed to different humidities and fed only pearled barley confirmed these calculations. The kangaroo rat is therefore a desert animal whose complete water balance is adequately accounted for. Water balance is maintained on the air-dried diet because of the utmost economy in water expenditure; a low evaporation, an extremely concentrated urine, and the formation of small amounts of faeces with a low water content.

12

OTHER RODENTS

SMALL rodents are the most abundant mammals in all deserts of the world. It would serve no useful purpose to list all these animals, for we would end up merely with a long catalogue of names, unfamiliar to many of us. Most of them have never been the subject of any kind of physiological study, and an enormous field is open for the investigator who cares to start.

Perhaps the greatest number of rodents is found in the Great Palae-arctic Desert, stretching from the west coast of Africa through Sahara, Arabia, up through Asia, and into central China. Large desert areas are also found in South Africa, the interior of Australia, and in North and South America, and they all have their characteristic rodent fauna. Many of these rodents eat dry seeds and other dry plant material and can live in captivity for months or years without water or moist food. These are of the same physiological type as the American kangaroo rats.

Other desert rodents depend on succulent plant material which they consume in various quantities. Two American desert rodents which belong to this group are the diurnal ground squirrel and the more nocturnal pack rat; both need food with a considerable moisture content. With one exception, the interesting North African rodent *Psam-momys*, we do not know which desert rodents in other parts of the world have similar needs for water in their food.

'DRY' RODENTS

The North American kangaroo rat is a good example of a mammal that can live entirely on dry food, and its water metabolism is better known than that of any other desert animal. Most of the work described in the preceding chapter referred to Merriam's kangaroo rat (*Dipodomys merriami*), but several other North American rodents have a similar physiology. They eat dry food by preference and can live for indefinite periods without additional moisture. This is true of several species of kangaroo rats, e.g. the Fresno kangaroo rat (*D. nitrotoides exilis*) (92). Two other kangaroo rats (*D. deserti* and *D. spectabilis*) have been kept in my own laboratory and conform to the overall picture of their model relative. The same is true of two species of pocket mouse (*Perognathus baileyi* and *P. penicillatus pricei*), which belong to the same family as the kangaroo rats, the Heteromyidae. The pocket mice are quite small and are not as easy to handle as kangaroo rats, so that what we know about them is more limited. They do excrete a highly concentrated urine, however, and live well without any moist food. In fact, they seem to be even more independent of moisture than the kangaroo rats. If some succulent fruit, such as a piece of watermelon, was offered to the kangaroo rats, they would occasionally nibble a little, but we never saw a pocket mouse display any interest in juicy foods. A third genus of the same family, the kangaroo mouse (*Microdipodops pallidus*), can also live on dry food without water (37, 138).

In the Old World deserts some of the commonest rodents are jerboas (family Dipodidae) which have an amazing external resemblance to the American kangaroo rat. This is a clear case of convergent evolution, for the animals belong to two different suborders of rodents.[1] Physiologically there is also considerable similarity.

African jerboas (*Jaculus jaculus*) are pleasant pets, and it has frequently been found that they get along well in captivity without water (74). We have had the same experience, both in the United States and in the Sahara. Although our animals did well on dry food, they did not thrive on the very simple diet that we used with kangaroo rats, dry pearled barley. Barley alone is nutritionally unsatisfactory; the protein and vitamin contents are low, and the mineral content is in some respects insufficient. With soybean meal as well, however, they did very well. jerboas did very well.

The jerboa in many respects seems like an exaggerated kangaroo rat. The hind legs are a little longer, the front legs smaller, and the whole animal seems more fragile. The kidneys, however, are more powerful than those of the kangaroo rat. The highest concentration of urea which we have found in jerboa urine was 4230 mM per litre (25·4 per cent), somewhat higher than the maximum of 3840 mM in kangaroo rats (see Table XXVI). Recently Kirmiz studied in detail the water balance of *Jaculus orientalis*, which also thrives on dry food (182). (Confusingly he uses the now obsolete name *Dipus aegyptius*, though Ellerman considers this synonymous with *J. jaculus*.)

Another Old World desert rodent that can live on dry food is the gerbil (*Gerbillus gerbillus*), a small rodent from Egypt that weighs some 20 to 25 grammes. The animal does well on dry pearled barley only, and its urine concentration of urea may be as high as 3410 mM/litre. By giving an extra salt load, the concentration of electrolytes in its urine has been brought to 1600 mM, about three times as high as sea water (73).

Other African animals that deserve mention are of the genus *Meriones*.

[1] The kangaroo rats (family Heteromyidae) belong to the suborder Sciuromorpha which includes such well-known animals as squirrels, gophers, and beavers. The jerboas (family Dipodidae) belong to the Myomorpha which includes ordinary rats, mice, hamsters, &c.

They are gerbils but have no common English names to distinguish them. They weigh up to 100 grammes or so and are normal-looking rodents which run on four legs. Two species from the Sahara have been examined. *Meriones libycus* was kept for extended periods on a dry diet without weight loss by the French zoologist, Petter (254), and a similar

TABLE XXVI

Maximal urine concentrations in various mammals

In many cases the listed figure is the highest available, although there is no certainty that it represents the concentration limit for that species. Maximal concentrations of urea and electrolytes usually do not occur in the same sample; therefore the values listed in the first two columns cannot be added to give the maximal osmotic concentration. When actual determinations are unavailable, the osmotic concentrations are estimates, judged to be reasonably accurate. (The electrolyte concentration is an approximation which in some cases refers to Na concentration, in others to electrolytic conductivity expressed as the equivalent NaCl solution)

	Urine urea, mM/l	Urine electrolyte, mEq/l	Urine osmotic conc., osm/l	Urine: plasma osmotic ratio
Man (204, 205)	792	460	1·43	4·2
Pack rat	1980	714	2·7 (est.)	7 (est.)
(*Neotoma albigula*) (290, 291)				
Sheep (209)	..	..	3·2	7·6
White rat (4, 22, 132, 206)	2160	760	2·9	8·9
Cat (265, 355)	2330	600	3·25	9·9
Camel (78)	..	1068	2·8	8
Ground squirrel	2860	1200	3·9	9·5
(*Citellus leucurus*) (33, 160, 309)				
Grasshopper mouse	..	..	4·0	12
(*Onychomys torridus*) (309)				
Kangaroo rat	3840	1200	5·5 (est.)	14 (est.)
(*Dipodomys merriami*) (290)				
Gerbil	3410	1600	5·5 (est.)	14 (est.)
(*Gerbillus gerbillus*) (73)				
Jerboa	4320	1530	6·5 (est.)	16 (est.)
(*Jaculus jaculus*) (309)				
Sand rat	2850	1920	6·34	17
(*Psammomys obesus*) (309)				

species *Meriones crassus*, that was caught for us by Petter near the oasis Béni Abbès, also lived well on dry food. It amazed us with its powerful kidney. One urine sample, collected from the urethral opening directly into a micropipette so that errors from evaporation were excluded, contained a total electrolyte concentration of 1793 mEq per litre. It thus appears that the exceptional kidney function is a characteristic of all those desert rodents that are able to subsist on dry food.

The various desert rodents are not equal in their ability to subsist on a dry regimen. Shkolnik has demonstrated a gradation by keeping seven different species on whole dry barley for a month at 30° C and 30 per cent relative humidity. He has permitted me to reproduce some of his unpublished results in Fig. 37. When these animals were offered water to drink after a month, a sequence emerged which clearly separated the least desert adapted species at the top of the list and the most pronounced desert species at the bottom (Table XXVII).

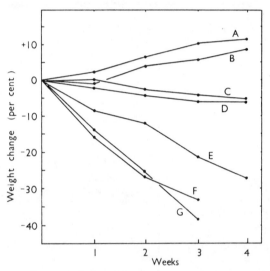

FIG. 37. Changes in body weight of seven species of desert rodents from Israel when kept for 4 weeks at 30° C and 30 per cent relative humidity. The animals were fed on whole barley. (A) *Gerbillus gerbillus*, (B) *G. dasyurus*, (C) *G. pyramidum*, (D) *Meriones crassus*, (E) *Acomys russatus*, (F) *Jaculus jaculus*, (G) *A. cahirinus*. The gerbil, *G. gerbillus*, is found in the most extreme desert habitat. (Shkolnik, personal communication.)

'MOIST' RODENTS

Of American desert rodents, the pack rat is more dependent on moist food than any other. As we saw in a preceding chapter, this animal is much less tolerant to dehydration than an ordinary laboratory rat and depends entirely on the intake of large quantities of succulent plant material, mostly cactus. Another American rodent that needs moist food but takes less of it and is more tolerant to dehydration is the ground squirrel. Whether any of the desert rodents from other parts of the world have a similar type of physiology is not yet known. It would seem very likely that this would be so. At least, in marginal areas there must be many animals that are not sufficiently independent of water to penetrate the more severe parts of the deserts, but still are more tolerant than their relatives in typically moist habitats. One can therefore expect that intermediate forms will be found, but it is impossible to point out particular examples because we lack knowledge of the many species and their physiology.

There is, however, one very interesting North African rodent that deserves mention, *Psammomys obesus*, properly called sand rat in English (315). This animal is restricted to places where the vegetation has a high

TABLE XXVII

Water consumption in various rodents from Israel after a month without water at 30° C and 30 per cent relative humidity (Shkolnik, personal communication)

	Water consumed, per cent of body weight
Acomys cahirinus	11·38
A. russatus	9·26
Jaculus jaculus	4·30
Meriones crassus	none
Gerbillus pyramidum	none
G. dasyurus	none
G. gerbillus	none

water content (253). The plant associations where it makes its nests are dominated by salt-loving plants, similar to the fleshy halophytes found at the edge of saline and brackish water all over the world. These plants are extremely abundant in some of the dried-out river beds where the soil remains moist between floods but still has a high salt content. Other plants do not grow in these places, but the halophytes thrive there, as the salt is a prerequisite for their growth.[1]

The juicy plants that the sand rat prefers to eat contain so much salt that they taste very salty. A few analyses made during the spring showed a salt content well above that of sea water (Table XXVIII). Further determinations were not made, and it is not known whether the salt concentration in the sap increases in summer. The sand rat eats great quantities of these plants, which contain between 80 and 90 per cent water. It must eat tremendous amounts in order to get enough nutrient from the watery flesh, and quantities of salty sap are an inescapable adjunct to the food.

[1] The commonest plants in the association where we obtained *Psammomys* were: *Traganum nudatum*, *Salsola foetida*, *Suaeda mollis*, *Suaeda pruinosa*, and *Arthrocnemum sp.* (253).

The sand rats are perfectly able to handle the salt; they produce about 1 ml of urine or more per hour (the animal weighs about 100 grammes). The highest urinary salt concentration we have measured is 1920 mEq per litre (see Table XXVI). This is not far from four times the concentration of sea water, and yet, we do not know whether this is the maximum limit for the animal. In the laboratory it has been kept on ordinary dry animal food with a 5 per cent sodium chloride solution for drinking and

TABLE XXVIII

Mineral composition of succulent halophytic plants from Wadi Saoura in the Sahara

(*All these plants belong to the same family, the Chenopodiacae, which also includes* Halogeton glomeratus, *a serious menace to sheep in the United States because of its high oxalic acid content.*) *Values are in milli-equivalents per kg fresh plant*

	Cl	Na	K	Oxalic acid
Arthrocnemum sp.	872	723	38	none
Traganum nudatum	61	706	153	421
Suaeda mollis	344	796	51	555
Sea water	548	470	10	none

in an exploratory study two individuals drank 8 per cent NaCl (1370 mEq per litre) for 10 days and 9 per cent NaCl (1540 mEq per litre) for 4 days without weight loss. In one of these animals the highest sodium concentration in the urine was 1890 mEq per litre, almost the same as in the wild animal mentioned above.

Another amazing finding concerning the sand rat was its tolerance to the large amounts of oxalic acid in the food (see Table XXVIII). Two plants which were part of its staple food contained about one-half normal oxalic acid in the sap, which is more than a 2 per cent solution. An animal eating 20 grammes of these plants would get about ½ gramme of oxalic acid, apparently without suffering any harm. In man, 5 grammes of oxalic acid will give a serious poisoning and may be lethal. The ability to eat with impunity plants that contain oxalic acid is similar to the tolerance of the American pack rat, but, as in that animal, we do not know whether the insensitivity is due to destruction of oxalic acid by intestinal bacteria or to its metabolism in the body. At the present time there is no indication whether or not the mechanism is the same in the two animals.

The similarity between pack rat and sand rat in the high intake of juicy food does not extend to their ability to excrete salt; in this respect they are at the opposite extremes among the animals we have discussed.

Whether any other desert animals are adapted to an extremely salty diet in the same way as the sand rat is unknown and would be worth study. It is also possible that rodents from an entirely different habitat, the salty marshes along oceanic coasts, may show similar adaptations to high salt intake. If this is found to be the case, the sand rat cannot be considered as uniquely adapted to the desert, but it utilizes a niche that other desert animals seem unable to fill.

Some small American rodents are particularly interesting because of their carnivorous diet. These are the grasshopper mice (*Onychomys*) which have obtained their name from one of their principal food items. Stomach analyses have shown that about 80 per cent of the food is insects and 90 per cent is of animal origin (19). In the laboratory we have kept *Onychomys torridus*, which weigh about 20 to 30 grammes, on a pure meat diet.

These animals maintain or gain weight when eating raw pork liver which contains 72 per cent water. Their urine concentrations may be quite high—in fact higher than in a carnivore such as the cat. If, however, the liver was boiled its water content decreased to 58 per cent and the grasshopper mouse could not remain in water balance. It may seem that this is a pronounced response to a moderate reduction in the water content of the diet. However, this is not so. The raw liver (78 per cent H_2O) contained 258 grammes H_2O per 100 grammes dry matter, while the boiled liver (58 per cent H_2O) contained only 138 grammes H_2O per 100 grammes dry matter. The water content was thus reduced almost to one-half by the boiling, if related to the nutritional value of the food. (In these experiments boiling *per se* had no effect for additional water would maintain the animals.) This information indicates that the renal function as well as the over-all water metabolism of the grasshopper mice is similar to that of other carnivorous animals.

The fauna of Australia is almost unknown in regard to the physiology of the smaller mammals. These are of two kinds, the native Australian rodents (which incidentally comprise about one-third of all Australian mammals), and a number of small marsupials which in size and general appearance are reminiscent of rodents. The species found in the arid interior are frequently known from only a few museum specimens, and some may be extinct. Foxes were introduced into Australia to provide sport for hunters and domestic cats have run wild. These are a menace to the small mammalian fauna, and it can be expected that the numbers will continue to decrease. One, the mulgara (*Dasycercus cristicauda*), which is carnivorous, will be discussed in a later chapter. Since virtually nothing is known about others, one cannot even make guesses about their physiology, either with respect to heat tolerance, water metabolism, evaporation, or excretion.

SUMMARY

Several rodents from the Old World deserts, notably jerboas and gerbils, are able to live on air-dried food without water. They appear to be similar in their physiological mechanisms to the better-known New World kangaroo rats (also rodents). In particular, the ability of their kidneys to withhold water is outstanding, as evidenced in high urine concentrations.

Other rodents take advantage of food with a high water content. One such rodent, the sand rat (*Psammomys*), has the most exceptional renal concentrating ability; it can produce a urine nearly four times as concentrated as sea water. Its normal food is juicy, salt-loving plants with a high salt content in the sap. Another example of a rodent which utilizes food with a high water content is the grasshopper mouse (*Onychomys*) which lives on an almost exclusively carnivorous diet. Its water metabolism is similar to that of other carnivorous desert animals.

Little information is available on Australian rodents or the rodent-like marsupials from the arid interior.

13

SOME AESTIVATING MAMMALS

What is aestivation?

THE word aestivation stands for sleep during the summer, in the same way that hibernation stands for winter sleep. The term is not well defined, and it is used loosely for all sorts of animals that spend a period during the warmer part of the year in a resting or torpid state. It has been applied to insects and plant seeds, to lung fish and mammals, to snails and beetles. Our concern in this chapter is the desert mammal that spends some part of the hot season in an inactive and lethargic state.

There are many reports of aestivation in desert mammals, particularly in ground squirrels. One of the most frequently quoted reports is that of Vorhies, who said that the round-tailed ground squirrel (*Citellus tereticaudus*) shares with other species of the same genus the curious habit of spending the late summer and early fall in aestivation (347). The animals disappear in late August and early September, and thus avoid the completely dry hot autumn period. The larger Columbian ground squirrel (*Citellus columbianus*) was observed over a number of years, and no animals were seen from late July or early August until the first days of March (312). When winter came the aestivation merged into hibernation, and the total duration of the period of inactivity exceeded 200 days. Reports on the natural history of other ground squirrels also contain frequent descriptions of inactivity and aestivation periods. For example, the Iranian *Citellus fulvus* shows a complete cessation of activity beginning between 5 and 15 June. The onset of aestivation is very sudden and coincides with a rapid desiccation of vegetation which is completely scorched by the sun before the first of July (226). Russian literature contains many references to rodents which begin aestivation in the arid regions of the south-eastern U.S.S.R. in the early summer. Many of these reports are mentioned by Kalabukhov in a review of the comparative ecology of hibernating and aestivating mammals (171).

The many reports about aestivation refer to this condition as a state of inactivity, but for years no information was accumulated that could contribute to an understanding of the phenomenon and its physiology. It has been known since early in the last century that hibernating animals when exposed to low temperatures, below, say, 10° C, permit their body temperatures to drop from the normal mammalian level about 38° C to approach that of the surroundings. This drop in body temperature involves a corresponding decrease in metabolic rate and other physiological processes, respiration, heart beat, and so on. The metabolic rate during hibernation is usually about 2 to 5 per cent of the rate at normal body temperature, and the greatly reduced level of energy expenditure permits the hibernators to survive on their body reserves through a long winter.

One difficulty in understanding aestivation is that this type of inactivity occurs during the warmest periods and therefore cannot be a response to cooling, as hibernation is. What external factors induce aestivation—temperature or lack of water? What physiological mechanisms control the aestivation? Does the aestivating animal have a reduced metabolic rate so that the energy reserves last correspondingly longer? What is the body temperature of the aestivating animal?

Body temperature in aestivation. Until 1955 no attempt had been made to study aestivation experimentally. In that year it was stated in a comprehensive review of hibernation that the body temperature of an aestivating animal had never been measured (202). However, in the same year, Petter, who kept a number of desert rodents in Paris, found that the gerbil (*Gerbillus gerbillus*) became lethargic in August and September (255). The rectal temperature fell from the usual 36° C or thereabouts to 25° C, and in the second week to 21·5°, 21·5°, and 22° C in three animals. I believe that these are the first temperature measurements in an aestivating animal, and they show that such animals can be dormant at air temperatures which do not permit a hibernator to enter its lethargic state—the hibernator requires much lower temperatures.

The first detailed report on the physiology of aestivation came from Bartholomew's laboratory (29). The object of study was the little pocket mouse (*Perognathus longimembris*) which was selected because it is one of the smallest North American rodents (6·5 to 10 grammes) and is a member of the same family as kangaroo rats (Heteromyidae), the most successful animals in the North American deserts. The usual range of rectal temperatures in normally active pocket mice is from 35° to 38° C, with a mean around 37° C. When the animals were kept for 2 to 3 weeks at temperatures varying between 2° and 9° C with food continually available, they maintained their weight and activity, and stayed in good condition. If the food was removed, however, they entered a state of dormancy or hibernation. Even if the drop in air temperature was more moderate, food deprivation would cause them to go into a condition of torpor.

It is interesting that, even with food available, individuals of the little pocket mouse would often allow the body temperature to drop to that of the environment when ambient temperatures were between 20° and 25° C. There was no difference in the condition of animals that were in

hibernation at low temperature and those that had become torpid at
25° C and later were cooled further. Bartholomew and Cade therefore
suggested that there is no real physiological difference between aestivation and hibernation (29, 337). They pointed out that there is a
continuous range of ambient temperatures between 2° and 25° C
where there is no sharp demarcation between the two states. However,
we habitually use the first term for the lower temperatures and the
second for the higher range. A more accurate description would be that
the animals are in a torpid state due to hypothermia and that this torpid
state in aestivating animals extends into a higher range of body temperatures (up to about 25° C) than in hibernators (up to about 10° or 15° C).

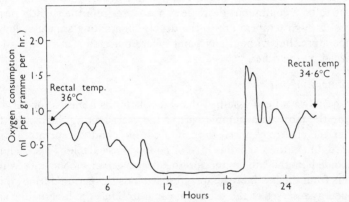

FIG. 38. Oxygen consumption during normal activity, during a short period of
'aestivation', and during and after spontaneous arousal in an adult Mohave ground
squirrel weighing 306 grammes. Ambient temperature between 23° and 26° C.
(Reproduced with permission from Bartholomew and Hudson (35).)

At a later time Bartholomew extended these studies to include
the Mohave ground squirrel, *Citellus mohavensis* (35), and the kangaroo
mouse, *Microdipodops pallidus* (37). The Mohave ground squirrel is,
like other ground squirrels, a diurnal rodent, and it undergoes prolonged
periods of aestivation and hibernation. Its distribution lies completely
within the range of the antelope ground squirrel (*Citellus leucurus*), but
the latter species neither hibernates nor aestivates and remains active
above ground at all times of the year. The Mohave ground squirrel
remains underground, and is presumably dormant, except during spring
and early summer. The studies of this animal included adequate determinations of metabolic rate, which went down from a normal level of
about 0·8 ml O_2 per gramme per hr. to between 0·1 and 0·2 ml O_2 per
gramme per hr. when animals were aestivating between 23° and 26° C
(see Fig. 38).

The entry into the torpid state is rapid, and the body temperature falls to within 1° C or less of ambient temperature. The animals can be dormant at body temperatures as high as 27° C, but they are completely normal when the temperature has reached 32° C. The dormant animals can be distinguished from sleeping animals by the pattern of respiration, they have prolonged periods with no visible respiratory movements, which animals sleeping normally do not have. The torpid animal with a body temperature of 25° C responds to touch with squeaking and is easily aroused. Below 21° C there is no vocalization but still fairly well co-ordinated movements. At body temperatures below 15° C the animals are unable to right themselves when placed on their backs, but even at body temperatures of 10° C they respond to touch by withdrawal. There seems to be a continuous decrease in response from the slightly torpid animal at high temperature to the deeply hibernating animal at lowest temperature, but without any point where one state can be said to be replaced by the other.

Advantages of aestivation

It has always been assumed that hibernation is a means for survival during the most unfavourable part of the year. During the cold of the winter the energy required to maintain a high body temperature is increased, but at the same time little or no food is available. This dilemma is avoided in the hibernator for the decreased metabolic rate which results from the low body temperature extends the period during which the energy reserves of the organism can last. Thus the hibernating animal can survive the long unfavourable period.

The aestivating desert rodent has much of the same advantage. It can escape the most difficult part of the year, and by dropping the metabolic rate to a low level it can extend its moderate energy reserves over long periods. In addition, with the reduced oxygen consumption there is a decrease in water loss.

The advantages of reduced energy expenditure are obvious, but the economy in water needs some further discussion. In addition to the general decrease in water expenditure that comes with the reduced level of all physiological processes, respiration, urea production, urine formation, and so on, the aestivating animal has a very specific advantage in being at the temperature of the surroundings instead of being warmer. This is the same advantage that all cold-blooded or poikilothermic animals have above the warm-blooded or homothermic animals, and it therefore merits special attention.

The simplest situation to consider is that of an animal in a burrow where the air is saturated with moisture, i.e. the relative humidity is 100 per cent. As the warm-blooded animal breathes, the air is warmed and becomes saturated with water vapour at a higher temperature. A certain amount of water vapour is therefore added to the respiratory air, the amount depending on the difference in temperature between inspired and expired air. The lower the temperature of the burrow, the less water vapour is present in the inspired air (although it is saturated), and more has to be added by the animal. We therefore have the seemingly paradoxical situation that a cool burrow with 100 per cent relative humidity is a greater drain on the water resources of the animal than a warmer burrow with the same high relative humidity.

The cold-blooded animal is in an entirely different situation. Its body temperature approaches that of the surroundings, and the air taken into the lungs is therefore not appreciably heated. If the inspired air is saturated, no further water is added in the lungs. This will be true in all saturated atmospheres, whether the temperature is 30°, 20°, or 10° C. The aestivating rodent is essentially a cold-blooded animal, its body temperature is less than 1° C above that of the environment, and in a moist atmosphere the evaporation from the lungs will be minimal and will, under ideal conditions, approach zero. Many desert animals plug their burrows during the hot time of the year, and this undoubtedly contributes to maintaining a high humidity inside. Our own measurements during the driest time of the year in Arizona showed that an enclosed air space at a depth of 30 cm had a relative humidity of 100 per cent, in spite of the completely dry appearance of the soil. In open burrows, however, the humidity was lower, but still considerably above that in the outside air (294).

In an atmosphere of less than 100 per cent relative humidity the evaporation will increase, both in the warm and in the aestivating animal. The situation becomes extremely complex for the warm-blooded animal, for both temperature and humidity of the inspired air influences the temperature of the expired air. The only reasonable approach to this problem is an experimental determination of evaporation at different humidities, such as has been started by Chew (81). In the aestivating animal the evaporation will still be moderate, for even the complete saturation of the expired air does not require as much water as it takes at higher temperatures. The curve for water content in saturated air has an increasingly steep inflection upwards as the temperature increases, but the aestivating animal is below the temperature range where this upturn reaches a magnitude that decides the balance between evaporation and available water in the warm animal.

It seems that to desert mammals this particular aspect is the most essential of the several advantages of the aestivation. The extension in time of energy reserves is, of course, valuable but probably not essential, for some food is still to be found or could have been stored in the burrow.

The reduced turn-over rate of water that goes with lower metabolic rate is merely an extension in time of the normal physiological activity; if the animal cannot remain in water balance under the given circumstances, the drawn-out time scale gives it a longer period before water loss becomes critical. The reduction in evaporation that follows with dropping to ambient temperature, on the other hand, is a radical departure from the high pulmonary water loss that otherwise is an obligatory result of being warm-blooded.

SUMMARY

Many observers have reported that certain desert rodents, notably ground squirrels, become inactive during the summer or early autumn. They enter a lethargic or torpid state, called aestivation, which is reminiscent of hibernation, but while hibernation occurs at temperatures below some $10°$ C, aestivation occurs at temperatures as high as $25°$ C.

In the torpid or aestivating animal the body temperature drops to within less than $1°$ C of ambient temperature, metabolic rate is reduced, respiratory frequency goes down, and there is a general reduction in the level of most physiological processes, similar to that which is seen in hibernation.

The state of aestivation has two major advantages. Firstly, the reduced metabolic rate prolongs the period during which the animal can live on its energy reserves, and, secondly, a considerable economy in water expenditure is achieved. The reduced ventilation of the lungs lowers the pulmonary evaporation of water, but, more importantly, the lowered temperature of the body means that less water is required to saturate the expired air.

The aestivating rodent is essentially a cold-blooded animal, with its body temperature approaching that of the surroundings. In a moist atmosphere the pulmonary evaporation will be very low, and as the humidity approaches 100 per cent the evaporation from the animal approaches zero.

In a dry atmosphere the evaporation will increase, both in the warm and in the aestivating animal. Still, the evaporation will be much lower in the aestivating animal because the respiratory air is not heated to the high temperature of the awake animal.

Thus, the state of aestivation has a profound effect in shifting the water balance of a mammal in a favourable direction.

14

MARSUPIALS

THE greater part of the native fauna of mammals in Australia belongs to the marsupials. These mammals range from the tropical coasts in the north to the temperate south, and many of them are characteristic of the vast semi-arid interior of the continent. We should expect these forms to be well adapted to life in an environment of excessive heat and water shortage. Unfortunately, very little is known about the physiology of the native Australian fauna, and an imaginative investigator can find many fascinating animals that are likely to prove rewarding objects of study. During recent years Australian biologists have realized the potential of the native fauna, but in spite of some striking contributions in various areas of marsupial physiology the entire field is still essentially unexplored.

The Australian marsupials comprise the most varied types, from the tree-climbing native-cats to blind, burrowing, marsupial-moles, from herbivores to ferocious carnivores, from small 10-gramme-size marsupial-mice and marsupial-rats to the large great-grey kangaroo which may weigh almost 100 kg (336). It would indeed be surprising if such a variety, almost as great as that in placental mammals, were not reflected in physiological differences as well.

It is often assumed that the marsupials represent a more primitive evolutionary level than the placental mammals. This concept, which originates in evidence of comparative anatomy, has led to the mistaken impression that functional characteristics should also be primitive. The fact is that the marsupials, after a separate evolutionary history of perhaps 100 million years, represent the same functional level as placental mammals, and with many striking similarities.

HEAT REGULATION

Late in the last century occasional measurements were made of the body temperatures of native Australian mammals, including the egg-laying monotremes Echidna and Platypus. It was found that the monotremes, which are generally regarded as extremely primitive mammals, had body temperatures much below what was considered normal for a mammal, while the marsupials had body temperatures only moderately below that in placentals. In line with the general run of thought of the times, the monotremes were classed as almost 'cold-blooded', while the marsupials were given an intermediate position between these and 'warm-blooded' placental mammals (327, 328).

The best-known and most frequently quoted authority for this viewpoint is C. J. Martin, later Professor of Pathology at the University of London. He made a study of the metabolic rate and the tolerance to high temperatures in the two monotremes mentioned above, in three marsupials, and in two placentals, the cat and the rabbit (218–21). In these experiments the observations were made at ambient temperatures from just above freezing to 40° C, and the entire range was covered in a single day. It is therefore impossible to use the observations for an evaluation of the tolerance of these animals to any particular temperature, or of their ability to regulate their body temperature under any particular external conditions. The animals were kept in a small chamber in a water bath, and the conditions for evaporation may have been poor. The determinations of metabolic rate suffer from the shortcoming that insufficient time was given to reach equilibrium conditions at any temperature. More seriously, the release of carbon dioxide was used to measure metabolic rate, but owing to the large pool of preformed carbon dioxide in the body this measurement is entirely unreliable when changes in respiration may occur. The material is unsuited for conclusions about tolerance to heat or ability to regulate body temperature, and it is unfortunate that it has been widely quoted in support of a 'primitive' mechanism for heat regulation.

The fact is that many marsupials are excellent heat regulators, and as a group they utilize the same mechanisms for evaporation as found in placental mammals—sweating, panting, and salivation.

The Quokka

The quokka (*Setonix brachyurus*) is a medium-sized marsupial which weighs about 3 to 4 kg and in many ways reminds one of a rabbit. Its hind legs are relatively short and it therefore moves in a running fashion, instead of jumping like a kangaroo. Its home is the coastal region of south-west Australia, where summers are hot and dry. Today, it is common only on some off-shore islands. The best known is Rottnest Island, so named by Dutch sailors who were impressed by animals reminiscent of huge rats which they found in great numbers on the island.

On Rottnest the annual rainfall is concentrated in the cool winter from April to October. During the dry summer the temperature frequently exceeds 38° C. A study by Bartholomew (28) of the ability of the quokka to tolerate a variety of external temperatures is therefore of considerable interest. Its body temperature was found to be remarkably constant. The average deep rectal temperature of animals resting during

PLATE 7

RED KANGAROO (*MACROPUS RUFUS*)

The large kangaroos move swiftly and easily over the semi-arid plains of central Australia. They can travel long distances to reach drinking water, but it remains unknown to what extent they depend on drinking

(*Courtesy, Australian News and Information Bureau, Canberra*)

the day was 37·0° C with less than one degree difference between the highest and lowest recorded. At night, when the animals were active and moving around, the average temperature of animals feeding quietly was about 0·5° C higher. Individuals that came to the drinking-places, presumably moving over some distance, had a mean body temperature of 38° C. The lowest temperature observed in the field was 36·7° C in a resting individual, and the highest 38·3° C in an active animal, a difference of only 1·6° C. This is a very narrow range for animals captured in

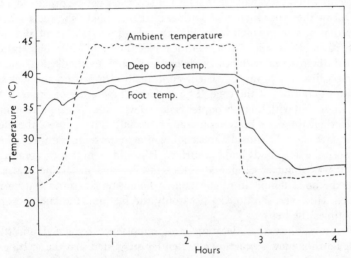

FIG. 39. The body temperature of the quokka remains almost constant at 38–39° C even when the ambient temperature is raised to 44° C. This shows an excellent ability of temperature regulation in this rabbit-sized marsupial. (Reproduced with permission from Bartholomew (28).)

the wild. Only in excited captive animals were temperatures as high as 39° C observed. These records, made on sixty-three animals, certainly do not suggest any instability of body temperature, and, as we shall see shortly, the quokka is an excellent temperature regulator.

When quokkas were exposed to temperatures from 3° to 44° C in the laboratory, it was found that they maintained their body temperature very well, both at the low and the high temperatures. In what follows we shall limit our discussion to the highest temperature to which the animals were exposed.

In one experiment, shown in Fig. 39, the animal had a slightly elevated initial temperature which was ascribed to the excitement connected with the initial insertion of thermocouples. However, throughout the 2 hours during which the air temperature was kept at 44° C, the rectal temperature remained virtually constant at 5° below ambient.

South-western Australia has summers in which temperatures above 38° C are common, but 44° C is practically never reached in the coastal areas. Since the quokka could easily resist this temperature under laboratory conditions, it should have little or no difficulty with problems of heat in its natural habitat, provided sufficient water is available. In the field as well as in captivity, quokkas drink regularly and copiously if water is available. On Rottnest Island, where the studies of the quokkas have been made, drinking-water does become a problem in summer. The possibility that they may use brackish or sea water will be discussed later.

During the exposure to high temperature the quokka showed a copious secretion of saliva, which it, by licking, spread over the front and hind feet, parts of the tail, and sometimes over the belly (28). The animals coated themselves with saliva deliberately and methodically, and so much saliva was produced that it continually dripped off the feet and fell to the bottom of the cage. The surface temperature of the feet and tail, measured with thermocouples fastened with adhesive tape, remained lower than the deep body temperature (rectal). The wetness therefore must have caused a considerable cooling due to the temperature gradient between the deep body and the surface. It would seem that this gradient, which was about 2° C, should suffice to eliminate metabolic heat and keep the body temperature constant if the entire skin surface were involved. However, the quokka licks only the feet and the tail, and only sometimes the belly.

The possibility that sweating is of importance remained unsettled after Bartholomew's experiments. Bentley suggested that the wetting of the feet and tail was due to sweating, only augmented by licking (46). Histological examinations revealed sweat glands in these areas of the skin, but not in other parts.[1] Of course, the presence of sweat glands does not prove anything about their function. In the dog, where sweat glands are found all over the body, their role in heat regulation seems insignificant. Information of a more decisive nature was obtained by equipping the animals with plastic collars which effectively prevented them from licking any part of the body. These animals were still able to maintain their body temperature below that of the environment equally as well as animals without collars (49).

Other findings also suggest that evaporation from the skin, without licking, is important. The naked young quokka from the pouch will maintain an internal body temperature of 4 degrees below that of the environment for an hour or longer when it is exposed to 44° C air temperature. This is not due to the licking response, which develops later, but presumably to evaporation from the moist, naked skin (28).

[1] Apocrine glands have been found in association with the hairs over the entire body surface of the quokka (133a).

These observations leave considerable uncertainty with respect to the effectiveness of salivation and licking. The licking response has been observed in other marsupials, such as the wallaby (*Petrogale penicillata*) and the wallaroo or euro (*Macropus robustus*) (280), and has been regarded as the typical marsupial mode. It would seem that the licking response would be a very uneconomical form for heat regulation. In the earlier discussion of sweating in the camel, it was stated how important it is for the water economy that the sweat evaporates from the surface of the skin, rather than from the surface of the fur. It would seem that the application of saliva to the outside of the fur, even if it is thoroughly wetted all the way through to the skin, would have the same disadvantage. Another biological disadvantage in the licking mechanism is that it cannot be employed except in the resting animal; a running animal pursued by a predator must utilize other means for evaporation. In this connexion it is of interest that at least some marsupials, for example, the common brush-tail possum (*Trichosurus vulpecula*), have sweat glands over the entire body (144).

The possible role of panting in the heat regulation of the quokka has not been clarified. Both Bartholomew and Bentley found that the respiratory rates might increase to nearly 200 respirations per minute when the animals were exposed to heat. What role this may have in heat regulation is uncertain. It would therefore be highly desirable to obtain separate quantitative determinations of water loss from the respiratory tract, from the skin when licking is prevented, and from salivation. At the present time the effectiveness of the salivation-licking mechanism cannot be estimated. It can, however, be stated unequivocally that the capacity of the quokka to control its body temperature is as great as, or greater than, that shown by most placental mammals of similar size.

Other marsupials

The knowledge of temperature regulation in other Australian marsupials is rather restricted, although information has been obtained about the reaction to hot atmospheres in some two dozen different species (280, 281). In the latter of these investigations, twenty-five species of Australian marsupials and four species of native Australian rodents were exposed for 6 hours to temperatures up to 40° C. The marsupials were of four different families and ranged in size from 11 grammes to 30 kg, while the rodents weighed from 38 to 700 grammes.

One of the most striking findings is that nineteen of the marsupials could tolerate the hot-room for the entire 6 hours and only six species had to be removed before this time. Only one of the four rodents could tolerate the full 6-hour exposure. The unfortunate complication in this experiment is that drinking-water was available to the animals throughout,

and many of them used it to wet their fur or for submersion of parts of
their bodies. Therefore, the apparent tolerance of some of the animals is
not a true indication of their physiological powers of heat regulation.

Two animals maintained body temperature between 37° and 38° C
throughout the exposure to 40° C (Fig. 40). These were the Tasmanian
devil (*Sarcophilus harrisii*) which weighs 6·7 kg and the red kangaroo
(*Megaleia rufa*=*Macropus rufus*) which weighs 30 kg. The great-grey
kangaroo (*Macropus major*), which is of about the same size as the red

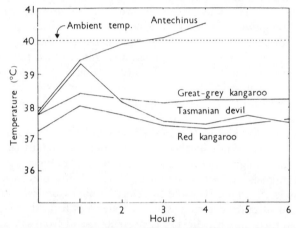

FIG. 40. Several marsupials, e.g. Tasmanian devil, red kangaroo, and
great-grey kangaroo are able to maintain their body temperature below
an ambient temperature of 40° C. Others, e.g. *Antechinus*, a small insectivorous marsupial-mouse, show little ability to resist heat. (Reproduced with permission from Robinson and Morrison (281).)

kangaroo, reacted in much the same way with a body temperature just
above 38° C. In the Tasmanian devil the only observable reaction to the
air temperature of 40° C was its high water consumption. Throughout
the period of exposure it showed no distress, there was no change
in respiratory rate, and no attempt was made to wet the coat. Since
this animal was able to maintain a virtually normal body temperature,
it seems that the only possible explanation is an effective sweating
mechanism. We therefore have a marsupial which seems to depend
exclusively on sweating for heat dissipation.

Many marsupials increased the respiratory rates during heat stress,
and shifted to breathing with an open mouth, reminiscent of panting. If
we arbitrarily select those animals that have respiratory rates during
heat exposure more than twice the control values, we find this change in
eight of the twenty-five marsupials, while none of the four true rodents
had it. Among those that were 'panting' according to this definition, we

find the two largest animals, the red and the grey kangaroos. These were also among the best temperature regulators, while others of the 'panting' animals had only fair tolerance to the high temperature. At the present time we have only these preliminary indications that panting may be an important means for heat dissipation in some of the marsupials, and further studies are sorely needed.

None of the small mouse-like marsupials had a good tolerance to high temperature (see Fig. 40). This is consistent with the general principle that small animals must evade heat stress, rather than combat it by evaporation.

Fat-tailed marsupials. The localized distribution of adipose tissue in the hump of the camel and the Indian cattle, and in the tail of the fat-rumped sheep, can be interpreted as advantageous to heat dissipation from the body (page 49). This interpretation is, however, difficult to apply to small animals that manage their heat problems in a different fashion. There are, however, characteristically fat-tailed desert rodents, such as the African *Pachyuromys* and *Steatomys* (170), and it is particularly challenging that some of the small marsupials from the arid interior of Australia likewise have fat tails. These include the fat-tailed marsupial-mouse (*Antechinus maculatus*) and the fat-tailed *Sminthopsis* (*Sminthopsis crassicaudata*). It is worth noting that some desert lizards also have a fat tail, for example, the Old World *Uromastix* and the American Gila Monster (*Heloderma*). An unexplained correlation between the locus for fat deposition and a desert habitat does not inevitably point to a causal relationship between the two. Until a fundamental connexion is found it is more prudent to view the phenomenon with curiosity and explanations with distrust.

WATER REQUIREMENTS

The information about water requirements in marsupials is extremely fragmentary. One interesting aspect of the problem can be observed on Rottnest Island, where the annual rainfall is about 750 mm, with more than 700 mm falling in winter between the end of March and the beginning of November. During the dry summer (November to March) the temperature may rise as high as 38° C, although the average daily maximum is below 30° C. The island consists of two parts, connected by a narrow strip, with separate quokka populations. The smaller part has no fresh water whatsoever, while the larger part in addition to salty lakes has some seepage of fresh water which is used for drinking by the quokkas (153).

The quokka population on the small, waterless part must either get along on the water content of the vegetation, which is low during the hot season, or the animals must drink sea water. When quokkas in the laboratory were given progressively increasing amounts of salt in their drinking-water they could be persuaded to drink solutions they would not take normally. Most animals could maintain their water balance on 2·5 per cent sodium chloride solution and remain in good condition. These animals had a very high intake of fluid; some drank as much as 500 ml per day. Since they weighed between 3 and 4 kg they drank about 15 per cent of their body weight and had a turnover of 10 to 15 grammes of sodium chloride per day. When the concentration was increased to 3 per cent NaCl, the intake decreased from 500 to between 350 and 400 ml per day. When the animals were presented with sea water, they all tasted it, but only one would drink any significant amount. This animal drank 30 ml in 24 hours and its urinary electrolyte concentration was 679 mEq per litre. This is significantly higher than the concentration of sea water, but the gain of water is not sufficient to maintain the animal in a positive water balance for any length of time (46).

Since only one individual drank sea water and only some of those drinking 3 per cent NaCl showed very high urine concentrations, Bentley (46) concluded that the wild quokka population as a whole did not depend on sea water for their water-supply, but that the water of the vegetation was sufficient. This conclusion is not entirely valid. On the dry laboratory feed, sea water was certainly inadequate for the quokkas, but if some water is available from the vegetation the situation is different. In the discussion of Wolf's experiments on cats (page 125) it was explained how sea water in combination with the water in the feed permits animals to remain in water balance, although each source of water may supply concentrations of excretory products too high to be tolerated alone.

The highest urine concentration observed in a quokka was 2188 mOsm, which occurred in an animal that had been dehydrated for 2 days and then loaded with sea water. The highest concentration in an animal collected in the field during a dry period was 1931 mOsm. We can therefore assume that the concentration limit in the quokka is about 2000 mOsm, or about five times the plasma osmotic concentration. A U/P ratio of five as the maximum urine concentration is not unusual among mammals. It is a far cry from the U/P ratio of 12 or 15 that can be attained by the kangaroo rat which can drink sea water with impunity.

The hill kangaroo. The euro, or hill kangaroo (*Macropus robustus*) is a large kangaroo which has been studied in the dry grazing country of Western Australia. It is considered a menace to sheep pastures, and there is strong pressure to reduce its numbers in the interest of the sheep owners. Since it easily jumps sheep fences these will not keep it out of the pastures, and control measures have centred around other possibilities. The euros come to watering places which are provided for livestock, and attempts have been made to poison them through the drinking-water. Probably the pastures would regenerate faster if the sheep were poisoned and the euros and the vegetation left alone.

Successful poisoning depends on the use of a suitable dosage. In order to determine the appropriate amount of poison to be added to the water it has been necessary to determine how much and how often each euro drinks. The water consumption of a grazing wild euro population in December, when the mean maximum temperature was $42°$ C, was 1·7 per cent of the body weight per day. Although this estimate was made on wild animals, it is quite accurate. The total water consumption was measured at the water trough, and the entire drinking population was afterwards trapped and weighed. If animals instead of grazing freely were kept in an enclosure with only scanty shade and fed on a dry diet, their daily water consumption was 5 per cent of the body weight (Ealey, personal communication). The wild animals spent the day in crevices in rock outcrops where they were in some measure protected against heat. This, in combination with a higher water content in their feed, evidently accounted for their lower water consumption.

The euros are elusive animals which come to drink only during the hot period preceding summer rains. They do not drink very often; even at the height of the summer they do not come to drink daily although water may be conveniently available. In this connexion it is interesting that a poisoning programme usually does not kill the entire euro population in a given area, perhaps because some animals do not drink at all. Estimates of the frequency with which the animals come to drink indicates that they go on the average for 2·7 days without water. There is, however, evidence that some go for very much longer and that they can withstand intense dehydration (112).

The urine concentrations in the euro are uniformly high, even when drinking-water is available. The highest concentrations have been found in dehydrated animals, which have shown values as high as 2730 mOsm. This suggests a maximum urine:plasma osmotic ratio of about 7 or 8, which is not indicative of any exceptional concentrating capacity of the kidney (cf. Table XXVI, page 181).

The larger red kangaroo (*Macropus rufus*) has the widest distribution of any kangaroo and occurs throughout the dry inland areas of Australia. Its biology is under investigation by Alan Newsome at Alice Springs, N.T., who has permitted me to quote some of his observations. From the analysis of a large number of urine samples a few results are given in Table XXIX. Apparently, the red kangaroo can produce a far more concentrated urine than the euro. In particular, the potassium concentration may be exceedingly high, and additional sodium brings the total electrolyte concentration to very unusual values. The concentrating capacity of its kidney is, in fact, in the range of such typical desert animals as the ground squirrel and the kangaroo rat. The indications are that the red kangaroo can go for long periods without drinking, but in hot dry periods its need for heat regulation apparently puts greater demands on its water resources than can be met unless it drinks occasionally.

TABLE XXIX

Urine concentrations in kangaroos during summer drought

	Na mEq/l	K mEq/l	Urea mM/l
Red kangaroo, mean*	126	950	500
Red kangaroo, maximum*	348	1333	593
Euro, maximum†	745	234	29

* Newsome, personal communication.
† Ealy, personal communication.

The Mulgara. The Australian fauna includes several small marsupial-mice and marsupial-rats, one being the mulgara, or crest-tailed marsupial-mouse (*Dasycercus cristicauda*). The animal weighs about 50 to 100 grammes, it inhabits the most arid central parts of the continent, and it lives predominantly or exclusively on carnivorous food with insects, small reptiles, and small rodents as major dietary components (169).

In the laboratory and in the absence of heat stress, the mulgara maintains its weight when fed on fresh meat or freshly killed whole mice. Young animals rapidly gain in weight on this diet, which apparently contains sufficient water. An earlier chapter in this book discussed the water balance of carnivores in general. It was shown that these animals, which produce large amounts of urea, depend on the ability to excrete urea in relatively high concentrations. The water content of their food then suffices for all physiological needs, provided water is not needed for heat regulation.

Urine samples obtained from mulgaras fed on whole mice were uniformly high in concentration, ranging from 522 to 674 mEq per litre of electrolytes, and from 1980 to 2610 mM per litre of urea. The total osmotic concentration of the most concentrated sample was calculated to be about 4000 mOsm. Whether the urine concentrations could be higher if the animal had to conserve water to its maximum ability is not known (308).

It is interesting that the most concentrated urine sample obtained from a mulgara had practically the same osmotic concentration as the most concentrated sample from a grasshopper mouse (*Onychomys torridus*) (see page 185). The latter animal, a rodent from the south-western United States, is predominantly carnivorous and therefore in much the same physiological situation as the mulgara. In both animals the large amounts of urea formed on a carnivorous diet can be excreted in a relatively small volume of urine, and the water found in the diet will suffice. Thus neither animal will have to resort to other sources for water, such as drinking or eating succulent plant material.

SUMMARY

Marsupials have incorrectly been accredited with a primitive type of heat regulation. Actually some marsupials are poor heat regulators, others are excellent, and this is exactly as among placental mammals.

Marsupials use the same mechanisms as placentals for regulation of their body temperature in hot surroundings; sweating, panting, and wetting of the fur with saliva.

Copious salivation with licking of the feet, tail, and belly is found in an excellent temperature regulator, the quokka, a rabbit-sized herbivorous marsupial. However, sweating may also be important in this animal. Indirect evidence (absence of panting and licking) indicates that sweating is the primary means of temperature regulation in the Tasmanian devil, a carnivorous marsupial which is an excellent heat regulator. Several marsupials show increased respiratory rates at high temperatures. Among these are the two largest kangaroos, the red and the great-grey kangaroos, which both tolerate high temperatures and can maintain their body temperature around $38°$ C at an ambient temperature of $44°$ C. When at rest, these animals display the salivation-licking response, a mechanism that would seem insufficient and impractical for a rapidly moving animal.

The small marsupials show a poor tolerance to high temperatures and are in this respect similar to small placental mammals.

The medium-sized quokka is known to live on hot coastal islands with no fresh water available. It cannot be sustained on sea water on a dry laboratory diet, but if some water is obtained from the vegetation, sea water could perhaps be used to supplement the supply.

The water requirement of the large kangaroos from the arid interior of Australia is low, but they do seek watering places during the hottest summer. Whether some individuals are independent of drinking-water is unknown.

In the absence of heat stress a carnivorous small desert marsupial, the mulgara, obtains sufficient water on a pure meat diet. Its kidney can produce urine as highly concentrated as that of some North American desert rodents.

The conclusion to be drawn from these diverse observations is that marsupials display a wide variety of physiological response in their heat and water metabolism. This reflects the multitude of biological forms which has evolved in the Australian fauna. The characteristic demands of the environment have been adequately met by responses comparable to those of placental mammals, and there is no reason to consider marsupials as physiologically primitive in these respects.

15

DESERT BIRDS

THERE are some differences between birds and mammals that have important implications for their life in desert areas. One of these is the greater mobility of birds. While a small rodent usually has a home range with a radius of less than 100 yards, birds can easily and rapidly fly several miles to a source of open water. They can also migrate over hundreds or thousands of miles, avoid the most unfavourable conditions, and seek out places where local rain has improved the availability of water and food.

Birds, to a greater extent than mammals, are diurnal and non-fossorial, and most are also of relatively small size. A notable exception is the ostrich (*Struthio camelus*) which may reach almost 100 kg. It so happens that this, the largest of living birds, is also a typical arid or desert form.

Reproduction raises some problems peculiar to birds. At times the danger to the eggs from overheating may be more important than the usual problem of keeping them warm. In particular, if the nests are placed on the ground, and many desert birds have this habit, the eggs must be shaded lest they become heated to temperatures fatal to the embryo. Likewise, the nestlings must be kept cool and provided with the water they need, often a major problem where food with a high water content is not easily available.

ADAPTATIONS OF BEHAVIOUR

Most desert birds are small and have the same problems in heat regulation that we met in small mammals; active heat regulation by evaporation requires large amounts of water. Accordingly, they avoid, as far as possible, excessive exposure.[1] In general, desert birds that are active throughout the day during the colder part of the year restrict their activity to the morning and early evening hours during the hot summer. This change in behaviour has, for example, been pointed out as a normal pattern for the Abert towhee (96) and the sparrow hawk (30).

An interesting difference between small and large birds in their selection of a suitable microclimate in which to spend the day was pointed out by Madsen (213). In east Sudan he observed that all birds

[1] Nighthawks and poor-wills (*Caprimulgidae*) are an interesting exception; they have the habit of spending the daylight hours, even in the desert, sitting quietly in the open. They also incubate their eggs on the ground where the embryos would rapidly be killed by the heat unless they were kept shielded by the adult bird (38, 89).

were feeding eagerly in the morning, immediately after sunrise. Later
in the day small birds were found with hanging wings and open beak
under the roof of houses or in dense trees. If disturbed, they would
move to another place in the shade, never in the sun. In the middle of the
day the air temperature was 38° to 45° C in the shade, but the microclimate
where the birds were found was not studied. What attracted attention
was that large birds did not hide in these places; they were circling high
in the sky at an estimated altitude of 700 to 1000 metres and remained
soaring at this height for the major part of the day. This behaviour seemed
to have no connexion with feeding, and the assumption was therefore
that it was an escape from the heat. At the indicated altitude the temperature should, due to adiabatic expansion, be 7° to 10° C below air temperature at the ground. If the soaring birds could ride on rising air currents,
which always occur over a heated plain, the energy expenditure would be
small and the behaviour an efficient selection of a suitable microclimate.

In dry years there is little possibility for many birds to nest and
raise the young successfully. In such years the birds of North Africa do
not reproduce, the gonads are atrophied, and there is no nest building
(192). In the arid interior of Australia the breeding of birds depends on
and is controlled by the amount of rain. During drought the gonads of
both male and female birds are of minimum size, and there is little or
no breeding behaviour. A good rain may change this completely; nest
building may begin within a week and ovulation in less than two. If the
rains are localized there is also likely to be a heavy influx of birds from
the surrounding areas resulting in a large breeding population. Coastal
birds do not respond this way, their breeding appears to be controlled
by day length, as in most birds (172).

An interesting detail in the nest-building behaviour of a weaver finch
(*Quelea quelea*) in Tanganyika assures that breeding begins only if conditions for raising the young are favourable. Successful nesting cannot
take place until the environment provides green grass with stems and
blades sufficiently long to be used by the males for weaving. This will
only happen if there has been enough rain to ensure the formation of
seeds and a crop of insects to feed the young (215).

These examples should serve to point out that the biology of birds
is sufficiently different from the mammalian pattern that the general
principles of the physiology of desert mammals cannot be applied to
birds without modifications.

TEMPERATURE REGULATION

Body temperature

The measurement of a 'normal' body temperature in birds meets with
technical difficulties. The small body size and high metabolic rate make

possible rapid fluctuations in temperature. In towhees (*Pipilo aberti*) with implanted thermocouples vigorous activity caused a temperature rise of 2° C in 3 minutes (96). It can be estimated that a violently struggling small bird may have a heat production high enough to increase its body temperature by 1 or 2 degrees in 1 minute. Many measurements made by inserting a thermometer into freshly caught or killed birds therefore give only an indication of the range of body temperature. Another difficulty is that birds, like mammals, have considerable diurnal temperature fluctuations, as well as changes associated with the pattern of activity. The usual diurnal cycles seem to be over a range of about 2° C (181).

Measurements of body temperature in a great variety of birds have been compiled and evaluated by King and Farner (181). In most of these cases there is reasonable assurance that satisfactory techniques were used and that the birds were relatively unexcited and as close to a 'normal' condition as compatible with laboratory conditions. In the great majority of species the temperature was found to be between 40° and 42° C, with small deviations to both sides of this range. This confirms the common textbook statement that birds mostly have a somewhat higher body temperature than mammals. The penguins are a notable exception, they seem to have a body temperature closer to the mammalian range, between 37° and 38° C.

In a hot environment a high body temperature is advantageous because it diminishes the heat load and thus the use of water in heat dissipation. Birds, therefore, have an *a priori* advantage over mammals, and if desert birds were to have body temperatures in a still higher range than other birds, the effect would be even greater.

Desert birds have not been subjected to extensive surveys of body temperature, but some good measurements are available for a few species, thanks to the work of Bartholomew and his collaborators. These measurements were well carried out with thermocouples permanently implanted deep in the pectoral muscle, so that continuous recording of temperatures was possible in birds that could move freely around in their cages. The measurements therefore yield reliable information about diurnal variations as well as variations with activity. The results of such measurements on four birds characteristic of desert areas of the south-western United States have been assembled in Table XXX. It is evident that in the absence of heat stress none of these birds has a body temperature outside the normal range for birds in general. An inherently high level of body temperature therefore is not a characteristic of these desert birds. At the Hebrew University in Jerusalem Jacob Marder has been working with the raven (*Corvus corax ruficollis*) which frequently occurs in deserts. When these birds were exposed to 45° C ambient temperature for 4 hours, they maintained their deep rectal temperature well below the ambient temperature throughout the experiment (personal communication). Marder's work is still in progress, and his further results can be anticipated with particular interest because the subject of study is a bird which is relatively large and completely black. (The black colour of some desert animals is a curious phenomenon, but since so little is understood of its role it will not be discussed in this book. (Cf. (61).)

TABLE XXX

Diurnal range in body temperature in some desert birds, measured in the absence of heat stress

		Body temp., °C
Quail (31)	*Lophortyx californicus;*	
	L. gambelii	39 to 41·5
Mourning dove (26)	*Zenaidura macroura marginella*	38·5 to 43
Sparrow hawk (30)	*Falco sparverius*	39 to 42
Towhee (96)	*Pipilo aberti dumeticolus*	39 to 42

Lethal body temperature. A passive resistance to a hot environment could be achieved if the lethal body temperature were sufficiently high. This would permit the animal to avoid the use of water to keep its body temperature down, a mechanism that would be most efficient for small organisms which, owing to their size, would otherwise have to evaporate large quantities of water to combat the environmental heat. Do desert birds have a higher than usual lethal body temperature?

The accurate determination of a lethal body temperature meets with some difficulties. An important factor is that the time of exposure plays a major role; a temperature that can be tolerated for a few minutes may not be compatible with life if it lasts for hours. We therefore have difficulties in comparing results obtained under different conditions and accurate figures for a lethal temperature cannot be given; it is only possible to indicate a general range.

Most measurements of the lethal temperature in birds have been done on the domestic chicken. It seems that a body temperature of 47° C invariably is fatal to this species (229, 359). A temperature of 46° C is critical, while 45° C apparently causes no major damage even if sustained for long periods. The critical range is therefore between 45° and 47° C. Since temperatures of about 45° C have frequently been measured in a variety of birds which afterwards appeared normal, and no reliable measurement exceeding 47° C has been made in any bird that survived, it is reasonable to consider this range as critical for birds in general.

The lethal temperature of desert birds, in the few cases where it has been measured, falls within the same limits. In the Abert towhee (*Pipilo aberti dumeticolus*), a resident of the very hot Colorado desert, the lethal body temperature has been established at 46·9° C (96). A sparrow hawk (*Falco sparverius*), which occurs in a wide variety of habitats including deserts, survived after the body temperature in a series of oscillations approached 46° C at the peaks. In the same species, a temperature of 45° C was tolerated repeatedly. Gambel's quail and California quail regularly display temperatures close to 45° C when exposed to heat stress, but the lethal limit has not been established (31). The mourning dove, which is common throughout the deserts of the south-western United States, can tolerate body temperatures at least as high as 45° C when exposed to high air temperatures, but temperatures much beyond this are not tolerated.

TABLE XXXI

Fraction of heat production dissipated by evaporation in two species of towhee

Figures expressed as per cent of total heat production. The surprising feature is that the relative importance of evaporation decreases with increasing temperature. In mammals the reverse holds true. From (96).

	Ambient temperature					
	36°	37°	38°	39°	40°	41°
Abert towhee	44·6	41·3	39·3	36·1	35·9	35·2
Brown towhee	30·5	30·9	30·2	29·3	27·6	26·9

Effect of body temperature on heat exchange

When the four desert birds which were discussed previously—quail, mourning dove, towhee, and sparrow hawk—were exposed to air temperatures of 40° C, their body temperature went up well beyond that of the environment and above what was normal for the species. These birds have the capacity to dissipate heat by the evaporation of water, and the rise is therefore presumably not due to an inability to keep the temperature down. It could instead be considered an adaptation that transfers the major part of the burden of heat dissipation from evaporation to conduction and radiation. (A rise in body temperature seems to be characteristic of birds generally when they are exposed to high temperature.)

The dependency on non-evaporative avenues for heat loss is reflected in the relatively small fraction of the total heat production that is dissipated by evaporation at high environmental temperatures. Table XXXI

gives some measurements made on two species of towhee and shows
that evaporation of water removes about one-third or less of the heat
production, the remainder presumably being lost by conduction and
radiation. The most surprising aspect of these figures is that the relative
importance of evaporation does not increase greatly at higher temperatures, as it does in mammals. Slightly higher figures have been found for
a number of non-desert species, but in no case did the fraction of the
resting heat production lost via evaporation exceed 50 per cent (181).
In the cardinal (*Richmondena cardinalis*), evaporative cooling accounts

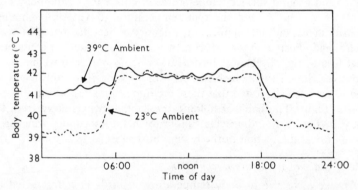

FIG. 41. Temperature curves for towhees kept at 23° C and at 39° C ambient temperature. Each curve represents the mean for seven birds. Light period 12 hours (from
06·00 to 18·00), dark period 12 hours. Drinking-water available. (Reproduced with
permission from Dawson (96).)

for about one-half the heat produced in metabolism at 41° C, although
the rate of evaporative water loss increases more than fivefold between
33° and 41° C (99). The poor-will (*Phalaenoptilus nuttallii*) and the
night-hawk (*Chordeiles minor*), however, can dissipate by evaporation
more heat than produced in metabolism at 41° C (38) (Dawson, personal communication).

When towhees were exposed to an ambient temperature of 39° C,
their mean day temperature (42° C) was not increased above the temperature for the same species at 23° C (see Fig. 41). However, the
diurnal fluctuation was reduced, for the night temperature did not fall
to the usual 39° C, but remained at 41° C. This again illustrates how a
passive rise in body temperature is a typical response in birds, permitting
an escape from the necessity of evaporating water to keep the body
temperature down.

The site of heat loss in birds at high ambient temperature has not been well
established. The general body surface is well insulated with feathers, the
legs being the only uninsulated parts of reasonable size. In the domestic

chicken the comb may be a major heat dissipating surface (359), but this viewpoint is not generally accepted (162) and further investigations are needed.

Birds with webbed feet can apparently utilize this large skin area relatively efficiently for heat dissipation. Howell and Bartholomew (158) observed that young albatrosses in the sun often sit on their heels with the main webbed part of the feet off the ground, shaded by the body. In this way they avoid contact with the hot surface of the ground, but, more importantly, they can lose heat to the air. At air temperatures of 29° to 31° C and ground surface temperatures of about 40° C, the body temperature was 39° C and the foot temperature 36° C. Although these measurements did not establish the quantity of heat dissipated from the feet, they indicate that the feet constitute a major avenue for conductive heat loss to the air. Desert birds, however, do not have webbed feet. However, the sides of many birds, beneath the wings, are thinly feathered and it has been suggested that these are important sites of heat dissipation in flight. The habit of holding the hanging wings away from the body in hot surroundings may indicate that these under-wing areas serve in heat dissipation in the resting bird as well.

Use of water in temperature regulation

An excessive rise in body temperature in birds is counteracted by evaporation of water. Birds have no sweat glands, and, furthermore, over most of the body the feathers form a barrier that impedes the passage of large quantities of water vapour. Thermoregulatory evaporation must therefore take place mainly from the respiratory tract, and birds do respond to elevated body temperatures by increasing the movement of air over the moist surfaces of the respiratory passages. The increased air movement can be achieved in two ways, by increased rate of respiratory movements or by a rapid flapping of the loose skin on the ventral surface of the throat. The latter, frequently described as gular fluttering, has not always been distinguished from an increased rate of respiration. Most publications on heat regulation in birds have merely discussed the phenomenon of 'panting' and it is therefore difficult to establish how common each type is. If gular fluttering occurs alone it is not likely to have much effect on the ventilation of the lungs, but panting by increased respiratory frequency must have profound effects on respiratory gas exchange, particularly on the loss of carbon dioxide resulting in alkalosis, For the purpose of achieving increased evaporation, it is probably of little significance whether one method or the other is employed.

It may, on the other hand, be important whether the energy require-ments are similar or different for the two types of mechanical movement. A superficial observation of a bird that displays gular fluttering at high temperature suggests that this process may be dependent on a resonant frequency, similar to that discussed for the panting of the dog, and may therefore have a relatively low energy requirement.

An increase in the respiratory rate in birds may or may not be energetically expensive—the air sac system is a complication that makes it even more difficult to evaluate the situation than in mammals. This is a field wide open for investigation.

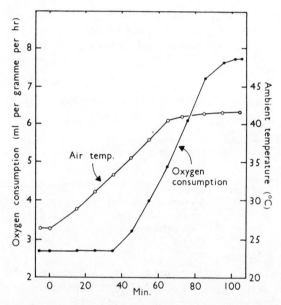

FIG. 42. Oxygen consumption in Abert towhee in response to rising environmental temperatures from 27° to 42° C. The oxygen consumption is increased about threefold at the high ambient temperature. It is probable that a considerable part of the increase in metabolism is due to the energy needed to maintain an increased rate of respiration. (Reproduced with permission from Dawson (96).)

There is an indication that panting may be expensive for birds in the observation that the oxygen consumption is greatly increased at high temperature (Fig. 42). When towhees were exposed to air temperatures close to the limit of their tolerance, about 42° C, their oxygen consumption increased to two or three times the usual value. It is possible that part of this increase was due to the direct effect of increased temperature on tissue metabolism. In most biological systems this increase is in the magnitude of a twofold increase for 10° C increase in temperature ($Q_{10} = 2$). It is therefore unlikely that the rise in oxygen consumption in the towhees, whose body temperature was raised by approximately

2° to 3° C, was due primarily to the temperature effect. To what extent the increase was due to the energy requirement for maintaining the panting activity remains unknown. It is, however, suggestive of a low efficiency of the panting mechanism in birds. This has been expressed quantitatively by Dawson who has estimated that in the cardinal at 40° C ambient temperature, 1·0 cal of every 2·5 cal dissipated was required to offset the thermogenesis associated with panting (personal communication).

On the other hand, the desert poor-will (*Phalaenoptilus nuttallii*) does not have a pronounced rise in oxygen consumption concurrent with the gular flutter at high temperature (38). This suggests a high mechanical

TABLE XXXII

The body temperature at which increased respiration or gular fluttering begins in various birds

Non-desert birds	Domestic pigeon (268)	42·5 to 43·2
	Domestic chicken (359)	42·5 to 43
	Domestic duck (279)	41·8
Desert birds	Quail (31)	43·5
	Mourning dove (26)	42·6
	Sparrow hawk (30)	·42·8 to 43
	Texas night-hawk (89)	42
	Poor-will (38)	41·5

efficiency of the gular fluttering, similar to that which the dog presumably achieves by panting at the resonant frequency of the respiratory system (91). Furthermore, the problem of heat dissipation in the poor-will appears simpler than in other birds for the reason that this bird has an exceptionally low metabolic rate—only about one-third of what could be expected in a bird of its size (38).

Critical temperature for panting. In many species the 'panting' seems to set in when the body temperature has reached a certain critical level. (For simplicity we will use the common term 'panting' for the two responses, gular fluttering and increased respiration. The term is used by most authors without any attempt at separating the two.)

Some observations on the body temperature at which the panting response first sets in during heat stress are tabulated in Table XXXII. The response occurs between 42° and 43° C in desert and non-desert birds alike; about 2 degrees below the point where a further increase might have serious or even fatal effects. In these few cases there is no indication that the panting response in desert birds differs from that in other birds.

Panting rates. The respiratory rate in chickens exposed to high temperature is increased some fourfold, from about 40 to 160 respirations per minute (359). Much higher rates have been observed in other birds. Flutter rates in excess of 400 per minute were reported for the mourning dove by Bartholomew and Dawson (26). In ravens (*Corvus corax ruficollis*) Marder has observed a rise in respiratory rates from a normal of about 28 to 30 per minute to about 200 per minute when the birds were exposed to 45° C ambient temperature. The highest rates measured were about 250 per minute (Marder, personal communication). In the domestic pigeon the rates may increase from a normal of 40 to 50 per minute to over 500, and single observations above 600 per minute have been recorded (288). It is perhaps of significance that many observations include intermediate rates, a fact that suggests the absence of a specific resonant frequency in this species.

The observations on the domestic pigeon also included determinations of tidal volume and respiratory minute volume. While the respiratory frequency increased some tenfold, the tidal volume decreased from about 4·5 to about 1·2 ml, and it was concluded that the respiratory minute volume increased at most three to four times. These figures should probably be considered as representing orders of magnitude only, for it is difficult to design apparatus for use with small animals which have well-functioning valves and a sufficiently small dead space to give accurate results. It is possible that the inevitable increase in dead space and resistance may have caused deeper respiration and therefore higher respiratory minute volumes than would be found in the undisturbed animal.

WATER METABOLISM

It is not possible to give as detailed discussion of the water metabolism of birds as could be done for small desert rodents. Sufficiently detailed data are not available for the various components of the water intake and water loss of any bird, be it a desert or non-desert species. However, available information suggests that most birds have a relatively high rate of water loss, even in the absence of heat stress, and as far as we know at the present time, no bird is able to subsist with oxidation water as the only source of water.

Rate of water loss

Urine. While mammals form urea as the end product of protein metabolism, birds form uric acid which has a low solubility and is excreted in crystalline form. The precipitation of the uric acid permits the withdrawal of most of the water from the urine, and the final product is a semi-solid paste with a low water content. Therefore, the excretion of metabolic end products requires only small amounts of water, compared with the amount necessary for excretion in mammals. (Birds with free access to water, in particular aquatic and marine species, excrete a dilute and liquid urine, but the uric acid is still present as a white precipitate.) This difference between mammals and birds (as well as reptiles) is one of the most frequently cited differences in the water metabolism of the two groups. It is therefore surprising to find that there is a lack of adequate information about the role of urinary water loss in terrestrial birds, in particular in species with limited access to water.

Evaporation. The evaporation of water from birds has, on the other hand, been studied in some detail. Presumably the loss of water from the skin is small, and the evaporation from the entire bird has therefore frequently been designated as respiratory loss. Whether or not this is correct is, for the moment, of minor consequence.

The evaporation of water in a number of birds, both desert and non-desert species, was determined by Bartholomew and Dawson (25), who also included in their considerations some determinations made by other investigators. They showed that the evaporation increases rapidly with diminishing size of the bird. Several later determinations of water loss in other birds have resulted in data of a similar nature, for example, in the mourning dove (36) and in the savannah sparrow (Poulson and Bartholomew, personal communication).

Although the general trend towards high evaporation in small birds has been adequately established, and is confirmed by high rates of drinking (27), more determinations are needed over a wider range of body weights. This would establish the basic relationship between evaporation and body size in birds, and deviations from the expected value could then be interpreted in terms of physiological mechanisms of water conservation.

As ambient temperature increases, evaporation increases too, and the greater use of water is reflected in the amount of drinking. In mourning doves kept at $39°$ C the amount of water drunk per day was 24 per cent of the body weight against 6·5 per cent at $23°$ C, almost a fourfold increase. It can be assumed that the main part of the added water intake is due to increased evaporative cooling. Accurate determinations of the evaporation from birds (measured as evaporation rather than water intake) have been made for only a few birds. The data plotted in Fig. 43 show that the evaporation in the Abert towhee increases about fivefold as the ambient temperature is raised to $44°$ C.

Water intake

Oxidation water. The amount of water formed in the oxidation of proteins is higher in birds than in mammals. The reason is that the end product, uric acid, has a lower hydrogen content than urea. While urea (CH_4ON_2) contains two hydrogen atoms per nitrogen atom the amount of hydrogen in uric acid ($C_5H_4O_3N_4$) is only half as great, one hydrogen per nitrogen. This increases the yield of oxidation water from 0·396 grammes H_2O per gramme protein when urea is formed, to 0·499 grammes H_2O per gramme protein when uric acid is the end product. This increase is, of course, not without value, but its magnitude is too small to be of much significance. Even though the yield of oxidation water from protein is 25 per cent higher in birds than in mammals, it is

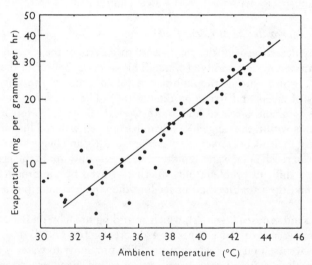

Fig. 43. The evaporative water loss of Abert towhee increases rapidly with rising environmental temperature. (Reproduced with permission from Dawson (96).)

still short of the amounts obtained in carbohydrate and fat metabolism. Compared to the quantities of water needed in heat regulation the difference in production of oxidation water in birds and mammals is completely insignificant and can be disregarded.

The formation of oxidation water was compared to the water loss by Dawson in his studies of the cardinal (99). Under basal conditions the metabolic rate was 12 to 13 kcal per 24 hours, which should be accompanied by the formation of between 1·2 and 1·8 grammes of oxidation water. However, the evaporative water loss of the cardinal under basal conditions was about 2·4 grammes per day. Hence, this bird could not, even in the absence of heat stress, offset evaporative losses by the production of oxidation water. The balance would be even less favourable if faecal and urinary losses were included in the account, and the use of water in heat regulation would be another unfavourable component in the balance. As a result, drinking-water or succulent food is required for the maintenance of water balance.

The indication is that all birds are in the same situation and need water, perhaps with a few exceptions. In a brief abstract, Bartholomew mentions that all birds so far studied lose weight steadily on a dry diet, 'except for a few individual savannah sparrows (*Passerculus sandwichensis*)'. However, in recent studies of this bird, it was shown that the minimum daily need for water was 26·8 per cent of the body weight in the subspecies with the lowest water requirement, *P. s. brooksi* (263).[1]

The need for water or succulent food

Many desert birds of the south-western deserts in the United States are restricted to the vicinity of water. This seems to be true of the Abert towhee, which during the summer is found only in the immediate vicinity of rivers and irrigation ditches (96). The mourning dove, one of the common birds in the south-western deserts, is much more numerous within the range of a few miles of open water. This bird may well need to drink only once every day or two (26), and being an excellent flier it can reach open water rapidly. The supply of water to the nestlings may be a difficult problem, but is perhaps solved by the production of crop milk, the usual method of feeding the young among pigeons and doves.

The sand grouse (*Pterocles*), which according to Heim de Balsac (149) is characteristic of the steppes and deserts of the Old World, never establishes itself out of reach of water. The proximity to water is always relative, the distance can probably exceed 50 km. Sand grouse are even better fliers than pigeons and since at certain times of the day they accumulate in large flocks at watering-places, it is obvious that they must be coming from considerable distances. Sand grouse normally stand in shallow water when drinking, and as their legs are short their breasts become saturated with water. Buxton (74) has suggested that from this has developed their very remarkable manner of supplying water to their chicks. Native hunters have always asserted that they carry water to their young in the hot, bare desert in their saturated breast plumage. The fascinating observations made by Meade-Waldo, who had sixty-one broods of sand grouse hatched in his aviaries, support this notion (223). He wrote:

[1] A recent study has examined the parakeet or budgerigah (*Melopsittacus undulatus*), which is a common seed-eating bird in the arid interior of Australia. The budgerigah has no particular tolerance to drinking salt solutions, but when deprived of all water it can exist with little weight loss for at least 38 days at 30° C. At lower temperature, 20° C, some individuals can apparently survive indefinitely without water (74a).

Water is conveyed to the young in the following curious manner, by the male only. The male rubs his breast violently up and down on the ground— a motion quite distinct from dusting—and when his feathers are awry gets into his drinking-water and saturates the feathers of his underparts. When soaked he goes through the motions of flying away, nodding his head, etc.; then, remembering his family is close by, he would run to the hen, make a demonstration, when the young run out, get under him, and suck the water from his breast—the appearance being that of a mammal suckling her young. The young pass the feathers through their bills, and keep changing places until the supply becomes exhausted.

Until the young can fly *they take water in no other way*, and the cock gives it to the young *only*.

It is difficult to imagine that the feathers of birds that fly many kilometres through the dry desert air should retain sufficient moisture for the young to obtain any water whatsoever in the way described by Meade-Waldo. My scepticism, however, was jolted when Dr. Mendelssohn of Tel Aviv University told me that chicks of sand grouse that he reared would die from thirst even if drinking-water was available to them, but that they would take water from wet cotton.

Some desert birds seem independent of free water. Quail can subsist by feeding on leaves, berries, and other succulent plant parts (344). Even in drought years it has been observed that Gambel's quail can raise its young on moisture derived from vegetation. A high proportion of the diet consists of succulent food such as leaves, buds, berries of mistletoe, and the succulent fruit of cacti (161). In captivity the house finch (*Carpodacus mexicanus*) has been kept indefinitely without drinking-water but with succulent vegetable food available (32). This is not very surprising since the water content of some of the food items, such as apples, may exceed 90 per cent.

More significant is the fact that the sparrow hawk (*Falco sparverius*) has been kept on meat without water (30). This shows that a purely carnivorous diet, at least in the absence of heat stress, makes this bird independent of open water. If the hawk remains inactive during the heat of the day and rests in places where the microclimate minimizes the heat stress, the water contained in its normal diet should suffice. For these animals the fact that uric acid requires only minimal amounts of water for excretion may be a more important factor in the water balance than it is in those birds which subsist mainly on vegetable material. A detailed study of the water balance in a predatory bird should therefore be worth while.

The great French ornithologist Heim de Balsac has discussed the need for water of desert birds (149). He considers that some of the birds of Sahara need water regularly. These include sand grouse (*Pterocles*), the rock pigeon (*Columba livia*), and the trumpeter bullfinch (*Bucanetes githagineus*). Others never drink or drink only occasionally, and among these he includes a number of small songbirds, the raven (*Corvus ruficollis*), and the bee-eater (*Merops apiaster*), a night-hawk (*Caprimulgus aegyptius*), the courser (*Cursorius cursor*), a partridge (*Alectoris barbara*), and the ostrich (*Struthio camelus*). Unfortunately, the information he gives about the birds and their natural history is insufficient. All of them can, of course, move over considerable distances, and their occurrence in unfavourable places may be restricted to certain parts of the year or to periods succeeding rain. However, this is not always the explanation. For example, the bee-eater feeds on insects and therefore also occurs more frequently near water. During a period of heat and extreme dryness the bee-eater was one of the rare species that did not come to drink at open water near Ain-Sefra in the Algerian Sahara. A partridge (*Alectoris*) occurs in places far from water, and this bird does not fly much. However, leaves and green plant material seem more important in its food than seeds. In Saharan areas this bird is restricted to bushy vegetation which can furnish shade as well as green fodder. It avoids denuded areas and true desert situations. In this respect it is probably quite similar to the American quail (161).

In conclusion we can say that some desert birds need drinking-water, some carnivorous birds can exist on a meat or insect diet, some plant-eating birds depend on the moisture in their food, but it remains unknown whether any desert bird can live on air-dried food without additional free water.

Tolerance to dehydration

Very little information is available about the tolerance to dehydration in birds. Although a weight loss is observed when the birds are deprived of drinking-water, this does not necessarily represent loss of water only. It is necessary to know the water content of the body in order to establish whether a decrease in weight is due to a reduction in tissue mass or in water. Since the metabolic rate of birds is high, tissue loss may be great, particularly in small species. The tolerance to weight loss varies markedly, the house finch (*Carpodacus mexicanus*) dies after losing 27 per cent of its body weight, while the California quail (*Lophortyx californicus*) may survive a weight loss of 50 per cent (34). Since the quail is larger than the house finch and loses water at a much lower rate (3·5 per cent of the body weight per day against 17·2 per cent in the house finch (25)), it should be able to withstand water deprivation approximately ten times as long.[1] It is, however, not justifiable to con-

---

[1] In more recent experimentation it was shown that the California quail when deprived of water had a mean daily loss of 1·6 ± 0·4 per cent of the initial body weight

clude that the 50 per cent weight loss in the quail represents a reduction in water content—white rats that died from water deprivation with
a weight loss of about 50 per cent still had 65 per cent water in their
bodies (see page 62). The amount of water that can be ingested in a
short time is large, but we do not know whether any desert bird has a
drinking capacity which approaches that of the camel and the donkey,
which can drink close to one-third of their body weight. The mourning dove has been observed to drink 17 per cent of its body weight in
10 minutes, a quantity about ten times as high as that which a man can
drink in the same time.

From his wide experience Bartholomew states (34) that no marked
differences have been found in the *ad libitum* water consumption between
desert and non-desert birds.

UTILIZATION OF SALINE WATER

The question of saline water for drinking is particularly important in
birds, for the avian kidney in general is unable to produce a urine anywhere near as concentrated as that of mammals. The bird kidney does
not have the characteristic Henle's loop, the structure that is responsible
for the high concentrating ability of the mammalian kidney. The loop
structure in the bird kidney is much less well developed, and the maximum concentration of bird urine is in the order of twice the plasma
concentration. In many birds the maximum urine concentration is
equivalent to about 300 mM NaCl, slightly more than one-half the
osmotic concentration of sea water.

Consumption of sea water should be impossible for birds if they had
only their kidney for elimination of salt. The ability of marine birds to
remain away from land and any possible source of fresh water for
months was one of the enigmas of biology until it was discovered that an
accessory gland in the head excretes sodium chloride in high concentrations. This nasal gland, or salt gland, which is found in all orders of
marine birds, can secrete a solution of up to 1000 mM NaCl. The
presence of the gland permits elimination of the excess salt present in
food or ingested sea water. Its existence does not prove that marine birds
do drink sea water, but only points out that they can do so with impunity
(121, 304, 306).

In terrestrial birds the nasal gland is generally much smaller than in
marine species, having a size about 1/10 to 1/100 that in equally large
marine species (330). There is no evidence that these small glands have

(*c.* 140 grammes). The mean survival time was over one month, and it was estimated
that as little as 2 grammes of water per day present in the food could maintain the
birds indefinitely (37*a*).

any role in salt excretion, and most terrestrial birds are quite intolerant to salt because their kidneys have a low concentrating ability. Do desert birds have a well-developed nasal gland, or is the role of the gland as insignificant as in other terrestrial birds?

The ability to tolerate salt has been examined in only a few desert birds. The mourning dove, for example, has only a moderate tolerance to salt. It will maintain its body weight when drinking 150 mM NaCl, but its *ad libitum* fluid consumption increases some $2\frac{1}{2}$-fold on this régime. When drinking 200 mM NaCl it loses weight, and on 250 mM NaCl the weight loss is almost as rapid as when it receives no water at all. Consumption of diluted natural sea water has approximately the same effect as corresponding solutions of NaCl (36).

The house finch (*Carpodacus mexicanus*) can tolerate slightly higher concentrations. It can maintain its weight on 250 mM NaCl, but not on 275 mM, which is within the range expected for terrestrial birds in general (32).

An entirely different magnitude of salt tolerance has been described in a few birds from arid zones. Farner (personal communication) has reported that the zebra finch (*Taeniopygia castanotis*), which is common in the arid interior of Australia, can tolerate 600 mM NaCl solution, slightly stronger than sea water and twice as concentrated as the expected limit for terrestrial birds generally. Farner has told me that he never noticed any discharge of fluid from the nose or mouth of zebra finches, an easily observed phenomenon which is characteristic of marine birds when they secrete from the salt gland. I could confirm this observation when I later had the opportunity to make similar experiments at Alice Springs in Central Australia. The birds were fed on dry seeds with NaCl solutions to drink. One of the birds survived and maintained its weight when drinking 700 mN NaCl.

Poulson and Bartholomew have studied the salt balance in the savannah sparrow (*Passerculus sandwichensis*), and have reported a considerable salt tolerance which differs in various subspecies (263). The highest tolerance was found in the subspecies *P. s. beldingi*, which lives and breeds in salt marshes. This subspecies could maintain its body weight when drinking 600 or 700 mM sodium chloride. Another subspecies, *P. s. brooksi*, which winters in salt marshes with *beldingi*, but breeds near fresh water, had a somewhat lower salt tolerance.

Bartholomew says that he has never observed any nasal discharge of fluids in these birds, and he has permitted me to dissect the head of one of his specimens. Its nasal gland was small, as in terrestrial birds generally, and had little similarity to the conspicuously large glands found in marine birds. Its salt tolerance is therefore not due to the same physiological mechanism as in marine birds.

The problem is clarified by the report that the urine concentration in *beldingi* may be as high as 960 mEq per litre of chloride. This amazing concentration is a sensation in avian renal physiology which is being pursued with further studies.

The urine: plasma concentration ratio in the savannah sparrow must obviously be higher than the maximum ratio of about 2 usually found in birds. However, when savannah sparrows drink salt solutions they do not maintain plasma concentrations at the usual low level. In some, the plasma chloride concentration was elevated to about 185 to 215 mEq per litre, and the plasma osmotic concentration to 490 to 610 mOsm per litre as compared with about 350 mOsm per litre in birds in general. This increase in plasma concentration permits the kidney to achieve a high final urine concentration without urine: plasma ratios as great as would otherwise be necessary. The osmotic U/P ratio reached 4·4, while a ratio of 7 or 8 would have been required to make the most concentrated urine in the absence of an elevated plasma concentration. A U/P ratio of 4·4, however, is still over twice as great as other bird kidneys can achieve, although far from the maximum concentration ratio of about 17 reached by the most efficient mammalian kidneys.

To what extent other desert birds may depend on an exceptionally powerful kidney deserves further study. An efficient kidney should be of particular advantage to birds that use little water for heat regulation, that is, birds which take advantage of microclimates that involve little or no heat stress. In these the water consumption is low, and they should be able to get along with relatively small amounts of water. A reduction in urinary loss would therefore represent a higher proportion of the total water turnover. This hypothetical type should correspond to the small desert rodent that avoids heat stress and manages its water balance thanks to a powerful kidney. It is possible that nocturnal insectivorous birds (for example, night-hawks) get along this way because of a relatively high moisture content in the food as well as the general advantage of producing uric acid instead of urea in protein metabolism (increased oxidation water and reduced water loss in urine). The real challenge to the physiological resources of the night-hawk is its habit of placing its nest directly on the ground in the open.

A powerful kidney should also enable birds to take advantage of the water in succulent salt-loving plants, such as *Salicornia* and similar halophytes. It has been reported that Pallas's sand grouse (*Syrrhaptes paradoxus*) feeds very largely on a desert chenopodiaceous plant, *Agriophyllum*, in Central Asia (74). Such succulents are common in dried-out river beds or wadis, and may be an important source of moisture where no open water is available.

The last bird that should be discussed from the viewpoint of salt tolerance is the ostrich. This giant bird was formerly common over large parts of the Sahara, but it is difficult to estimate to what extent its disappearance is due to excessive hunting or to general aridity, for this great desert has become increasingly dry even during historical times. The ostrich is an excellent runner and could easily move over considerable distances to reach water. Its food consists of plant material, insects, lizards, &c., i.e. the diet of a voracious omnivore, and it could probably be independent of open water when heat regulation does not put too high demands on the water resources.

There is, however, some indication that the ostrich may be in a different category. It is the only terrestrial bird that is known to have a large nasal gland, as large as the salt gland of some marine birds (330). The function of the gland has not been studied, but if it is similar to that in marine birds, it opens interesting possibilities. First, the ostrich might be able to take advantage of saline waters, too concentrated to be tolerated by other birds and most mammals. Another source of water available to a bird with a powerful salt-excreting organ is the succulent salt-loving vegetation.[1]

The former presence of ostriches throughout the Sahara is still evident from scattered fragments of ostrich egg shells on the ground where they have been nesting. One place where I found many such fragments was in the vicinity of Wadi Saoura. The nesting sites had been within easy reach of the wadi, which usually carries water for some weeks during the winter and has a rich vegetation of salty succulents during the remain-

---

[1] In collaboration with A. Borut and P. Lee I have recently obtained evidence for nasal excretion of salt in several terrestrial reptiles and birds, both in desert forms (*Dipsosaurus, Uromastyx, Ammoperdix, Struthio*) and in the humid-tropical *Iguana*. It thus seems possible that the mechanism may be present in terrestrial birds and reptiles in general. The well-known excretion of salt from the nasal gland of marine birds and reptiles would then represent a more highly developed form of this general mechanism.

We should like to suggest that extra-renal excretion of salt may be connected with the efficient withdrawal of water from the cloacal contents in the following way: In the cloaca salts are withdrawn by active transport from the liquid urine which has entered from the ureters. This makes the cloacal contents hypotonic to the blood, and due to the concentration difference water now leaves the cloaca by passive diffusion. If soluble salts were to remain in the cloaca in appreciable quantities, the urine would remain liquid and it would be impossible to produce a solid, almost dry urine without invoking an extremely efficient transport of water. So far active transport of water has not been demonstrated with certainty in any animal, and, furthermore, for theoretical reasons active transport of water would probably require an energy expenditure several hundred fold higher than necessary if the same net effect were achieved by the transport of a cation such as sodium, followed by a passive diffusion of water.

It could be suggested that an extra-renal excretion of salts not only is an integral part in the process of withdrawal of water from the urine, but that it may be essential to the efficient utilization of uric acid excretion as a water conserving mechanism in birds and reptiles. It should, in fact, be considered whether the mechanism may have been a prerequisite for the original evolution of terrestrial forms among these animals.

ing part of the year. At least one subspecies of ostrich (*Struthio camelus massaicus*) is particularly fond of the neighbourhood of soda and salt lakes (212)—do they drink the salty water or seek the succulent food?[1]

The ostrich should be a most interesting bird for further studies. Because of its size it cannot take advantage of microclimates that reduce or eliminate heat stress for smaller birds. In all likelihood the ostrich is in a physiological situation similar to that of the camel. It probably is tolerant to some increase in body temperature and to dehydration, but it is almost imperative that it should also have efficient mechanisms for heat dissipation by evaporation of water.

TORPIDITY AND AESTIVATION

Although folklore is rich in tales about torpidity in wintering swallows and swifts, scientists have been reluctant to acknowledge the occurrence of this phenomenon. A change in the attitude took place when a torpid desert poor-will was found by a class of students while on a field trip in the California deserts (165). The observation that humming-birds reduce their high rate of energy turnover by permitting the body temperature to drop during the night contributed to the acceptance of torpidity as a natural phenomenon in birds (244). Later on, torpidity has been well documented for night-hawks (caprimulgids), swifts (micropodids), and humming-birds (trochilids) (246). To what extent hypothermia and torpidity occur in birds in general remains to be elucidated, but it does not seem probable that the phenomenon should be restricted entirely to the families mentioned.

The torpidity that has been reported so far has always been in response to low temperatures. The ambient temperature does not have to be as low as for most hibernators, for example, the poor-will (*Phalaenoptilus nuttallii*) showed torpor at 17° to 19° C (157). To what extent torpidity could occur in birds in a manner similar to the aestivation of mammals remains to be seen. *A priori* it does not seem likely that torpidity with an appreciable decrease in metabolic rate could occur unless the ambient temperature dropped considerably below the usual body temperature of birds, say below 30° C. Rodents can achieve this in their underground burrows, but it seems unlikely that birds during the hot summer would find places where the microclimate is sufficiently favourable, and torpidity in birds, similar to aestivation in mammals, is probably not utilized extensively as a means for survival in the desert.

---

[1] The cactus family is native to the New World. The ostrich has therefore evolved in areas where this source of relatively salt-free water was unavailable.

SUMMARY

Most birds are diurnal and active during the day. Under conditions of extreme heat, however, their activity is mostly restricted to morning and late afternoon hours. Part of the adaptation to desert conditions is therefore behavioural; they avoid the most extreme heat stress.

Reproduction in desert birds involves some difficulties as it is necessary to shield the eggs and nestling young against overheating and supply the nestlings with water. Breeding is therefore commonly restricted to the most favourable periods and during extreme drought there is no reproductive activity. In some desert birds the endocrine control of reproduction seems to depend directly upon rainfall, rather than upon day-length, which controls breeding in many other birds.

The usual body temperature in most birds is in the range of 40° to 42° C, somewhat higher than in mammals. In those desert birds where information is available, the body temperature is similar to non-desert species. The lethal body temperature in desert birds is likewise similar to that in non-desert species, between 45° and 47° C. Desert birds are therefore not more tolerant to increased body temperatures than their non-desert relatives.

The fact that birds in general have a higher level of body temperature than mammals permits them to rely to a greater extent upon the dissipation of heat by conduction and radiation. During heat stress the body temperature may be further increased by several degrees, so that a favourable gradient from the body to the surroundings is maintained until the ambient temperature exceeds 40° to 41° C.

Birds depend on evaporation of water to prevent body temperature from rising to a critical level. They have no sweat glands, and evaporation from the respiratory tract seems to be the main avenue of water loss. The passage of air over the moist surfaces is increased by increasing the respiratory rate or by a rapid fluttering of the soft skin under the throat (the gular flap), or by a combination of both. This reaction appears when the body temperature reaches about 43° C, both in desert and in non-desert species.

Some desert birds seem independent of drinking-water and depend on the free water in the food. Under experimental conditions this is true, for example, for a predatory bird (sparrow hawk) and for a plant eater (quail). Many birds, on the other hand, are restricted to the vicinity of open water, and some depend on a rapid and powerful flight for moving to drinking-places miles away.

Terrestrial birds in general have a low tolerance to saline waters, and some desert birds are in this category (mourning dove, house finch). At least one desert bird (zebra finch) and one that normally lives and nests in saline marshes (savannah sparrow) have a tolerance to saline waters more concentrated than sea water. Among non-marine birds this is unique. While marine birds depend on an accessory gland in the head for the excretion of salt, the savannah sparrow has a kidney that can produce a highly concentrated urine, about three times as high as the maximum limit for birds in general.

Besides physiological specialization, the adaptation of birds to deserts involves a combination of behavioural and ecological factors. If they do not move entirely out of the desert area when conditions become unfavourable, they can utilize microclimates to avoid extreme heat stress.

16

LIZARDS, SNAKES, AND TORTOISES

REPTILES are a conspicuous and important element in the desert fauna. Lizards are most frequently seen because of their great number and diurnal habits. Snakes, although common, are more secretive and nocturnal, while tortoises occur only in relatively small numbers. The fourth living order of reptiles, the crocodiles, is amphibious and has no truly terrestrial representative. Most desert reptiles are carnivorous, the smaller forms prey on insects, but turtles and a few lizards are plant-eaters.

In many respects reptiles are quite different from mammals and birds, the most-featured contrast being that reptiles are 'cold-blooded' or poikilothermic, while mammals and birds are 'warm-blooded' or homothermic.[1] As we shall see, this is a misleading simplification. During much of their active lives reptiles have a fairly constant body temperature which may differ greatly from that of the surroundings. In the hibernating mammal or bird, on the other hand, the body temperature fluctuates widely with that of the environment and often approaches freezing. The usual textbook division into 'cold-blooded' and 'warm-blooded' is therefore not only inadequate but also misleading.

Mammals and birds usually have relatively high metabolic rates, and their body temperature can be maintained in cold surroundings by internal heat production. These animals can therefore be called *endothermic*. Reptiles, in general, have low metabolic rates, but they can utilize external heat sources such as solar radiation to elevate their body temperature to levels as much as 30° C above the ambient air. They can therefore properly be called *exothermic* (90). Thus, the endothermic animal maintains an elevated body temperature by producing its own heat, while the exothermic animal can realize a high body temperature only when an external heat source is available.

In many reptiles the main nitrogenous excretory product is uric acid. Reptiles therefore enjoy the same savings in renal water expenditure as

[1] The words *homothermic* and *homoiothermic* are used interchangeably, but neither conveys the accurate meaning of the physiological concept for which it stands. The Greek *homos* = like, and *homoios* = similar, give no linguistic basis for a distinction between the two. The simpler *homothermic* is widely used and is my own preference, but the longer *homoiothermic* has history on its side, for it was used by the Byzantine writer Tzetzes in the twelfth century A.D. My colleagues in the Department of English tell me that the ending *'ous'* entered English via Latin and that the hybrid 'homothermous' therefore should be avoided.

birds, a situation far more advantageous in water economy than the mammalian mode of urea excretion.

Desert reptiles are relatively small animals; they have a very limited range and never move over great distances. This means that they must be adapted to life in their immediate environment, they cannot move away as birds and large mammals can when conditions are unfavourable. Evasion is still possible, and all desert reptiles, whether diurnal or nocturnal, take advantage of shelter or underground burrows during the hottest time of the day.

The low metabolic rate of reptiles, which decreases further at low temperature, permits extended periods of inactivity and lethargy.

TABLE XXXIII

Range of body temperatures in normally active individuals of two species of spiny lizard. From (63)

	Altitude metres	Air temp. mean	Body temp.	
			Range	Mean
Sceloporus formosus malachiticus	1500 to 2200	19·1	30·0 to 35·8	32·9 ± 0·38
Sceloporus variabilis variabilis	150	29·5	33·6 to 40·0	36·9 ± 0·24

BODY TEMPERATURE

Normal activity range

It is well known that, within limits, reptiles become more active at high temperatures. It is less well recognized that many reptiles during periods of normal activity maintain their body temperature within fairly narrow limits in spite of fluctuations in external temperature. The main factor in this regulation is based on the utilization of solar radiation to elevate the body temperature, and by appropriate adjustments in behaviour relative to microclimatic conditions the animals can achieve a surprisingly accurate regulation. Ten different species and subspecies of spiny lizards (*Sceloporus*) in the United States and Mexico had mean body temperatures during normal activity which varied only from 32·9° to 36·9° C although they were at altitudes from 60 to 2200 metres (63). The data for the two extremes, one from the arid lowlands of Mexico and the other from the cooler high altitudes, are given in Table XXXIII. The activity range of body temperature for the other eight species fell within the limits of these two. Evidently the spiny lizards, when active and abroad, maintain their body temperature within close limits, in spite of wide variations in air temperature.

PLATE 8

DESERT IGUANA (*DIPSOSAURUS DORSALIS*)

After a cool night the desert iguana rapidly warms itself in the morning sun. During the day its temperature remains surprisingly constant within a few degrees of 40° C. This is achieved by carefully adjusted behaviour, including reduced exposure to sun and avoidance of the hottest part of the desert surface

(*Photo, Dr. C. M. Bogert, courtesy the American Museum of Natural History*)

PLATE 8

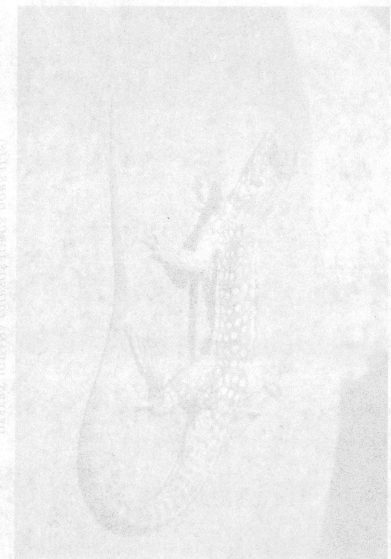

DESERT ICTIDOSAURUS DORSALIS

This should not be taken to imply that spiny lizards have no leeway in temperature. They can be fully active within a range of about 30° to 40° C in body temperature, but most individuals are found closer to the mean. Fig. 44 shows the distribution of body temperatures observed in two species of *Sceloporus*, and when they were normally active in their native desert habitat.

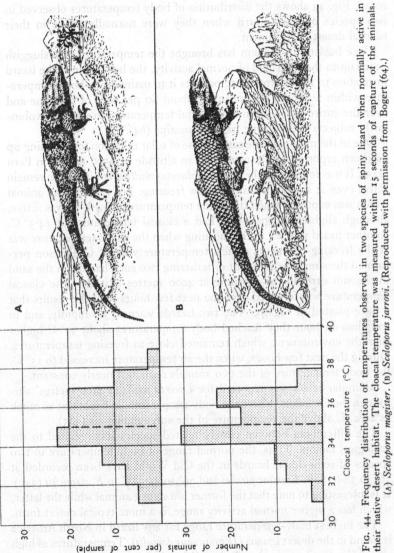

FIG. 44. Frequency distribution of temperatures observed in two species of spiny lizard when normally active in their native desert habitat. The cloacal temperature was measured within 15 seconds of capture of the animals. (A) *Sceloporus magister*. (B) *Sceloporus jarrovi*. (Reproduced with permission from Bogert (64).)

This should not be taken to imply that spiny lizards have no leeway in temperature. They can be fully active within a range of about 30° to 40° C in body temperature, but most individuals are found closer to the mean. Fig. 44 shows the distribution of body temperatures observed in two species of spiny lizard when they were normally active in their natural desert environment.

Once basking in the sun has brought the temperature of a sluggish lizard up to the threshold of normal activity, the behaviour of the lizard in relation to the microclimate permits it to maintain its body temperature within 2·5° C of the mean for about 80 per cent of the time and over the entire range of environmental temperature to which it voluntarily subjects itself during its daily routine (64).

One of the most extreme cases of use of solar radiation for warming up has been reported by Pearson from an altitude of 4500 metres in Peru (245). It was found that the lizard *Liolaemus multiformis* is able to remain active even at air temperatures below freezing. For example, an animal which was captured when the shade temperature was 4·5° C was active, although slightly sluggish, and had a cloacal temperature of 14·5° C. Another lizard was hot in the morning when the shade temperature was at the freezing-point—its cloacal temperature was 31° C. Pearson performed the simple experiment of tethering two such lizards on the sand in the sun early in the morning at 4000 metres altitude. The cloacal temperature was followed over the next few hours with the results that I have plotted in Fig. 45. The two lizards warmed up rapidly, and in less than an hour they reached body temperatures about 30° C higher than the environment, which remained close to freezing temperatures. During the next few hours, when the air temperature increased to 13° C, the body temperature of the two animals remained nearly constant.

A similar result was reported for *Lacerta agilis* at 4100 metres' altitude in the Caucasus, where the body temperature at times was as much as 29·2° C above the temperature of the surrounding air (325).

The differences between closely related species seem related to the ecological factors. Thus, the normal range of body temperature in two species of semi-desert lizards in the Old World have been recorded at 36° to 38·6° C in *Eremias pleskei* and 39° to 41·5° C in *E. strauchii* (340). It is interesting to note that the former is a steppe animal while the latter, which has a higher normal activity range, is a more typical desert form.

The highest body-temperature range for any lizard in North America is found in the desert iguana (*Dipsosaurus dorsalis*). Temperatures as high as 44° C are not unusual and 46·4° C has been recorded in a normally active individual (239). Since the lethal body temperature in this lizard is about 47° to 49° C, its normal activity temperature is amazingly close to the tolerable thermal limit.

Keeping warm—keeping cool

The ability of lizards to maintain a body temperature within narrow limits in spite of wide variations in external conditions depends primarily on the selection of an appropriate microclimate. Internal heat production and evaporation from the animal are of little importance in the heat budget. The main items are three avenues of heat exchange with the environment: (*a*) conduction to or from the air; (*b*) conduction to or from the substratum; and (*c*) radiation from the sun. Of these, conduc-

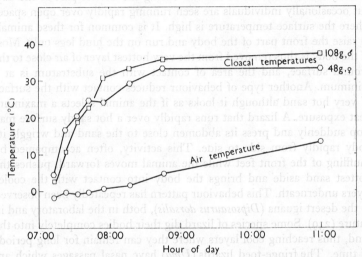

Fig. 45. The increase in cloacal temperature in two lizards (*Liolaemus multiformis*) tethered in the sun at 4000 metres' altitude in southern Peru. (Data from Pearson, (245).)

tion between the animal and the surrounding air seems to play a minor role, as we have seen in the preceding, and it appears that the other two factors are far more important.

Contact with the substratum. Many investigators have shown that the body temperature of lizards frequently is more closely related to the surface temperature of the substratum than to the simultaneous air temperature (see, for example (289)). However, it is necessary to be cautious in the evaluation of such observations for some measurements of soil-surface temperature are quite inaccurate. For example, a mercury thermometer gives only the roughest indication of the true surface temperature. Small thermocouples or thermistors give more precise results. However, the measurement of the radiation temperature in the infra-red range is the most accurate of any available method because it eliminates the need for any contact with and disturbance of the surface.

In cool air a lizard can absorb a considerable amount of heat from a warm soil or rock surface. In experiments where a substratum of sand was heated while cold air was circulated above the lizards, it was shown that the body temperature always followed that of the substratum (85). Animals of small size heat up much faster than larger ones, and can therefore attain an optimal temperature in a much shorter time.

In the desert, during the day, the temperature of the surface may exceed 70° C and this is far beyond the tolerable limit for any lizard. Usually lizards stay out of the sun during the hottest part of the day, but occasionally individuals are seen running rapidly over open spaces where the surface temperature is high. It is common for these animals to raise the front part of the body and run on the hind legs only. Most of the body is thus removed from the very hottest layer of air close to the ground surface, and the area of contact with the substratum is at a minimum. Another type of behaviour reduces contact with the surface of very hot sand 'although it looks as if the animal selects a maximum heat exposure. A lizard that runs rapidly over a hot sandy surface may stop suddenly and press its abdomen close to the sand and wriggle its body rapidly from side to side. This activity, often accompanied by shuffling of the front feet while the animal moves forward, pushes the hottest sand aside and brings the body into contact with the cooler layers underneath. This behaviour pattern has repeatedly been observed in the desert iguana (*Dipsosaurus dorsalis*), both in the laboratory and in nature (239). Some species of lizard dig their bodies completely into the sand, thus reaching cool layers where they can remain for long periods of time. The fringe-toed lizards (*Uma*) have nasal passages which are looped and U-shaped so that sand does not enter when the animal breathes, submerged in sand to the level of the nostrils (321).

Solar radiation. In the desert solar radiation is the most important heat source for reptiles. When they warm up by basking in the sun during the morning hours, both the direct radiation and the heat conducted from the substratum are derived from the sun. While the animal is heating up and is still sluggish it is useful that the temperature should rise as rapidly as possible; later in the day when the animal is warm and air temperature is high, further heating of the body should be avoided. Some kind of regulation or adjustment of the heat gain is therefore desirable.

Heat gain can be varied several ways. The animal may move from sun to shadow, thus eliminating solar radiation completely (although re-radiation from nearby surfaces may remain). In shade the surface temperature of the substratum will also be lower, thus further reducing the heat gain. Even if the animal remains in the sun, the heat gain can be varied by assuming different positions. If it orients itself perpendicularly to the rays of the sun and presses itself firmly down, it exposes a maximum surface. By selecting a different slope and posture, it can greatly reduce the surface exposed to incident radiation.

Recently it has been brought out that the parietal eye (pineal eye) may have an interesting function. This organ, which is located on the very top of the head of lizards and snakes, has long been a puzzle to zoologists. Stebbins and Eakin have removed the parietal organ from desert lizards of three different genera, with the result that all of them remained exposed to sunlight for longer periods than unoperated controls. Covering the eye with a light-tight shield had the same effect. However, the body temperature of all the lizards remained the same as in the controls—the prolonged exposure did not result in higher temperatures (322).

The conclusion to be drawn from these experiments is that the parietal eye seems to help regulate the duration of exposure to sunlight. There is some indication that the mechanism may act via the endocrine system. Stebbins and Eakin failed to find any nerve connexion between the 'eye' and the brain, and the 'retina' appeared to be secretory. The thyroid gland showed hypertrophy and loss of colloid, suggesting a relationship between thyroid activity and the increased locomotory activity observed in the parietalectomized animals.

Skin colour. Another factor to be considered in connexion with heat balance is the colour of the animal. The lightness or darkness of the skin indicates whether reflectance is high or low in the visible range of the spectrum. Absorbed radiation is transformed to heat, and since roughly one-half of the total energy of solar radiation is in the visible range, skin reflectance would seem important in the heat balance. (It is probable that in most of the infra-red range lizard skin, like most other non-metallic surfaces, is essentially a black body with a reflectance close to zero.) A particularly interesting aspect is that the reflection of visible light can be changed by the animal. It has many times been observed that when the body temperature of a lizard rises to a level which can barely be tolerated, its skin turns lighter (18, 85, 241).

It appears that the reflectance is higher in desert species than in other lizards. In sixteen species from widely different areas it was found that the average reflectance of both dorsal and ventral skin was highest in the desert lizards and decreased, in order, through semi-desert, plains, and temperate forest to tropical rain forest species (163). These determinations were made on isolated skin from 320 mμ (ultra-violet) through the visible range (400 to 700 mμ) to 1100 mμ in the near infra-red. The average reflectance varied from 6·2 per cent in a tropical form (*Iguana iguana*) to 35 per cent in the desert horned lizard (*Phrynosoma platyrhinos*). When the estimated heat gain from solar radiation was calculated for these two forms, it was found to be in the proportion of 1 to 0·7.

The quantitative importance of skin colour in heat gain is therefore not as great as suggested by the more than fivefold higher reflectance in the desert form. This follows simply from the complement value of reflectance, the absorption. For the two species mentioned the absorbed radiation is 94 per cent and 65 per cent respectively, that is, in the proportion of 1 to 0·7.

The change in reflectance that occurs when the skin of a lizard blanches as the body temperature approaches a critical high level should

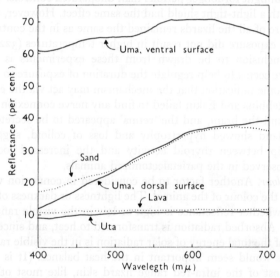

FIG. 46. The reflectance of visible light from the dorsal skin of a fringe-toed lizard (*Uma n. notata*) is very close to that of the surrounding sand. The reflectance from the black *Uta stansburiana* closely matches the black lava background where it normally lives. The reflectance from the white belly of *Uma* is high, but the colour of the ventral surface is probably of minor importance in heat regulation. (Reproduced with permission from Norris (241).)

be measured quantitatively not only for visible light, but in the entire range of the solar spectrum. Measurements have been made in the visible range, of 400 to 700 mμ, but the difference in reflectance was only a few per cent between a cold and a heated *Uma* (fringe-toed lizard). On the other hand, in all the wavelengths measured the reflectance of the dorsal skin of *Uma* remained close to that of the substratum, an indication of excellent colour matching (see Fig. 46) (241).

The ventral surface of many lizards is almost white and has a high reflectance in the visible range. Is this of any significance in reducing heat flow from a hot substratum? The usual interpretation is that the white ventral surface breaks up and reduces the optical effect of the shadow under the animal, and that it therefore is a form of protective coloration. The high reflectance will, of course, also reduce the absorption of reflected solar light and to a minor extent the heat load on the animal. However, most of the radiation from the hot sand is in the middle to far infra-red, and in all likelihood the white ventral skin is a completely black body in the range of substratum emission. Any assumption that the light belly is an advantage in heat balance is unwarranted unless actual measurements show this to be true.

Protective coloration is evidently quite important in lizards. A subspecies of *Sceloporus* from White Sands in New Mexico is almost white and remains fully as white as at the time of capture after remaining in captivity for 2 years (240). Similarly, a near-black subspecies of *Uta*, which matches the black background colour of the lava where it lives, has a low reflectance of 10 per cent throughout the visible range. This again emphasizes that colour matching is much more important in the coloration of desert reptiles than is heat regulation. This is in itself not very surprising, for although an adjustment in visible colour has some influence on heat exchange, the same result can much more easily be achieved by moving from sun to shade or by entering an underground burrow.

Effect of temperature on metabolic rate

The metabolic rate of an animal varies with its temperature. Within the range of body temperature normally tolerated by the animal, an increase by $10°$ C is often accompanied by approximately a twofold increase in metabolic rate and oxygen consumption. The increase that occurs with a $10°$ C temperature rise is called the Q_{10} (page 45).

Many studies have been made of the effect of temperature on metabolic rate in reptiles, one of the most detailed being that of Benedict (44). The Q_{10} of reptiles in general is usually in the range between 2 and 3. This means that at low temperatures the metabolic rate and energy turnover are quite low, all physiological processes are slowed down, and the animals are slow and sluggish. As the temperature increases all rates increase roughly in proportion to the oxygen consumption, that is, two or threefold for each 10 degree rise in temperature. At the normal activity temperature, between $30°$ and $40°$ C for most reptiles, the metabolic rate is high and the animals can move at top speed.

An interesting characteristic of some desert lizards was pointed out by Cook (86). At relatively low temperatures their oxygen consumption is highly temperature dependent with a Q_{10} of about 3. At higher temperature levels (up to $36°$ C) the metabolism is much less temperature dependent, and it was suggested that this is useful for animals which normally are active in very warm surroundings. These lizards were three species from the deserts of southern California, *Xantusia vigilis*, *Uma notata*, and *Cnemidophorus tessellatus*. On the other hand, the most heat-tolerant American lizard, the desert iguana (*Dipsosaurus dorsalis*), shows no depression in the Q_{10} at the highest temperatures it can tolerate, close to 46° C (Fig. 47) (100). This may be connected with the fact that *Dipsosaurus* has significantly lower rates of oxygen consumption between 20° and 40° C than other desert species. This is consistent

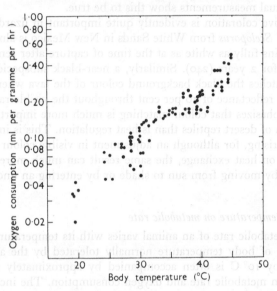

FIG. 47. Oxygen consumption in the desert iguana (*Dipsosaurus dorsalis*) increases with increasing body temperature up to the maximum temperature tolerated, 45° C. (Reproduced with permission from Dawson and Bartholomew (100). Copyright 1958 by the University of Chicago.)

with the remarkable temperature tolerance possessed by *Dipsosaurus* and should probably be regarded as a metabolic adjustment for operation at high temperatures (101).

Reptiles in general have a much lower metabolic rate at 37° C than do mammals of the same size. A comparison between *Dipsosaurus* and two desert rodents of a similar size (kangaroo rat and antelope ground squirrel) showed that the metabolism of the lizard at 37° C was about one-seventh that of the mammals. Even with the further increase that takes place when the lizard's temperature approaches the tolerable maximum, its metabolic rate still remains less than a third of that in the mammal at 37° C (100).

Other physiological rates. As oxygen consumption increases, other physiological processes also increase in rate. Several physiological functions were studied by Dawson and Bartholomew, and the results on the desert iguana are particularly illuminating (100). The rate of respiration (i.e. frequency of breathing) increases logarithmically with temperature, and the Q_{10} is about 2·5, the same order of magnitude as the Q_{10} for oxygen consumption. The heart-rate increases similarly with increasing body temperature. When these data are plotted on a semi-logarithmic scale, they fall on a straight line between 20° and 45° C, the slope giving a Q_{10} of 2·5. (Between 5° and 20° C the change with temperature was more rapid with a Q_{10} of about 4·8). The fact that heart-rate changes in exactly the same proportion as oxygen consumption suggests that the increased demands on the circulation are met by an increase in heart frequency only and that stroke volume remains unchanged. The unusual aspect of this reaction becomes evident if we compare it to the corresponding response in man. If the metabolic rate in man is increased, say, tenfold, the increased demand for oxygen is met by an increase of about threefold in heart-rate and a similar threefold increase in stroke volume. The suggestion that only the heart-rate increases in the lizard is, however, not a certain conclusion, for information is lacking about the arterio-venous oxygen difference. If it proves correct that the heart of the desert iguana regulates cardiac output by changes in rate only, this heart would be most interesting for further studies of cardiac physiology.

The excised heart of Dipsosaurus studied *in vitro* shows similar characteristics. The auricle contracts spontaneously over a wide range of temperatures and the Q_{10} is between 2·5 and 3. This suggests that the change in rate is inherent in the heart muscle, and that it does not depend on extracardiac control via the cardiac nerves. At the highest temperatures, between 40° and 45° C, the rate in the isolated preparation did not increase, but since it does increase in the living animal, it is probably an artifact due to lack of oxygen in the excised heart. Experiments at higher oxygen concentrations might settle the question as to whether or not the depression is due to inadequate oxygen supply.

The tension of isolated heart muscle has also been studied. The isometric tension developed in response to a single electrical stimulus showed a maximum around 25° C with a rapid decline at both lower and higher temperatures. The tension decreased to about one-fifth as the temperature rose from 25° to 45° C. At first glance this seems surprising, for other physiological performance generally increases at high temperature in the desert iguana. However, the recorded tension was that of a single twitch developed in response to a single electric stimulus. The tension of a muscle twitch is directly related to the duration of the action potential and since the action potential is of shorter duration at higher temperature, the tension in response to the single stimulus should also decrease with increasing temperature.

Acclimation to different temperatures

The metabolic rate of a lizard at a given temperature depends to some extent on the thermal history of the individual. Acclimation to temperature takes place in the sense that animals that have been maintained at relatively high temperatures show a lower metabolic rate than animals kept at a low temperature, if the metabolic rates of the two groups are

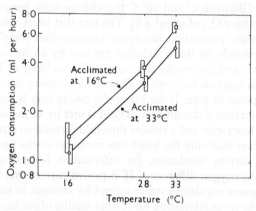

FIG. 48. Oxygen consumption in relation to temperature in the lizard *Sceloporus occidentalis* acclimated for 5 weeks at 16° C and at 33° C. At any given temperature the warm acclimated animals had a lower metabolic rate than the cold acclimated animals. Vertical bars represent two standard errors on each side of the mean. (Reproduced with permission from Dawson and Bartholomew (98). Copyright 1956 by the University of Chicago.)

compared point by point over a certain temperature range. This has, for example, been demonstrated for *Sceloporus occidentalis* (see Fig. 48) (98).

This phenomenon is not unexpected, it is characteristic for most cold-blooded animals that a considerable degree of thermal acclimation takes place. Further studies along this line in various species may, however, reveal interesting differences that may be meaningful when related to the thermal environment of desert and non-desert species.

One interesting and puzzling effect of thermal acclimation has been observed in *Sceloporus occidentalis*. If the animals are placed in a thermal gradient where they can settle at any preferred temperature, the selected temperature depends on their previous thermal history. In one such study (353) animals were kept for 14 days at constant temperatures of 12°, 25°, and 35° C. It might be expected that those animals which were acclimated at the highest temperature would show a preference for high ambient temperature. However, surprisingly, the opposite was found to be the case. While the animals kept at 12° and 25° C selected an environment where the body temperature was maintained at a mean level of 33° to 34° C, the animals acclimated at 35° C had a lower preferred temperature with a mean of 30·1° C (see Table XXXIV).

TABLE XXXIV

Influence of previous thermal acclimation on preferred body temperature in the lizard Sceloporus occidentalis

The difference between animals acclimated to 35° C and to lower temperatures was statistically significant (P<0·01). From (353).

Acclimation temp.	No. of animals	No. of readings	Preferred temperature, combined means ±S.E.
12° C	43	344	33·7±0·43
25° C	25	220	33·2±0·06
35° C	52	382	30·1±0·65

Lethal body temperature

The desert iguana (*Dipsosaurus dorsalis*) is normally active at body temperatures as high as 44° to 45° C (88, 239). This activity temperature exceeds that tolerated by any other New World reptile for which data are available. A temperature of 44° or 45° C is deleterious or lethal to many other lizards, including several desert species of the genus *Sceloporus* (85).

The desert iguana can tolerate a body temperature of 46° C or slightly above for extended periods (100, 239). If, however, the temperature increases slightly above this level it is rapidly fatal to the animal. Thus, the desert iguana normally lives under conditions which bring its body temperature surprisingly close to the lethal limit.

A great deal of information has been accumulated on the lethal temperatures for a variety of reptiles, but the results are not always directly comparable. First of all, many investigators have placed lizards or snakes in open sun and have shown that these animals tolerate such direct exposure for a short time only, perhaps 10 or 20 minutes, depending on the conditions. If a thermometer is now inserted in the cloaca of a dying animal this gives only the roughest estimate of the lethal temperature.

In order to make accurate observations of body temperatures it is necessary to have the animals in a uniform environment rather than placed on a hot substratum with solar radiation and a steep gradient to the air adding to the complexity of the environment. Another important factor is that the time of exposure to a given near-lethal temperature determines how much damage is done. It is therefore necessary to ascertain what the exact body temperature is and how long this temperature is maintained. Reliable and accurately calibrated measuring devices are also necessary, and mercury thermometers are not ideal for this purpose for a number of reasons which include their slow response and large heat capacity. There is therefore no reason to compile lists of 'lethal temperatures' as they have been obtained with various techniques under a variety of more or less well-defined conditions.

Although direct comparisons between the results of different investigators are difficult to make, many interesting conclusions can be drawn from the available material. A consistent report is that snakes generally have a lower temperature tolerance than lizards. For example, Cowles and Bogert (88) reported that the critical maximum temperature for the sidewinder rattlesnake (*Crotalus cerastes*) is 41·6°, while lizards from the same desert areas have critical maxima of 45° to 47·5° C. The same relationship is expressed by Saint-Girons and Saint-Girons, who make the general statement that the maximum lethal temperature is about 43° to 44° C in all snakes and in lizards from temperate and cold zones, while lizards from hot zones have a lethal maximum of 48° to 49° C (289). It can be assumed that this is related to the fact that snakes usually are nocturnal animals, while most lizards are diurnal and often exposed to higher temperatures.

The actual cause of thermal death in animals, whether from desert or temperate environments, remains essentially unknown. No single factor has been pinpointed, but it seems that derangement in the function of the central nervous system is a major factor. In many animals thermal death occurs far below a temperature where coagulation of proteins or denaturation of enzymes should take place. It is probable that the cause of death in these animals is related to the lack of physiological co-ordination which occurs when various rate processes are influenced to different degrees by temperature. In desert animals, on the other hand, where the lethal temperature may be between 45° and 50° C, the cause of thermal death could be connected with direct effects on tissue proteins and enzymes. For example, muscle from the desert lizard, *Eremias strauchii*, loses its excitability after 5 minutes' exposure to 48·5° C while muscle from the related *Eremias pleskei*, a steppe animal, loses its excitability at 47·4° C (340).

The temperature tolerance of the tissues of the desert iguana (*Dipsosaurus dorsalis*), the most tolerant lizard for which data are available, is amazingly high. The heart muscle was able to respond to electric stimulation after a 5-minute exposure to 50·2° C (100).

The maximum temperature tolerated under laboratory conditions is not necessarily identical with the temperature the animal can survive when exposed in its native habitat. Cowles (87) has pointed out that when snakes or lizards are exposed to high temperatures they lose their capacity for co-ordinated locomotion at a body temperature which they would survive without permanent damage if removed from the exposure. If the animals reach this point in their natural surroundings, they are unable to escape and will therefore remain exposed to the heat and perish. For practical purposes the point where organized and purposeful

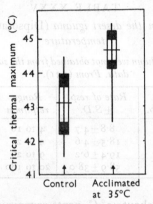

Fig. 49. Critical thermal maxima for the lizard *Uta ornatus linearis* acclimated at 35° C. Horizontal lines represent means, white rectangles two standard errors on each side of the mean, and one black and one white rectangle combined, one standard deviation. (Reproduced with permission from Lowe and Vance (201).)

locomotion is lost constitutes the lethal limit of exposure. Cowles has therefore suggested that this point be designated as the 'critical maximum temperature,' a point which is actually more useful for ecological considerations than the absolute lethal temperature.

Acclimation and lethal temperature. The maximum lethal temperature and its relation to the previous exposure of animals has received a great deal of attention (71, 166). It is therefore surprising that little attention has been given to this phenomenon in desert reptiles. It has, however, been shown that both the critical thermal maximum and the survival time at high temperature are increased by exposure to non-lethal high temperature of the lizard *Uta ornatus linearis* (201). In this investigation the control animals were freshly caught in the field and had been maintained for 1 or 2 days at room temperature prior to testing. The experimental animals were kept at a constant temperature of 35° C for 7 to 9 days, which sufficed for a highly significant increase in their thermal tolerance (Fig. 49).

Prevention of overheating, panting, and evaporation

When lizards are exposed to environments that cause critical over-heating, they attempt to escape, as was described earlier in this chapter. If unable to remove themselves from exposure, are lizards able to oppose actively a rise in body temperature?

Reptiles have no sweat glands, and evaporation of water for heat regulation is probably restricted to the respiratory tract. Dawson and Bartholomew have described how the desert iguana, when the body

TABLE XXXV

Rate of respiration in the desert iguana (Dipsosaurus dorsalis) *at high temperature*

The figures in the last column were not obtained from the same specimens as the other data. From (331).

Cloacal temp.	Rate of resp. $\pm S.D.$	Range resp./min	Evaporation mg $H_2O/g/hr$
32° C	8·8±4·7	4 to 16	0·86±0·23
36° C	18·5±4·6	9 to 25	1·16±0·25
40° C	19·4±6·2	9 to 26	2·08±0·44
44° C	58·9±38·0	20 to 180	3·64±0·93

temperature exceeds about 43° C, pants conspicuously with the tongue partly extruded and engorged with blood (100). This panting, however, is not an abrupt acceleration of the breathing-rate, as in certain mammals and birds. As was shown above there is a continuous acceleration of respiration as metabolic rate increases, and the temperature coefficient is of the same magnitude as that for oxygen consumption. Similar 'panting' has been observed for other lizards, but it is not universal. In the skink *Eumeces obsoletus*, the rate of respiration does not increase to the same extent as oxygen consumption, and Dawson states that panting is not observed even at temperatures high enough to be injurious to the animals (101).

In contrast, the increase in respiratory rate in the desert iguana is more conspicuous (331). The mean rate of respiration at a cloacal temperature of 40° C was 19 and at a cloacal temperature of 44° C the rate had increased to 59 respirations per minute (Table XXXV) with a range in the observed rates of 9 to 26 at 40° C and 20 to 180 at 44° C. This shows an appreciable capacity for increase in the respiratory rate, but the effect on the water loss did not seem to be as great as suggested by the respiratory rate. This indicates that panting is a relatively in-efficient mechanism for increasing evaporation. It will receive a more detailed treatment later in this chapter.

It would be interesting to study panting and evaporation at high temperatures, and even closer to the critical limit, in lizards of widely different body size. Various large lizards, such as *Varanus* in the Old World and Australian deserts, should be suitable for such studies. Evaporation as a means of heat regulation should theoretically be much more efficient in large animals. Furthermore, since the Old World deserts are geologically much older than those in the New World, it can be expected that the lizards in these areas may display more highly developed physiological responses to their desert habitat.

WATER METABOLISM

Normally reptiles have a water content in their bodies similar to that in mammals, or perhaps slightly higher. This has long been known, and has recently been confirmed for a few typical desert species (174, 176, 342). The fairly high water content found in the lizards *Uromastyx* and *Varanus* compared to mammals is partly due to the lower fat content in the two lizards.

For an animal to remain in water balance the water content of the body should be maintained, and the losses which occur through faeces and urine and by evaporation should be covered by a corresponding water intake. This intake is derived from the usual three sources, drinking, free water in the food, and oxidation water.

Free water for drinking is only rarely found in the desert, and most reptiles live in surroundings where no water-supply is available. It is possible that dew may play some role, in particular for animals of small body size. Very small animals might, on mornings with heavy dew, lick up droplets and thereby secure an adequate supply. However, dew usually occurs only on cool or cold nights and evaporates again in the morning before most lizards have had time to warm up in the sun and become active. It has been reported that snakes lick up droplets of dew as they rapidly stick out their tongue against rocks, leaves, &c., on cool mornings. Unfortunately, the appearance of licking up dew does not answer the question of whether or not they do so. Another possibility that also deserves attention is whether the contact of the skin with surfaces covered by dew could permit absorption of water through the skin.

At the University of Tel Aviv Mendelssohn has tried to demonstrate absorption of water through the skin, but if drinking was prevented he found no weight increase. He tried this with the three desert lizards *Agama*, *Acanthodactylus*, and *Uromastyx* (personal communication).

On the other hand, a lizard from the desert regions of Australia, *Moloch horridus*, has been reported to soak up water through the skin

(74). Quite recently, it has been demonstrated that the water does not enter *through* the skin but moves by capillarity along fine open channels in the outer keratinized layer of the epidermis. If an animal is placed with its belly in water, the skin works like blotting-paper, and an advancing front of water can even be seen moving over the skin. When the water reaches the mouth the animals move their jaws and take in water. If the jaws were held together with adhesive tape the weight gain was no greater than what was supposedly due to capillary absorption in the skin, but if the tape was removed the jaws started to move and a further weight gain ensued. As a confirmation, an animal deficient in water was allowed to lie in water containing the dye Evans blue. Later the dye was found in the stomach although drinking in the ordinary way was never seen (50).

When reptiles are given water in captivity they usually drink some, and may even immerse themselves more or less completely. Quantitative studies of drinking are virtually non-existent, but I know about one impressive report of water intake by the desert tortoise (*Gopherus agassizii*), which has been reported to increase by over 40 per cent in weight by drinking (356). An interesting way of water intake has been suggested for the Florida worm lizard (*Rhineura floridana*) by Bogert and Cowles (62). These investigators showed that the worm lizard loses water relatively rapidly if it is kept in dry sand, but if returned to moist sand it gains weight again. They stated that the sand was not sufficiently wet for the lizard to ingest water by way of the mouth, and that the most reasonable conclusion is that water was absorbed through the skin. It would be useful to repeat these experiments under well-controlled conditions, and also to extend them to other species, in particular to desert species.

Most desert reptiles are carnivorous and their food therefore contains a fairly high amount of water. As long as water is not used for heat regulation the animals should be in a quite favourable water balance, for urine production requires little water in animals that mainly excrete uric acid. Rattlesnakes, for example, have been kept in captivity for long periods of time without any drinking-water and are obviously able to subsist on the water of the food (183). Mendelssohn has told me that he kept a snake from the Negev, *Spalerosophis diadema*, for 5 years without water, fed on live mice only. During 9 months one snake consumed 21 mice and gained in weight from 123 to 132 grammes.

The amounts of oxidation water formed in metabolism are the same in reptiles as in other animals, but it should be remembered that proteins yield a slightly higher amount of oxidation water in animals that eliminate uric acid instead of urea (see page 215).

Evaporation of water

The evaporation from reptiles has not been a subject of sufficient attention. One can expect tremendous variations in the amount of water evaporated from reptiles depending on air temperature and humidity.

When a poikilothermic animal with its relatively low metabolic rate remains in a cool underground burrow, its body temperature is very close to that of the surroundings. If the air has a high relative humidity, as we have seen it frequently has in underground air spaces, the evaporation should be quite low and approach zero. This gives the same advantage that the aestivating mammal enjoys when its body temperature is permitted to drop towards that of the environment, as was discussed in a previous chapter (page 190). Even if the air in the underground retreat should be below the saturation point, evaporation would still be low because the respiratory air remains cool and will hold only a moderate amount of water vapour, even when it becomes saturated in the respiratory tract.

When the desert reptile is active, being warmed by the sun to its normal activity range, it is essentially in the same situation as a mammal. Of course, it makes no difference whether the heat is derived from external sources in the exothermic lizard or from internal metabolism in the endothermic mammal. In each case the amount of water vapour added to the air in the respiratory tract depends on the temperature and humidity of the inspired and the expired air.

If the ambient temperature exceeds the tolerable body temperature, the only means of preventing a rise to the lethal limit is evaporation (unless the animal can remove itself to more favourable conditions). We do not know to what extent desert reptiles can use water for heat regulation, but if they were to resort to this mechanism they would be in much the same situation as mammals. Large reptiles would heat up fairly slowly and have a high thermal inertia and, since their surface is relatively small, the use of water in heat regulation might be efficient. Most desert reptiles, however, are small or very small, and the use of water for heat regulation would be very expensive. Accordingly, we can expect that most desert lizards do not employ evaporation as a major mechanism in combating high temperatures, but have to rely mostly or exclusively on the ability to avoid lethal or near lethal exposure.

Rate of water loss in reptiles. The skin of reptiles is dry and covered with a thick keratin layer. It could be expected that evaporation from this dry surface would be very small. Compared to evaporation from the moist skin of amphibians, the evaporation is indeed very low, as can be seen from the fact that the temperature of reptiles remains very close to that of the environment, while amphibians, due to the rapid evaporation of water, are cooled to several degrees below the ambient temperature, in particular at low humidities (see Fig. 50). However, as we shall see, there is strong evidence for a relatively high evaporation in reptiles as compared to that in mammals.

Any attempt at evaluating the rate of evaporation from reptiles meets with the difficulty that the few determinations made by various investigators have been obtained on different species under widely different conditions. It is necessary to know the temperature of the air as well as

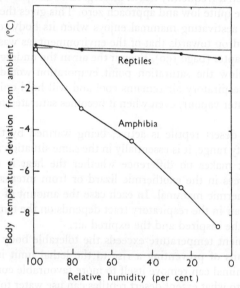

FIG. 50. The evaporation from moist amphibian skin causes a cooling of the animal below the ambient temperature, with the temperature difference increasing as the air becomes drier. Evaporation from the dry skin of reptiles is low and the cooling effect is very small. (Reproduced with permission from (139).)

its humidity. The temperature is important, not only for the amount of water the air can contain, but also because the metabolic rate of the animal is affected. A rise from 20° to 40° C should involve a five or tenfold increase in metabolic rate, and evaporation from the respiratory tract could be expected to be closely related to oxygen consumption and the ventilation of the lungs. The size of the animal is important because evaporation from both skin and respiratory tract should be more closely related to body surface than to body weight. Finally, any appreciable temperature difference between the animal and the surrounding air should, of course, be known.

In order to obtain an approximate idea about the importance of various factors, primarily the body size, I have plotted in Fig. 51 some observations made for terrestrial reptiles by various investigators. This figure is by no means complete, it is merely an attempt at bringing together a number of observations made on reptiles of widely different size.

It is apparent that evaporation, when expressed in per cent of the body weight, is larger in the small animal. This could indeed be expected, for

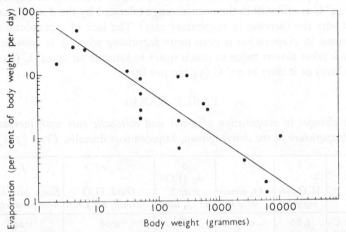

FIG. 51. When observations on water loss in various reptiles are related to their body weight, it appears that small animals have a higher rate of evaporation than larger ones. The increase in evaporation in the small reptiles is greater than predicted from their greater relative surface (see text). Selected data from (44), (47), (62), (331).

the small animal has a larger relative surface, a higher metabolic rate, &c., than the large animal. However, the line in Fig. 51 has a slope of -0.67, and if we were dealing with a strict surface-related function the slope should be only half as great, -0.33.

A compilation of this kind should be viewed with extreme caution for the data were obtained with widely different techniques, often without control of atmospheric humidity, and on a variety of animal species. Much more information is necessary, uniform technique is desirable, and, wherever possible, observations for different species should be treated separately. (It is interesting, however, that there seems to be a uniform pattern for the evaporation in reptiles from different terrestrial orders, and that the evaporation from an alligator, normally an aquatic animal, exceeds by one order of magnitude that of other reptiles (62).)

The particular data for the desert iguana, *Dipsosaurus dorsalis* show an increase in water loss with increasing temperature. The rate of oxygen consumption was determined in the same animals, and the observations are therefore particularly well suited for a discussion of evaporation relative to metabolic rate. In Table XXXV (page 240) it was shown that the rate of respiratory movements increased almost sevenfold between 32° and 44° C. Since evaporation remained nearly proportional to the oxygen consumption, the increase in respiration was not followed by a corresponding increase in water loss. In other words, the 'panting' seems quite inefficient and pointless when no effect towards heat dissipation is apparent. Perhaps increased evaporation could not be expected, for 44° C is still within the normal range tolerated by the desert iguana. But why the increase in respiratory rate? The lack of a proportionate increase in evaporation is even more surprising when it is considered that it takes almost twice as much water to saturate air at 44° C (63 mg per litre) as it does at 32° C (34 mg per litre).

TABLE XXXVI

The changes in evaporation of water and metabolic rate with increasing temperature in the desert iguana, Dipsosaurus dorsalis. *From (331)*

a	b	c	d	e	f
	H_2O *loss* mg/g hr	O_2 *cons.* ml/g hr	mg H_2O *evap./* ml O_2 *used*	*Oxid.* H_2O *formed, mg/g hr*	*Evap. heat loss/ heat production*
32° C	0·86	0·10	8·6	0·06	1·04
36° C	1·16	0·18	6·5	0·11	0·78
40° C	2·08	0·24	8·7	0·14	1·05
44° C	3·64	0·35	10·4	0·21	1·26

The relatively constant evaporation per oxygen consumed (column *d*, Table XXXVI) makes it possible to compare water loss in desert reptiles with that in desert mammals. When the evaporation in small desert rodents was calculated on this same basis, it was found that their evaporation was in the order of magnitude of 0·6 mg water per ml oxygen used, or less than one-tenth of that in the lizard. If, for the moment, we assume that the ventilation of the lungs in reptiles is similar to that in mammals, the figures indicate that perhaps only one-tenth of the evaporation takes place from the respiratory tract and the remaining nine-tenths from the skin. As far as I know, the only attempt at determining separately the evaporation from the skin and the respiratory tract in reptiles has been made by Chew, who found that the evaporation from the head was related to the evaporation from the body in the ratio 2:1 (81). The unexpectedly high figures quoted above indicate that further studies might yield extremely informative results.

It has commonly been assumed that evaporation from reptilian skin is low, but the tentative results quoted here indicate the opposite. The figures in Table XXXVI are not the only information available, observations made by Benedict on snakes and tortoises weighing between 2·6 and 10·2 kg gave water losses ranging from 3·5 to 9 mg water per ml oxygen used (44). In other words, large-size snakes and tortoises evaporate in the same order of magnitude, relative to metabolism, as Templeton's lizards, and far above the evaporation found in mammals. Benedict himself considered that his figures demonstrated an appreciable loss of water through the shell of the turtle and from the skin of snakes, an opinion that was supported by the observation that the snakes consistently showed a somewhat lower temperature than that of the surroundings.

In the discussion of the kangaroo rat it was shown that the evaporation from the respiratory tract in completely dry air is close to the amount of oxidation water formed at the same time. The amount of oxidation water formed in the lizards is given in column e of Table XXXVI. This shows that the evaporation from the desert iguana in dry air is ten to fifteen times as high as the amount of oxidation water formed in the same period of time. This is indeed unexpectedly high, but since the same order of magnitude is indicated by Benedict's results for larger reptiles, snakes as well as tortoises, we can assume that the order of magnitude is correct, at least until more detailed studies come out differently.

One further interesting circumstance is brought out in Table XXXVI. Column f indicates the relationship between heat removed by evaporation and the simultaneous heat production in the lizard. These two processes are of about the same order of magnitude throughout the temperature range measured, giving a ratio close to 1. Thus, heat is being removed by evaporation at the same rate as it is being formed, even at the highest temperature. It would be interesting to know whether this relationship still holds for temperatures 1 or 2 degrees higher, in the narrow range between normal activity temperature and the lethal limit for the desert iguana. Although water is not used for heat regulation at 44° C, it might occur at 45° or 46° C to prevent a rise to the lethal limit for body temperature.

Urine

Uric acid. In 1822 Vauquelin (341) reported that reptilian urine is composed almost entirely of uric acid, and it has since been commonly accepted that uric acid excretion is correlated with the lack of water and the need for water conservation in terrestrial and arid habitats. The excretion of uric acid in terrestrial reptiles and in birds has been confirmed many times, and it has further been found that aquatic reptiles, such as crocodiles and marine turtles, excrete mainly urea and ammonia (318). The correlation between uric-acid excretion and habitat is apparent also within more closely related species. For example, some urea was found in the urine of eight species of chelonian reptiles, but while the amphibious species excreted primarily ammonia and urea the xerophilous terrestrial species excreted mainly uric acid as their major nitrogenous product (232).

The fact that reptiles can form and excrete both uric acid and urea has attracted considerable interest. There has been some confusion as to whether any given species excretes mainly one or the other. It turns out that there can be variations within a species. In the tortoise, *Testudo leithii*, even one individual can change from predominantly uric acid to urea excretion, or vice versa (175). The cause of the shift between urea and uric acid excretion in another species of tortoise, *Testudo mauritanica*, is apparently a direct function of temperature and hydration of the animal, with the formation of uric acid increasing when water balance is less favourable (109). The underlying mechanism controlling such a shift in biochemical activity is unknown and would be worth study.

The fact that uric acid is precipitated from the urine and is excreted as a semi-solid mass permits a high degree of water economy. It was found by Marshall (216) that uric acid is not only filtered in the glomerulus of the kidney, but is also added to the urine by active secretion as the fluid passes down the renal tubule. Marshall's results indicated that in the lizard *Iguana iguana* 6 per cent of the uric acid entered the urine by filtration, while 94 per cent was added by tubular secretion. Further studies of the nitrogen metabolism and excretion in other typically terrestrial and arid zone reptiles should be worth while.

Urine concentration. It is well known that only mammals and birds can produce a urine more concentrated than the blood-plasma in total osmotic concentration. Reptiles have no ability to form a urine which is highly concentrated, and this makes the uric acid mechanism particularly valuable. When it comes to such substances that remain dissolved in the urine, water is necessary for their excretion. Since the osmotic concentration of the urine cannot exceed the plasma concentration, it can be assumed that reptiles cannot tolerate the consumption of salty water or plants with a high salt concentration, unless they have some extra-renal mechanism for salt excretion.

The problem of extra-renal salt excretion has been solved by marine birds. When these animals, whose kidney is unable to cope with the salt of sea water, ingest food with a high salt content or drink sea water, a nasal gland secretes the excess salt. This salt-secreting gland is active only when there is an osmotic load on the organism; in the gull it is located on top of the skull and ducts carry the secretion to the nasal cavity from where it runs out the nares and drips off from the tip of the beak. The secreted fluid is a highly concentrated solution of almost pure sodium chloride (306). A similar mechanism for salt excretion has been demonstrated with certainty in marine turtles (whose salt gland is located in the orbit of the eye) and in the marine iguana (which has a nasal salt gland) and it is probable that a similar mechanism occurs also in the marine sea snakes (303). It is difficult to make predictions about the existence of extra-renal electrolyte excretion in desert reptiles and the subject ought to receive more attention than it has so far. I have made a few experiments with the desert tortoise (*Gopherus aggassizi*) which I gave injections of hypertonic sodium chloride solutions and methacholine to stimulate gland activity, but no secretion was observed that was comparable to the salty 'tears' that are produced by marine turtles in response to osmotic loads. However, an iguana (*Iguana iguana*) kept as a laboratory pet has consistently secreted from the nose a fluid containing sodium and potassium salts with equal amounts present as chloride and as bicarbonate.

Studies of water and electrolyte excretion in the Australian lizard *Trachysaurus rugosus* gave some information about responses that are likely to be found in other arid forms as well (47, 48). Urine samples collected in the field during the summer had a mean osmotic concentration of 334 ± 15 mOsm, while the mean concentration of the plasma in five animals was 350 ± 25 mOsm. This plasma concentration is normal for a reptile, and the fact that the urine concentrations nearly equalled the plasma concentrations shows that the animals had no excess of water for urine formation. In animals that were fed on meat and kept without water for 2 weeks, the freezing-point of the urine was 247 ± 70 mOsm, which indicates that these animals were in positive water balance and therefore could manage on a carnivorous diet without utilizing the full concentrating power of the kidney.

Attempts at increasing the flow of urine by the injection of hypertonic sodium chloride solutions gave negative results. Repeated injections of 6 per cent NaCl solution caused the plasma sodium concentration to increase from about 150 mN to about 230 mN. This represents a high tolerance to elevated plasma concentrations, and in this way urine concentrations can be increased somewhat above what is normal for the animal. In specimens collected in the field during the dry summer, sodium plasma concentrations as high as 195 were observed, showing that the animals probably were short of water and surviving with increased plasma concentrations.

The kidney of *Trachysaurus* has a relatively small glomerular volume but a normal kidney weight. The urine flow is low, and water loads are excreted only slowly. The Egyptian lizard *Varanus griseus* shows even less response to water loads; after injection of water in an amount of 15 per cent of the body weight, there was no increase in urine volume (177).

When water was administered to *Trachysaurus* in an amount of 15 per cent of the body weight, the urine flow increased to a mean of 1·31 ml per 100 grammes per hour, which is a considerable increase above the mean urine flow of non-hydrated lizards (0·024 ml per 100 grammes per hour). The animals respond to the injection of pitressin with a reduction in urine flow, and their hypophysis contains agents that cause marked antidiuresis in hydrated lizards. It can therefore be assumed that the water excretion is under hormonal control, as it is in higher vertebrates. The slow response to water loads could be due to the persistence of a high concentration of antidiuretic substance in the blood or to the fact that metabolic processes in general are slower in cold-blooded than in warm-blooded animals. This is an area where a comparison of arid forms with others, including semi-aquatic species such as the Galapagos iguana, is likely to contribute valuable information to comparative physiology and a better understanding of those adaptations that are characteristic for desert species.

SUMMARY

Of the four living orders of reptiles the lizards, snakes, and tortoises have many representatives in desert regions while crocodiles are restricted to semi-aquatic environments.

All reptiles are poikilothermic animals, and the rates of metabolism and other physiological processes vary with the body temperature. At low temperature these animals are sluggish, but at higher temperatures they become increasingly active.

When the air temperature is low, desert lizards, and probably to a lesser extent snakes, use solar radiation to warm their bodies to levels above the surrounding air. By adjustments in their behaviour lizards are able to maintain their body temperature relatively constant in the range of 30° to 40° C. Certain species of lizards may have a body temperature of 30° C while the air temperature is at the freezing-point.

When warm, reptiles avoid further exposure, first by seeking shade, and under hot conditions by retreating underground. Most desert lizards are diurnal and can move swiftly over hot ground, but if they are kept exposed to the sun on a hot desert surface they soon perish. Snakes are more nocturnal and avoid day-time exposure to heat more than lizards do.

The lethal body temperature for lizards is probably around 48° C for most desert species, while snakes have a somewhat lower lethal temperature, in the range of 43° to 44° C.

If lizards are exposed to lethal or near lethal temperatures there is an increase in respiratory rate which has been called panting. However, the increase seems to be due to the rise in oxygen consumption which is caused by the elevated body temperature. There is, as yet, little evidence that the 'panting' involves significant use of water for heat regulation, even when body temperature approaches the fatal limit.

Reptiles have no sweat glands, but the few measurements that have been made indicate that the evaporation from the skin is appreciable. This is probably true for lizards, as well as snakes and tortoises. Where measurements have been made, total evaporation was found to be in the order of ten times as high as the amount of oxidation water formed in the same period of time. Evaporation increases with increasing temperature at about the same rate as metabolic rate increases. Small reptiles have a higher rate of water loss per unit body weight than large ones, the difference apparently being related to the larger relative surface in small animals.

In reptiles from arid and desert areas, uric acid is the main nitrogenous excretory product. It is excreted in crystalline form as a semi-solid white paste. Therefore, only relatively small amounts of water are expended in formation of urine.

The reptilian kidney is unable to produce a urine with a higher osmotic concentration than the blood-plasma, and unless these animals have an extra-renal mechanism for salt elimination, they should be unable to tolerate the ingestion of salty water or plants with a high mineral content. Preliminary observations indicate the presence of a nasal secretion of salts in some lizards.

One main physiological advantage of desert reptiles is their poikilothermic nature. This permits a relatively high metabolic rate when the animal is active, and a decrease when the animal retreats underground to cooler surroundings. Furthermore, when the body temperature approaches that of the surroundings, evaporation of water decreases, a decrease which is particularly great if the atmosphere of the cool retreat has a high relative humidity. Although some excellent studies have been made, we lack really adequate quantitative studies of water metabolism in reptiles.

REFERENCES

1. ADAMSONS, KARLIS, JR., ENGEL, S. L., DYKE, H. B. VAN, SCHMIDT-NIELSEN B., and SCHMIDT-NIELSEN, K. 'The distribution of oxytocin and vasopressin (antidiuretic hormone) in the neurohypophysis of the camel', *Endocrinology*, **58**, 272–8 (1956).
2. ADOLPH, E. F., and DILL, D. B. 'Observations on water metabolism in the desert', *Amer. J. Physiol.* **123**, 369–78 (1938).
3. ——'Heat exchanges of man in the desert', ibid. **123**, 486–99 (1938).
4. —— 'Do rats thrive when drinking sea water?', ibid. **140**, 25–32 (1943).
5. —— *et al. Physiology of man in the desert.* Interscience: New York (1947), 357 pp.
6. —— and RAHN, H. Résumé of the investigation', in ADOLPH. E. F. *et al.*, *Physiology of man in the desert.* Interscience: New York (1947), pp. 5–15.
7. —— 'Urinary excretion of water and solutes', in ADOLPH, E. F. *et al.*, *Physiology of man in the desert.* Interscience: New York (1947), pp. 96–109.
8. —— 'Blood changes in dehydration', in ADOLPH, E. F. *et al.*, *Physiology of man in the desert.* Interscience: New York (1947), pp. 160–71.
9. —— 'Signs and symptoms of desert dehydration', in ADOLPH, E. F. *et al.*, *Physiology of man in the desert.* Interscience: New York (1947), pp. 226–40.
10. AMES, ROSE G., and VAN DYKE, H. B. 'Antidiuretic hormone in the urine and pituitary of the kangaroo rat', *Proc. Soc. Exp. Biol.* **75**, 417–20 (1950).
11. —— —— 'Antidiuretic hormone in the serum or plasma of rats', *Endocrinology*, **50**, 350–60 (1952).
12. ANDERSSON, BENGT, and McCANN, S. M. 'A further study of polydipsia evoked by hypothalamic stimulation in the goat', *Acta physiol. Scand.* **33**, 333–46 (1955).
13. ANDREWS, ROY CHAPMAN. 'Living animals of the Gobi Desert', *Nat. Hist.* **24**, 150–9 (1924). (Amer. Mus. 3rd Asiatic Exped.)
14. ANREP, G. V., and HAMMOUDA, M. 'Observations on panting', *J. Physiol.* **77**, 16–34 (1933).
15. AOKI, T., and WADA, M. 'Functional activity of the sweat glands in the hairy skin of the dog', *Science*, **114**, 123–4 (1951).
16. ARMSTRONG, D. G., BLAXTER, K. L., GRAHAM, N. McC., and WAINMAN, F. W. 'The effect of environmental conditions on food utilisation by sheep', *Anim. Prod.* **1**, 1–12 (1959).
17. ARNOLD, J. F. 'Forage consumption and preferences of experimentally fed Arizona and antelope jack rabbits', *Univ. Arizona Tech. Bull.* No. 98, 51–86 (1942).
18. ATSATT, S. R. 'Color changes as controlled by temperature and light in the lizards of the desert regions of Southern California', *Univ. Calif. Publ. Biol. Sci.* **1**, 237–76 (1939).
19. BAILEY, V., and SPERRY, C. C. 'Life history and habits of grasshopper mice, genus *Onychomys*', *U.S. Dept. Agric. Tech. Bull.* **145**, 1–19 (1929).
20. BALDWIN, ERNEST. *An introduction to comparative biochemistry*, Cambridge University Press (1949), 164 pp.

21. BARKER, J. P., ADOLPH, E. F., and KELLER, A. D. 'Thirst tests in dogs and modifications of thirst with experimental lesions of the neurohypophysis', *Amer. J. Physiol.* **173**, 233–45 (1953).

22. —— —— 'Survival of rats without water and given seawater', ibid. **173**, 495–502 (1953).

23. BARKER, ROBERT. 'The process of making ice in the East Indies', *Phil. Trans. Royal Soc. Lond.* **65**, 252–7 (1775).

24. BARTHE, M. L. 'Composition du lait de chamelle', *J. de Pharm. et de Chim.*, Sér. 6, **21**, 386–8 (1905).

25. BARTHOLOMEW, G. A., and DAWSON, W. R. 'Respiratory water loss in some birds of southwestern United States', *Physiol. Zool.* **26**, 162–6 (1953).

26. —— —— 'Body temperature and water requirements in the mourning dove, *Zenaidura macroura marginella*', *Ecology*, **35**, 181–7 (1954).

27. —— and CADE, TOM J. 'Water consumption of house finches', *Condor*, **58**, 406–12 (1956).

28. —— 'Temperature regulation in the macropod marsupial, *Setonix brachyurus*', *Physiol. Zool.* **29**, 26–40 (1956).

29. —— and CADE, TOM J. 'Temperature regulation, hibernation, and aestivation in the little pocket mouse, *Perognathus longimembris*', *J. Mammal.* **38**, 60–72 (1957).

30. —— —— 'The body temperature of the American kestrel, *Falco sparverius*', *Wilson Bull.* **69**, 149–54 (1957).

31. —— and DAWSON, W. R., 'Body temperatures in California and Gambel's quail', *Auk*, **75**, 150–6 (1958).

32. —— and CADE, TOM J. 'Effects of sodium chloride on the water consumption of house finches', *Physiol. Zool.* **31**, 304–10 (1958).

33. —— and HUDSON, JACK W. 'Effects of sodium chloride on weight and drinking in the antelope ground squirrel', *J. Mammal.* **40**, 354–60 (1959).

34. —— 'The physiology of desert birds', *Anat. Rec.* **137**, 338 (1960).

35. —— and HUDSON, JACK W. 'Aestivation in the Mohave ground squirrel *Citellus mohavensis*', *Bull. Mus. Comp. Zool. Harv.* **124**, 193–208 (1960).

36. —— and MACMILLEN, R. E. 'The water requirements of mourning doves and their use of sea water and NaCl solutions', *Physiol. Zool.* **33**, 171–8 (1960).

37. —— —— 'Oxygen consumption, estivation and hibernation in the kangaroo mouse, *Microdipodops pallidus*', ibid. **34**, 177–83 (1961).

37a. —— —— 'Water economy of the California quail and its use of sea water', *Auk*, **78**, 505–14 (1961).

38. —— HUDSON, J. W., and HOWELL, T. R. 'Body temperature, oxygen consumption, evaporative water loss, and heart rate in the poor-will', *Condor*, **64**, 117–25 (1962).

39. BAZETT, H. C. 'Physiological responses to heat', *Physiol. Rev.* **7**, 531–99 (1927).

40. —— 'The regulation of body temperatures', in *Physiology of heat regulation* (ed. L. H. Newburgh), Saunders, Philadelphia (1949), pp. 109–92.

41. BEAKLEY, W. R., and FINDLAY, J. D. 'The effect of environmental temperature and humidity on the respiration rate of Ayrshire calves', *J. Agric. Sci.* **45**, 452–60 (1955).

42. BEDFORD, T., and WARNER, C. G. 'The globe thermometer in studies of heating and ventilation', *J. Hyg.* **34**, 458–73 (1934).

43. BELLOWS, R. T. 'Time factors in water drinking in dogs', *Amer. J. Physiol.* **125**, 87–97 (1939).

44. BENEDICT, FRANCIS G. 'The physiology of large reptiles with special reference to the heat production of snakes, tortoises, lizards and alligators', Carnegie Inst. Washington, Publ. No. 425 (1932), 539 pp.

45. —— 'Vital energetics: A study in comparative basal metabolism', ibid. Publ. No. 503 (1938), 215 pp.

46. BENTLEY, P. J. 'Some aspects of the water metabolism of an Australian marsupial *Setonyx brachyurus*', *J. Physiol.* **127**, 1–10 (1955).

47. —— 'Studies on the water and electrolyte metabolism of the lizard *Trachysaurus rugosus* (Gray)', ibid. **145**, 37–47 (1959).

48. —— 'Effects of elevated sodium concentration on sodium and potassium in the erythrocyte of the lizard *Trachysaurus rugosus* (Gray)', *Nature*, **184**, 1403 (1959).

49. —— 'Evaporative water loss and temperature regulation in the marsupial *Setonyx brachyurus*', *Austr. J. Exp. Biol. Med. Sci.* **38**, 301–5 (1960).

50. —— and BLUMER, W. F. C. 'Uptake of water by the lizard *Moloch horridus*', *Nature*, **194**, 699–700 (1962).

51. BIANCA, W. 'The effect of thermal stress on the acid-base balance of the Ayrshire calf', *J. Agric. Sci.* **45**, 428–30 (1955).

52. —— 'The relation between respiratory rate and heart rate in the calf subjected to severe heat stress', ibid. **51**, 321–4 (1958).

53. —— 'The effect of clipping the coat on various reactions of calves to heat', ibid. **52**, 380–3 (1959).

54. BLAGDEN, CHARLES. 'Experiments and observations in an heated room', *Phil. Trans. Roy. Soc. Lond.* **65**, 111–23 (1775).

55. —— 'Further experiments and observations in an heated room', ibid. 484–94 (1775).

56. BLAXTER, K. L., GRAHAM, N. McC., WAINMAN, F. W., and ARMSTRONG, D. G. 'Environmental temperature, energy metabolism and heat regulation in sheep. II. The partition of heat losses in closely clipped sheep', *J. Agric. Sci.* **52**, 25–40 (1959).

57. —— —— —— 'Environmental temperature, energy metabolism and heat regulation in sheep. III. The metabolism and thermal exchanges of sheep with fleeces', ibid. 41–49 (1959).

58. BLIGH, JOHN. 'A comparison of the temperature of the blood in the pulmonary artery and in the bicarotid trunk of the calf during thermal polypnoea', *J. Physiol.* **136**, 404–12 (1957).

59. —— 'The receptors concerned in the thermal stimulus to panting in sheep', ibid. **146**, 142–51 (1959).

60. BLOOMFIELD, A. L., and TAINTER, M. L. 'Vitamin B deprivation and spontaneous activity in white rats', *Fed. Proc.* **2**, 75 (1943).

61. BODENHEIMER, F. S. 'Problems of animal ecology and physiology in deserts', in *Desert Research*, Res. Council of Israel, Special Publ. No. 2, Jerusalem (1953), pp. 205–29.

62. BOGERT, C. M., and COWLES, R. B. 'Moisture loss in relation to habitat selection in some Floridian reptiles', *Amer. Mus. Novitates*, No. 1358, 1–34 (1947).

63. —— 'Thermoregulation and eccritic body temperatures in Mexican lizards of the genus *Sceloporus*', *Anales del Inst. de Biol. Mexico*, **20**, 415–26 (1949).

64. —— 'How reptiles regulate their body temperature', *Sci. Amer.* **200**, No. 4, 105–20 (1959).

65. BONSMA, J. C. 'The influence of climatological factors on cattle. Observations on cattle in tropical regions', *Farming in S. Africa*, **15**, 373–85 (1940).

66. BONSMA, J. C., and PRETORIUS, A. J. 'Influence of colour and coat cover on adaptability of cattle', *Farming in S. Africa*, **18**, 101–20 (1943).
67. BRODY, SAMUEL. *Bioenergetics and Growth*, (1945), 1023 pp. Reinhold: New York.
68. BROOK, A. H., and SHORT, B. F. 'Sweating in sheep', *Austral. J. Agric Research*, **11**, 557–69 (1960).
69. BROWN, A. H. 'Water shortage in the desert', in ADOLPH, E. F. *et al.*, *Physiology of man in the desert*. Interscience: New York (1947), pp. 136–59.
70. —— 'Dehydration exhaustion', in ADOLPH, E. F. *et al.*, *Physiology of man in the desert*. Interscience: New York (1947), pp. 208–25.
71. BULLOCK, T. H., 'Compensation for temperature in the metabolism and activity of poikilotherms', *Biol. Rev.* **30**, 311–42 (1955).
72. BURCH, GEORGE E., and WINSOR, TRAVIS. 'Rate of insensible perspiration (diffusion of water) locally through living and through dead human skin , *Arch. Internal Med.* **74**, 437–44 (1944).
73. BURNS, THOMAS W. 'Endocrine factors in the water metabolism of the desert mammal, *G. gerbillus.*, *Endocrinology*, **58**, 243–54 (1956).
74. BUXTON, P. A. *Animal life in deserts, a study of the fauna in relation to the environment*, Arnold, London (1923), 176 pp., reprinted 1955.

74a. CADE, TOM J., and DYBAS, J. A., Jr. 'Water economy of the budgerygah', *Auk*, **79**, 345–64 (1962).
75. CALDWELL, G. T. 'Studies in water metabolism of the cat. The influence of dehydration on blood concentration, thermoregulation, respiratory exchange, and metabolic-water production', *Physiol. Zool.* **4**, 324–59 (1931).
76. CAPOT-REY, ROBERT. *Le Sahara français*. Presses Univ. de France, Paris (1953), 564 pp.
77. CHARNOT, YOLANDE. 'A propos de l'écologie des camélidés', *Bull Soc. Sci. nat. et phys. Maroc*, **39**, 29–39 (1959).
78. —— 'Répercussion de la deshydration sur la biochimie et l'endocrinologie du dromadaire', *Travaux de l'Inst. Sci. Chérifien.*, Sér. zool. No. 20, Rabat (1960), 168 pp.
79. CHEW, ROBERT M. 'The water exchanges of some small mammals', *Ecol. Monogr.* **21**, 215–25 (1951).
80. —— 'Water metabolism of desert-inhabiting vertebrates', *Biol. Rev.* **36**, 1–31 (1961).
81. —— and DAMMANN, A. E. 'Evaporative water loss of small vertebrates, as measured with an infrared analyzer', *Science*, **133**, 384–5 (1961).
82. CLARK, R., and QUIN, J. I., 'Studies on the water requirements of farm animals in South Africa. I. The effect of intermittent watering on Merino sheep', *Onderst. J. Vet. Sci.* **22**, 335–43 (1949).
83. CLAUSHEN, A. 'Mikroskopische Untersuchungen über die Epidermalgebilde am Rumpfe des Hundes mit besonderer Berücksichtigung der Schweißdrüsen', *Anat. Anzeiger*, **77**, 81–97 (1933).
84. CLELAND, J. B. 'Diurnal variations in the temperatures of camels', *Proc. Linn. Soc. of New South Wales*, **34**, Part 2: 268–71 (1909).
84a. CLOUDSLEY-THOMPSON, J. L. (ed.). *Biology of Deserts*, Institute of Biology, London (1954), 224 pp.
85. COLE, LaMONT C. 'Experiments on toleration of high temperature in lizards with reference to adaptive coloration', *Ecology*, **24**, 94–108 (1943).
86. COOK, S. F. 'Respiratory metabolism of certain reptiles and amphibia', *Univ. of Calif. Publ. Zool.* **53**, 367–76 (1949).

87. COWLES, R. B. 'Additional implications of reptilian sensitivity to high temperatures', *Amer. Naturalist*, **74**, 542–61 (1940).

88. —— and BOGERT, C. M. 'A preliminary study of the thermal requirements of desert reptiles', *Bull. Amer. Mus. Nat. Hist.* **83**, 261–96 (1944).

89. —— and DAWSON, W. R. 'A cooling mechanism of the Texas nighthawk', *Condor*, **53**, 19–22 (1951).

90. —— 'Semantics in biothermal studies', *Science*, **135**, 670 (1962).

91. CRAWFORD, EUGENE C., Jr. 'Mechanical aspects of panting in dogs', *J. Appl. Physiol.* **17**, 249–51 (1962).

92. CULBERTSON, A. E. 'Observations on the natural history of the Fresno kangaroo rat', *J. Mammal.* **27**, 189–203 (1946).

93. CZERNY, A. 'Versuche über Bluteindickung und ihre Folgen', *Arch. f. exper. Path. u. Pharm.* **34**, 268–80 (1894).

94. DALE, H. E., BURGE, G. J., and BRODY, SAMUEL. 'Environmental physiology and shelter engineering with special reference to domestic animals. XXXIX. Environmental temperature and blood volume', *Univ. Mo. Agr. Exp. Sta. Res. Bull.*, No. 608: 1–20 (1956).

95. DALY, R. A., and CARTER, H. B. 'The Fleece growth of young Lincoln, Corriedale, Polwarth and fine Merino maiden ewes under housed conditions and unrestricted and progressively restricted feeding on a standard diet', *Austr. J. Agric. Res.* **6**, 476–513 (1955).

96. DAWSON, W. R. 'Temperature regulation and water requirements of the Brown and Abert Towhees, *Pipilo fuscus* and *Pipilo aberti*', *Univ. Calif. Publ. Zool.* **59**, No. 4, 81–124 (1954).

97. —— 'The relation of oxygen consumption to temperature in desert rodents', *J. Mammal.* **36**, 543–53 (1955).

98. —— and BARTHOLOMEW, G. A. 'Relation of oxygen consumption to body weight, temperature, and temperature acclimation in lizards *Uta stansburiana* and *Sceloporus occidentalis*', *Physiol. Zool.* **29**, 40–51 (1956).

99. —— 'Relation of oxygen consumption and evaporative water loss to temperature in the cardinal', ibid. **31**, 37–48 (1958).

100. —— and BARTHOLOMEW, G. A., 'Metabolic and cardiac responses to temperature in the lizard *Dipsosaurus dorsalis*', ibid. **31**, 100–11 (1958).

101. —— 'Physiological responses to temperature in the lizard *Eumeces obsoletus*', ibid. **33**, 87–103 (1960).

102. DEKEYSER, P. L., and DERIVOT, J. *La vie animale au Sahara*. Collection Armand Colin, No. 332, Section Biologie, Paris (1959), 220 pp.

103. DENTON, D. A. 'The study of sheep with permanent unilateral parotid fistulae', *Quart. J. Exp. Physiol.* **42**, 72–95 (1957).

104. DILL, D. B., BOCK, A. V., and EDWARDS, H. T. 'Mechanisms for dissipating heat in man and dog', *Amer. J. Physiol.* **104**, 36–43 (1933).

105. —— JONES, B. F., EDWARDS, H. T., and OBERG, S. A. 'Salt economy in extreme dry heat', *J. Biol. Chem.* **100**, 755–67 (1933).

106. —— *Life, heat and altitude. Physiological effects of hot climates and great heights*, Harvard University Press: Cambridge, Mass. (1938), 211 pp.

107. DOWLING, D. F. 'The hair follicle and apocrine gland populations of Zebu (*Bos indicus* L.) and shorthorn (*B. taurus* L.) cattle skin , *Austr. J. Agric. Res.* **6**, 645–54 (1955).

108. —— 'The thickness of cattle skin', ibid. 776–85 (1955).

109. DRILHON, A., and MARCOUX, F. 'Étude biochimique du sang et de l'urine d'un chélonien: *Testudo mauritanica*', *Bull. Soc. Chim. Biol. Paris*, **24**, 103–7 (1942).

110. DUBOIS, E. F. *Fever and the regulation of body temperature*, C. C. Thomas: Springfield, Ill. (1948), 68 pp.

111. DUKES, H. H. *The physiology of domestic animals*, Comstock: Ithaca, New York (1937), 695 pp.

112. EALEY, E. H. M., and SUIJDENDORP, H. 'Pasture management and the Euro problem in the North-west of Western Australia', *J. Agric. W. Austr.* **8**, 273–86 (1959).

113. EDERSTROM, H. E. 'Blood flow changes in the dog during hyperthermia', *Amer. J. Physiol.* **176**, 347–51 (1954).

114. EICHNA, L. W., ASHE, W. F., BEAN, W. B., and SHELLY, W. B. 'The upper limits of environmental heat and humidity tolerated by acclimatized men working in hot environments', *J. Indust. Hygiene and Toxicol.* **27**, 59–84 (1945).

115. —— BERGER, A. R., RADER, B., and BECKER, W. H. 'Comparison of intracardiac and intravascular temperatures with rectal temperatures in man', *J. Clin. Invest.* **30**, 353–9 (1951).

116. EIMER, K. 'Untersuchungen über das Wesen der Perspiration', *Archiv exp. Path. Pharmak.* **125**, 150–80 (1927).

117. ENCYCLOPEDIA OF SCIENCE AND TECHNOLOGY. Volume **12**, 244–9, McGraw-Hill: New York (1960).

118. EULER, CURT VON. 'Physiology and pharmacology of temperature regulation', *Pharmacol. Rev.* **13**, 361–98 (1961).

119. EVANS, J. V. 'Water metabolism in the sheep', *Nature*, **180**, 756 (1957).

120. FAIRBANKS, B. W., and MITCHELL, H. H. 'The availability of calcium in spinach, in skim milk powder, and in calcium oxalate', *J. Nutrition*, **16**, 79–89 (1938).

121. FÄNGE, RAGNAR, SCHMIDT-NIELSEN, KNUT, and ROBINSON, MARYANNE. 'Control of secretion from the avian salt gland', *Amer. J. Physiol.* **195**, 321–6 (1958).

122. FINDLAY, J. D. 'The effects of temperature, humidity, air movement and solar radiation on the behaviour and physiology of cattle and other farm animals', *Hannah Dairy Res. Inst. Bull.* No. 9, 1–178 (1950).

123. —— and YANG, S. H. 'The sweat glands and Ayrshire cattle', *J. Agric. Sci.* **40**, 126–33 (1950).

124. —— 'The climatic physiology of farm animals', *Meteorol. Monog.* **2**, 19–29 (1954).

125. —— and JENKINSON, D. M. 'The morphology of bovine sweat glands and the effect of heat on the sweat glands of the Ayrshire calf', *J. Agric. Sci.* **55**, 247–9 (1960).

126. FLINN, F. B. 'Some effects of high environmental temperatures on the organism', *U.S. Public Health Rep.* **40**, 868–96 (1925).

127. FRENCH, M. H. 'The effect of infrequent water intake on the consumption and digestibility of hay by Zebu cattle', *Emp. J. Exp. Agric.* **24**, 128–36 (1956).

127a. GAUTHIER-PILTERS, HILDE, *see* PILTERS, GAUTHIER-, HILDE.

128. GEIGER, RUDOLF. *The climate near the ground*, Harvard University Press: Cambridge, Mass. (1957) (Rev. ed., 2) xxi–494 pp.

129. GEYER, R. P., GEYER, B. R., DERSE, P. H., ZINKIN, T., ELVEHJEM, C. A., and HART, E. B. 'Growth studies with rats kept under conditions which prevent coprophagy', *J. Nutrition*, **33**, 129–42 (1947).

130. GJÖNNES, BJÖRN, and SCHMIDT-NIELSEN, K. 'Respiratory characteristics of kangaroo rat blood', *J. Cell. Comp. Physiol.* **39**, 147–52 (1952).

131. GOSSELIN, R. E. 'Rates of sweating in the desert', in ADOLPH, E. F. *et al.*, *Physiology of man in the desert*. Interscience: New York (1947), pp. 44–76.

132. GOTTSCHALK, CARL, and MYLLE, M. 'Micropuncture study of the mammalian urinary concentrating mechanism: evidence for the countercurrent hypothesis', *Amer. J. Physiol.* **196**, 927–36 (1959).

133. —— 'Osmotic concentration and dilution in the mammalian nephron', *Circulation*, **21**, 861–8 (1960).

133a. GREEN, LORNA M. A. 'Sweat glands in the skin of the quokka of Western Australia', *Austr. J. Exp. Biol. Med. Sci.* **39**, 481–6 (1961).

134. GREGERSEN, MAGNUS I. 'A practical method for the determination of blood volume with the dye T-1824', *J. Lab. Clin. Med.* **29**, 1266–86 (1944).

135. —— and RAWSON, RUTH A. 'Blood volume', *Physiol. Rev.* **39**, 307–42 (1959).

136. GUERRANT, N. B., and DUTCHER, R. A. 'The influence of exercise on the growing rat in the presence and absence of Vitamin B_1', *J. Nutrition*, **20**, 589–98 (1940).

137. HALDANE, J. S. 'Salt depletion by sweating', *Brit. Med. J.* **2**, 469 (1929).

138. HALL, E. R., and LINSDALE, J. M. 'Notes on the life history of the kangaroo mouse (*Microdipodops*)', *J. Mammal.* **10**, 298–305 (1929).

139. HALL, F. G., and ROOT, R. W. 'The influence of humidity on the body temperature of certain poikilotherms', *Biol. Bull.* **58**, 52–58 (1930).

140. —— DILL, D. B., and GUZMAN BARRON, E. S. 'Comparative physiology in high altitudes', *J. Cell. Comp. Physiol.* **8**, 301–13 (1936).

141. HANSEN, ANKER, and SCHMIDT-NIELSEN, K. 'On the stomach of the camel with special reference to the structure of its mucous membrane', *Acta Anatomica*, **31**, 353–75 (1957).

142. HARDY, JAMES D. 'Heat transfer', in *Physiology of heat regulation and the science of clothing* (L. H. Newburgh, ed.). Saunders: Philadelphia (1949), pp. 78–108.

143. —— 'Physiology of temperature regulation', *Physiol. Rev.* **41**, 521–606 (1961).

144. HARDY, M. H. 'The group arrangement of hair follicles in the mammalian skin, Part 1', *Proc. Roy. Soc. Queensland*, **58**, 125–48 (1947).

145. HARGITAY, B., and KUHN, W. 'Das Multiplikationsprinzip als Grundlage der Harnkonzentrierung in der Niere', *Zeitschr. f. Elektrochem. u. angewandte physik. Chem.* **55**, 539–58 (1951).

146. HART, J. S. 'Calorimetric determination of average body temperature of small mammals and its variation with environmental conditions', *Canadian J. Zool.* **29**, 224–33 (1951).

147. HAWBECKER, A. C. 'Food and moisture requirements of the Nelson antelope ground squirrel', *J. Mammal.* **28**, 115–25 (1947).

148. HAYWARD, J. S. 'The ability of the wild rabbit to survive conditions of water restriction', *CSIRO Wildlife Res.* **6**, 160–75 (1961).

149. HEIM DE BALSAC, HENRI. 'Biogéographie des mammifères et des oiseaux de l'Afrique du Nord', *Bull. Biol. de France et Belgique*, Suppl. 21 (1936), 447 pp.

150. HEMINGWAY, ALLAN. 'The panting response of normal unanesthetized dogs to measured dosages of diathermy heat', *Amer. J. Physiol.* **121**, 747–54 (1938).

151. —— RASMUSSEN, T., WIKOFF, H., and RASMUSSEN, A. T. 'Effects of heating hypothalamus of dogs by diathermy', *J. Neurophysiol.* **3**, 329–38 (1940).

152. HERZFELD, C. M., and HARDY, J. D. (eds.). *Temperature. Its measurements and control in science and industry*, Volume 3, Part III, *Biology and Medicine.* Reinhold: New York (1963), pp. 683.

153. HODGKIN, E. P., and SHEARD, K. 'Rottnest Island: the Rottnest Biological Station and recent scientific research', *J. Roy. Soc. of Western Austral.* **42**; Part 3, 65–95 (1959).

154. HOME, EVERARD. 'Observations on the camel's stomach respecting the water it contains and the reservoirs in which that fluid is enclosed; with an account of some peculiarities in the urine', *Phil. Trans. Roy. Soc. Lond.* 357–84 (1806).

155. HOUPT, T. RICHARD. 'Utilization of blood urea in ruminants', *Amer. J. Physiol.* **197**, 115–20 (1959).

156. HOWELL, A. B., and GERSH, I. 'Conservation of water by the rodent *Dipodomys*', *J. Mammal.* **16**, 1–9 (1935).

157. HOWELL, T. R., and BARTHOLOMEW, G. A. 'Further experiments on torpidity in the poor-will', *Condor*, **61**, 180–5 (1959).

158. —— —— 'Temperature regulation in Laysan and black footed albatrosses', ibid. **63**, 185–97 (1961).

159. HUDSON, JACK W. 'Water requirements and thermoneutrality in the antelope ground squirrel, *Citellus leucurus*', *Anat. Rec.* **138**, 357–8 (1960).

160. —— 'The role of water in the biology of the antelope ground squirrel *Citellus leucurus*', *Univ. Calif. Publ. Zool.* **64**, 1–56 (1962).

161. HUNGERFORD, CHARLES R. 'Water requirements of Gambel's quail', *Trans. of 25th North Amer. Wildlife Conf.* (March 1960), pp. 231–40.

162. HUTCHINSON, J. C. D. 'Heat regulation in birds', in *Progress in the physiology of farm animals*, **1**, 299–362, Butterworths, London (1954) (J. Hammond, ed.)

163. HUTCHISON, VICTOR, and LARIMER, J. L. 'Reflectivity of the integuments of some lizards from different habitats', *Ecology*, **41**, 199–209 (1960).

164. IRVING, L., FISHER, K. C., and McINTOSH, F. C. 'The water balance of a marine mammal, the seal', *J. Cell. Comp. Physiol.* **6**, 387–91 (1935).

165. JAEGER, EDMUND C. 'Does the poor-will "hibernate"?' *Condor*, **50**, 45–46 (1948).

166. JOHNSON, FRANK H. (ed.). *Influence of temperature on biological systems*, Amer. Physiol. Soc.: Washington, D.C. (1957), 275 pp.

167. JOHNSON, HAROLD D., CHENG, C. S., and RAGSDALE, A. C. 'Environmental physiology and shelter engineering with special reference to domestic animals. XLVI. Comparison of the effect of environmental temperature on rabbits and cattle. Part 2. Influence of rising environmental temperature on the physiological reactions of rabbits and cattle', *Univ. Mo. Agric. Exp. Sta. Res. Bull.* No. 648 (1958), 27 pp.

168. JOHNSON, R. E., PITTS, G. C., and CONSOLAZIO, F. C. 'Factors influencing chloride concentration in human sweat', *Amer. J. Physiol.* **141**, 575–89 (1944).

169. JONES, F. W. *The mammals of South Australia, Part I*, Government Printer: Adelaide (1923), 131 pp.

170. KACHKAROV, D. N., and KOROVINE, E. P. *La vie dans les déserts. Edition française par Théodore Monod.* Payot: Paris (1942), 360 pp.

171. KALABUKHOV, N. I. 'Comparative ecology of hibernating animals', *Bull. Mus. Comp. Zool. Harv.* **124**, 45–74 (1960).

172. KEAST, ALLEN. 'Australian birds: their zoogeography and adaptations to an arid continent', *Biogeography and Ecol. in Austral.* **8**, 89–114 (1959).

173. KEETON, ROBERT W. 'The peripheral water loss in rabbits as a factor in heat regulation', *Amer. J. Physiol.* **69**, 307–17 (1924).

174. KHALIL, FOUAD, and ABDEL-MESSEIH, G. 'Water content of tissues of some desert reptiles and mammals', *J. Exp. Zool.* **125**, 407–14 (1954).

175. —— and HAGGAG, G. 'Ureotelism and uricotelism in tortoises', ibid. **130**, 423–32 (1955).

176. —— and ABDEL-MESSEIH, G. 'Water, nitrogen and lipides content of tissues of *Varanus griseus*, Daud', *Zeitschr. f. vergl. Physiol.* **42**, 403–9 (1959).

177. —— —— 'The storage of extra water by various tissues of *Varanus griseus* Daud', ibid. 415–21 (1959).

178. KIBLER, H. H., BRODY, S., and WORSTELL, D. M. 'Environmental physiology with special reference to domestic animals. IV. Influence of temperature, 50° to 105° F., on heat production and cardiorespiratory activities in dairy cattle', *Univ. Mo. Agric. Exp. Sta. Res. Bull.* No. 435 (1949), 32 pp.

179. —— —— 'Environmental physiology with special reference to domestic animals. XIX. Relative efficiency of surface evaporative, respiratory evaporative, and non-evaporative cooling in relation to heat production in Jersey, Holstein, Brown Swiss and Brahman cattle, 5° to 105° F.', ibid. No. 497 (1952), 31 pp.

180. —— —— 'Environmental physiology with special reference to domestic animals. XIII. Influence of increasing temperature, 40° to 105° F., on heat production and cardiorespiratory activities in Brown Swiss and Brahman cows and heifers', *Univ. Mo. Agric. Exp. Sta. Res. Bull.* No. 473 (1951), 16 pp.

181. KING, JAMES R., and FARNER, DONALD S. 'Energy metabolism, thermoregulation and body temperature', in *Biology and comparative physiology of birds*, **2** (A. J. Marshall, ed.), Academic Press: N.Y. (1961), pp. 215–88.

182. KIRMIZ, JOHN P. *Adaptation de la gerboise au milieu désertique. Étude comparée de la thermorégulation chez la gerboise* (Dipus aegyptius) *et chez le rat blanc*, Soc. Publ. Égyptiennes: Alexandria, Egypt (1962), 154 pp.

183. KLAUBER, LAURENCE M. *Rattlesnakes: Their habits, life histories and influence on mankind*, Vol. I, University of California Press (1956), 708 pp. (Vol. II, pp. 709–1476).

184. KNAPP, B. J., and ROBINSON, K. W. 'The role of water for heat dissipation by a Jersey cow and a Corriedale Ewe', *Austral. J. Agric. Res.* **5**, 568–77 (1954).

185. KON, S. K., and COWIE, A. T. (eds.). *Milk: the mammary gland and its secretion*, Volume II. Academic Press: N.Y. (1961), 423 pp.

186. KROGH, AUGUST. *Osmotic regulation in aquatic animals*, Cambridge University Press (1939), 242 pp.
187. KUNO, YAS. *Human perspiration*. Amer. Lecture series, publ. No. 285, Springfield, Ill: Chas. C. Thomas, 1956, 416 pp.

188. LADELL, W. S. S., WATERLOW, J. C., and HUDSON, M. F. 'Desert climate. Physiological and clinical observations', *Lancet*, **2**, 491–7 (1944).
189. —— —— —— 'Desert climate. Physiological and clinical observations. Heat exhaustion Type II; ibid. 527–31 (1944).
190. —— 'Thermal sweating', *Brit. Med. Bull.* **3**, 175–9 (1945).
191. —— 'The changes in water and chloride distribution during heavy sweating', *J. Physiol.* **108**, 440–50 (1949).
192. LAVAUDEN, L. 'Quelques effets de la sécheresse sur les vertébrés supérieurs de l'Afrique du Nord', *C.R. Acad. Sci. Paris*, **185**, 1210–12 (1927).
193. LEDGER, H. P. 'A possible explanation for part of the difference in heat tolerance exhibited by *Bos taurus* and *Bos indicus* beef cattle', *Nature*, **184**, 1405–6 (1959).
194. LEE, DONALD G., and SCHMIDT-NIELSEN, KNUT. 'The skin, sweat glands and hair follicles of the camel (*Camelus dromedarius*)', *Anat Rec.* **143**, 71–77 (1962).
195. LEE, DOUGLAS H. K., ROBINSON, K., and HINES, H. J. G. 'Reactions of the rabbit to hot atmospheres', *Proc. Roy. Soc. Queensland*, **53**, 129–44 (1941).
196. —— —— 'Reactions of the sheep to hot atmospheres', ibid. **53**, 189–200 (1941).
197. —— 'Studies of heat regulation in the sheep with special reference to the Merino', '*Austral. J. Agric. Res.* **1**, 200–16 (1950).
198. LEES, A. D. 'The water balance in *Ixodes ricinus* L. and certain other species of ticks', *Parasitology*, **37**, 1–20 (1946).
199. LEONARD, ARTHUR GLYN. *The camel. Its uses and management*, Longmans, Green: London (1894), 335 pp.
200. LEROUX, C. *Aspects de la régulation thermique des animaux du désert. Observations personnelles chez le dromadaire*, Ecole Nationale Vétérinaire de Lyon, No. 27 (1960), 84 pp.
201. LOWE, CHARLES H., Jr., and VANCE, V. J. 'Acclimation of the critical thermal maximum of the reptile *Urosaurus ornatus*', *Science*, **122**, 73–74 (1955).
201a. —— and NORRIS, K. S. 'A subspecies of the lizard *Sceloporus undulatus* from the White Sands of New Mexico', *Herpetologica*, **12**, 125–7 (1956),
202. LYMAN, C. P., and CHATFIELD, P. O. 'Physiology of hibernation in mammals', *Physiol. Rev.* **35**, 403–25 (1955).
203. —— and DAWE, A. R., (eds.), 'Mammalian hibernation', *Bull. Mus. Comp. Zool. Harvard*, **124**, 1–549 (1960).

204. McCANCE, R. A., and YOUNG, W. F. 'The secretion of urine during dehydration and rehydration', *J. Physiol.* **102**, 415–28 (1944).
205. —— 'The excretion of urea, salts and water during periods of hydropaenia in man', ibid. **104**, 196–209 (1945).
206. —— and WILKINSON, E. 'The response of adult and suckling rats to the administration of water and of hypertonic solutions of urea and salts', ibid. **106**, 256–63 (1947).

REFERENCES 263

207. McDonald, Janet, and Macfarlane, W. V. 'Renal function of sheep in hot environments', *Austr. J. Agric. Res.* **9**, 680–92 (1958).
208. McGee, W. J. 'Desert thirst as disease', *Interstate Med. J.* **13**, 279–300 (1906).
209. Macfarlane, W. V., Morris, R. J., and Howard, B. 'Water economy of tropical Merino sheep', *Nature*, **178**, 304–5 (1956).
210. —— —— —— 'Heat and water in tropical Merino sheep', *Austr. J. Agric. Res.* **9**, 217–28 (1958).
211. —— Robinson, K., Howard, B., and Kinne, R. 'Heat, salt and hormones in panting and sweating animals', *Nature*, **182**, 672–3 (1958).
212. Mackworth-Praed, C. W., and Grant, C. H. B. 'Birds of eastern and north eastern Africa', *African Handb. of Birds*, Ser. 1, Vol. 1, Longmans, Green: London (1957), 806 pp.
213. Madsen, Harry. 'Quelques remarques sur la cause pourquoi les grands oiseaux au Soudan planent si haut au milieu de la journée', *Vidensk. Medd. Dansk Naturhist. Foren. Kbh.* **88**, 301–3 (1930).
214. Marais, E. N. 'Notes on some effects of extreme drought in Waterberg, South Africa', *Annual Report Smithsonian Inst.* (1914), pp. 511–22.
215. Marshall, A. J., and Disney, H. J. de S. 'Experimental induction of the breeding season in a xerophilous bird', *Nature*, **180**, 647–9 (1957).
216. Marshall, E. K., Jr. 'Kidney secretion in reptiles', *Proc. Soc. Exp. Biol.* **29**, 971–3 (1932).
217. —— 'The comparative physiology of the kidney in relation to theories of renal secretion', *Physiol. Rev.* **14**, 133–59 (1934).
218. Martin, C. J. 'Thermal adjustment and respiratory exchange in monotremes and marsupials. A study in the development of homoeothermism', *Phil. Trans. Roy. Soc. London*, B, **195**, 1–37 (1903).
219. —— 'Thermal adjustment of man and animals to external conditions. Lecture I', *Lancet*, **2**, 561–7 (1930).
220. —— 'Thermal adjustment of man and animals to external conditions. Lecture II', ibid. 617–20 (1930).
221. —— 'Thermal adjustment of man and animals to external conditions. Lecture III', ibid. 673–8 (1930).
222. Mather, G. W., Nahas, G. G., and Hemingway, A. 'Temperature changes of pulmonary blood during exposure to cold', *Amer. J. Physiol.* **173**, 390–2 (1953).
223. Meade-Waldo, E. G. B. 'Observations on the sand-grouse', *Bull. British Ornithol. Club*, **42**, 69–70 (1921).
224. Mickelsen, Olaf, and Keys, Ancel. 'The composition of sweat, with special reference to the vitamins', *J. Biol. Chem.* **149**, 479–90 (1943).
225. Milne, A. H. 'The humps of East African cattle', *Emp. J. Exp. Agric.* **23**, 234–9 (1955).
226. Misonne, Xavier. 'Analyse zoogéographique des mammifères de l'Iran', *Bruxelles, Inst. Royal des Sci. Nat. de Belgique, Mémoires*, 2ᵐᵉ sér. **59** (1959), 157 pp.
227. Molnar, G. W. 'Man in the tropics compared with man in the desert', in Adolph, E. F. et al., *Physiology of man in the desert*. Interscience: New York (1947), pp. 315–25.
228. Monod, Théodore. 'Majâbat al-Koubrâ. Contribution à l'étude de l' "Empty Quarter" ouest-Saharien', *Mémoires Inst. Franç. d'Afrique Noire*, No. 52, IFAN-Dakar (1958), 407 pp.

229. MORENG, R. E., and SCHAFFNER, C. S. 'Lethal internal temperatures for the chicken, from fertile egg to mature bird', *Poultry Sci.* **30**, 255–66 (1951).
230. MORRISON, PETER R., and RYSER, F. A. 'Weight and body temperature in mammals', *Science*, **116**, 231–2 (1952).
231. MOSS, K. NEVILLE. 'Some effects of high air temperatures and muscular exertion upon colliers', *Proc. Roy. Soc. Lond.*, B, **95**, 181–200 (1924).
232. MOYLE, VIVIEN. 'Nitrogenous excretion in chelonian reptiles', *Biochem. J.* **44**, 581–4 (1949).

233. NAGAYAMA, T. 'Experimentelle Studien über die Perspiratio insensibilis und den respiratorischen Gaswechsel. (I. Mitteilung) Die Versuche unter verschiedenen atmosphärischen Bedingungen', *Okayama-Igakkai-Zasshi — Mitt. med. Ges. Okayama*, **44**, 1891–1908 (1932). Mit deutscher Zusammenfassung, pp. 1891–2.
234. NAY, T., and HAYMAN, R. H. 'Sweat glands in Zebu (*Bos indicus* L.) and European (*B. taurus* L.) cattle. I. Size of individual glands, the denseness of their population and their depth below the skin surface', *Austr. J. Agric. Res.* **7**, 482–94 (1956).
235. NEWBURGH, L. H. (ed.). *Physiology of heat regulation and the science of clothing*. W. B. Saunders: Philadelphia (1949), 457 pp.
236. NICHOLS, J. 'Effects of high sodium diet and of high potassium diet on the adrenals and kidney of the desert kangaroo rat and domestic albino rat', *Exp. Med. and Surg.* **7**, 366–76 (1949).
237. NICHTER, RICHARD. 'The effect of variation in humidity and water intake on activity of *Dipodomys*', *J. Mammal.* **38**, 502–12 (1957).
238. NIELSEN, MARIUS. 'Die Regulation der Körpertemperatur bei Muskelarbeit', *Skand. Arch. f. Physiol.* **79**, 193–230 (1938).
239. NORRIS, K. S. 'The ecology of the desert iguana *Dipsosaurus dorsalis*', *Ecology*, **34**, 265–87 (1953).
240. —— and LOWE, CHARLES H., Jr. See 201a.
241. —— 'The evolution and systematics of the iguanid genus *Uma* and its relation to the evolution of other North American desert reptiles', *Bull. Amer. Mus. Nat. Hist.* **114**, 247–326 (1958).

242. OTIS, ARTHUR B., FENN, W. O., and RAHN, H. 'Mechanics of breathing in man', *J. Appl. Physiol.* **2**, 592–607 (1950).

243. PACE, NELLO, and RATHBUN, EDITH N. 'Studies on body composition. III. The body water and chemically combined nitrogen content in relation to fat content', *J. Biol. Chem.* **158**, 685–91 (1945).
244. PEARSON, O. P. 'The daily energy requirements of a wild Anna hummingbird', *Condor*, **56**, 317–22 (1954).
245. —— 'Habits of the lizard *Liolaemus multiformis multiformis* at high altitudes in Southern Peru', *Copeia*, **2**, 111–16 (1954).
246. PEARSON, OLIVER. 'Torpidity in birds', *Bull Mus. Comp. Zool. Harv.* **124**, 93–103 (1960).
247. PECK, E. F. 'Salt intake in relation to cutaneous necrosis and arthritis of one-humped camels (*Camelus dromedarius* L.) in British Somaliland', *Vet. Rec.* **51**, 1355–60 (1939).
248. PEIRCE, A. W. 'Studies on salt tolerance of sheep. I. The tolerance of sheep for sodium chloride in the drinking water', *Austr. J. Agric. Res.* **8**, 711–22 (1957).

249. PEIRCE, A. W. 'Saline content of drinking water for livestock', *Vet. Rev. and Annotations*, **3**, 37–43 (1957).
250. —— 'Studies on salt tolerance of sheep. II. The tolerance of sheep for mixtures of sodium chloride and magnesium chloride in the drinking water', *Austr. J. Agric. Res.* **10**, 725–35 (1959).
251. —— 'Studies on salt tolerance of sheep. III. The tolerance of sheep for mixtures of sodium chloride and sodium sulphate in the drinking water', ibid. **11**, 548–56 (1960).
252. PETRI, J. 'Notiz über den Harnstoffgehalt des Kamelharns', *Zeitschr. Physiol. Chem.* (Hoppe-Seyler), **166**, 125–7 (1927).
253. PETTER, F. 'Note préliminaire sur l'éthologie et l'écologie de *Psammomys obesus* Cretzschmar', *Mammalia*, **16**, 137–47 (1952).
254. —— 'Note préliminaire sur l'éthologie et l'écologie de *Meriones libycus* (Rongeurs, Gerbillides)', ibid. **17**, 281–94 (1953).
255. —— 'Note sur l'estivation et l'hibernation observées chez plusieurs espèces de rongeurs', ibid. **19**, 444–6 (1955).
256. —— 'Eléments d'une révision des lièvres européens et asiatiques du sousgenre Lepus', *Zeitschr. f. Säugetierkunde* **26**, 1–64 (1961).
257. PHILLIPS, RALPH W. 'The cattle of India', *J. Heredity,* **35**, 273–88 (1944).
258. PIERRE, FRANKLIN. *Écologie et peuplement entomologique des sables vifs du Sahara nord-occidental*, Publications du Centre de Recherches Sahariennes, Série Biol. No. 1: 1–332 (1958).
259. PILLIET, A. 'Structure de la portion gaufrée de l'estomac du chameau', *Bull. Soc. Zool. France*, **10**, 40–41 (1885).
260. PILTERS-GAUTHIER, HILDE. 'Quelques observations sur l'écologie et l'éthologie du dromadaire dans le Sahara nord-occidental', *Mammalia*, **22**, 140–51 (1958).
261. —— 'Observations sur l'écologie du dromadaire dans le Sahara nord-occidental', ibid. **25**, 195–280 (1961).
262. POTTIER, J. 'Étude sur les possibilités d'utilisation des plantes marines tunisiennes pour la nourriture du bétail', *Ann. Inst. Océanogr.* **6**, 321–62 (1929).
263. POULSON, THOMAS L., and BARTHOLOMEW, G. A. 'Salt balance in the savannah sparrow', *Physiol. Zoöl.* **35**, 109–19 (1962).
264. PRECHT, H., CHRISTOPHERSEN, J. and HENSEL, H. *Temperatur und Leben*, Springer-Verlag: Berlin (1955), 514 pp.
265. PRENTISS, P. G., WOLF, A. V., and EDDY, H. A. 'Hydropenia in cat and dog. Ability of the cat to meet its water requirements solely from a diet of fish or meat', *Amer. J. Physiol.* **196**, 625–32 (1959).
266. PREVOST, JEAN, and BOURLIÈRE, FRANÇOIS. 'Vie sociale et thermorégulation chez le manchot empereur *Aptenodytes forsteri*', *Alauda*, **25**, 167–73 (1957).
267. PROUTY, L. R. 'Heat loss and heat production of cats at different environmental temperatures', *Fed. Proc.* **8**, 128–9 (1949).
268. RANDALL, W. C. 'Factors influencing the temperature regulation of birds', *Amer. J. Physiol.* **139**, 56–63 (1943). ,
269. —— and McCLURE, W. 'Quantitation of the output of individual sweat glands and their response to stimulation', *J. Appl. Physiol.* **2**, 72–80 (1949).
270. READ, B. E. 'Chemical constituents of camel's urine', *J. Biol. Chem.* **64**, 615–17 (1925).

271. RHOAD, A. O. 'Absorption and reflection of solar radiation in relation to coat color in cattle', *Proc. Amer. Soc. Anim. Prod.* **33**, 291–3 (1940).
272. —— 'The Iberia heat tolerance test for cattle', *Tropical Agric.* **21**, 162–4 (1944).
273. RICE, H. A., and STEINHAUS, A. H. 'Studies in the physiology of exercise. V. Acid-base changes in the serum of exercised dogs', *Amer. J. Physiol.* **96**, 529–37 (1931).
274. RIEK, R. F., HARDY, M. H., LEE, D. K. H., and CARTER, H. B. 'The effect of the dietary plane upon the reactions of two breeds of sheep during short exposures to hot environments', *Austr. J. Agric. Res.* **1**, 217–30 (1950).
275. RIEMERSCHMID, G., and ELDER, J. S. 'The absorptivity for solar radiation of different coloured hairy coats of cattle', *Ond. J. Vet. Sci.* **20**, 223–34 (1945).
276. RITZMAN, E. G., and BENEDICT, F. G. *Nutritional physiology of the adult ruminant*, Washington, D.C.: Carnegie Inst. Publ. No. 494, 1938, 200 pp.
277. ROBINSON, K., and LEE, D. H. K. 'Reactions of the cat to hot atmospheres', *Proc. Roy. Soc. Queensland*, **53**, 159–70 (1941).
278. —— —— 'Reactions of the dog to hot atmospheres', ibid. 171–88 (1941).
279. —— —— 'Animal behaviour and heat regulation in hot atmospheres', *Univ. Queensland Papers, Dept. Physiol.* **1**, 1–8 (1946).
280. —— Heat tolerance of Australian monotremes and marsupials. *Austr. J. Biol. Sci.* **7**, 348–60 (1954).
281. —— and MORRISON, P. R. 'The reaction to hot atmospheres of various species of Australian marsupial and placental animals', *J. Cell. Comp. Physiol.* **49**, 455–78 (1957).
282. ROBINSON, SID. 'Physiological adjustments to heat', in *Physiology of heat regulation and the science of clothing* (L. H. Newburgh, ed.), W. B. Saunders: Philadelphia (1949), pp. 193–231.
283. —— GERKING, S. D., TURRELL, E. S., and KINCAID, R. K. 'Effect of skin temperature on salt concentration of sweat', *J. Appl. Physiol.* **2**, 654–62 (1950).
284. ROTHMAN, STEPHEN. *The physiology and biochemistry of the skin*, University of Chicago Press (1954), 741 pp.
285. ROTHSTEIN, A., and TOWBIN, E. J. 'Blood circulation and temperature of men dehydrating in the heat', in ADOLPH, E. F. *et al., Physiology of man in the desert*. Interscience: New York (1947), pp. 172–96.
286. —— ADOLPH, E. F., and WILLS, J. H., 'Voluntary dehydration', in ADOLPH *et al., Physiology of man in the desert*. Interscience: New York (1947), pp. 254–70.
287. RYTAND, D. A. 'The number and size of mammalian glomeruli as related to kidney and to body weight, with methods for their enumeration and measurement', *Amer. J. Anat.* **62**, 507–20 (1938).

288. SAALFELD, E. VON. 'Untersuchungen über das Hacheln bei Tauben. I. Mitteilung', *Zeitschr. f. vergl. Physiol.* **23**, 727–43 (1936).
289. SAINT-GIRONS, H., and SAINT-GIRONS, M.-C. 'Cycle d'activité et thermo-régulation chez les reptiles (Lézards et Serpents)', *Vie et Milieu*, **7**, 133–226 (1956).

290. SCHMIDT-NIELSEN, BODIL, SCHMIDT-NIELSEN, K., BROKAW, ADELAIDE, and SCHNEIDERMAN, H. 'Water conservation in desert rodents', *J. Cell. Comp. Physiol.* **32**, 331–60 (1948).

291. SCHMIDT-NIELSEN, K., SCHMIDT-NIELSEN, B., and BROKAW, A. 'Urea excretion in desert rodents exposed to high protein diets', ibid. 361–80 (1948).

292. SCHMIDT-NIELSEN, BODIL, and SCHMIDT-NIELSEN, KNUT. 'Do kangaroo rats thrive when drinking sea water?', *Amer. J. Physiol.* **160**, 291–4 (1950).

293. —— —— 'Pulmonary water loss in desert rodents', ibid. **162**, 31–36 (1950).

294. —— —— 'Evaporative water loss in desert rodents in their natural habitat', *Ecology*, **31**, 75–85 (1950).

295. —— —— 'A complete account of the water metabolism in kangaroo rats and an experimental verification', *J. Cell. Comp. Physiol.* **38**, 165–82 (1951).

296. SCHMIDT-NIELSEN, KNUT, and SCHMIDT-NIELSEN, B. 'Water metabolism of desert mammals', *Physiol. Rev.* **32**, 135–66 (1952).

297. —— 'Heat regulation in small and large desert mammals', in *Biology of deserts* (ed. J. L. Cloudsley-Thompson), Inst. of Biology: London (1954), pp. 182–7.

298. —— 'Animals and arid conditions: Physiological aspects of productivity and management', in *The future of arid lands* (G. F. White, ed.), Washington, D.C.: Amer. Assoc. Adv. Sci. Publ. No. 43 (1956), pp. 368–82.

299. SCHMIDT-NIELSEN, B., SCHMIDT-NIELSEN, KNUT, HOUPT T. R., and JARNUM, S. A. 'Water balance of the camel', *Amer. J. Physiol.* **185**, 185–94 (1956).

300. SCHMIDT-NIELSEN, KNUT, SCHMIDT-NIELSEN, B., HOUPT, T. R., and JARNUM, S. A. 'The question of water storage in the stomach of the camel', *Mammalia*, **20**, 1–15 (1956).

301. —— ——, JARNUM, S. A., and HOUPT, T. R. 'Body temperature of the camel and its relation to water economy', *Amer. J. Physiol.* **188**, 103–12 (1957).

302. SCHMIDT-NIELSEN, BODIL, SCHMIDT-NIELSEN, K., HOUPT, T. R., and JARNUM, S. A. 'Urea excretion in the camel', ibid. 477–84 (1957).

303. SCHMIDT-NIELSEN, KNUT, and FÄNGE, RAGNAR. 'Salt glands in marine reptiles', *Nature*, **182**, 783–5 (1958).

304. —— 'Salt glands', *Sci. Amer.* **200**, 109–15 (1959).

305. —— 'The physiology of the camel', ibid. **201**, 140–51 (1959).

306. —— 'The salt-secreting gland of marine birds', *Circulation*, **21**, 955–67 (1960).

307. SCHMIDT-NIELSEN, BODIL, and O'DELL, ROBERTA. 'Structure and concentrating mechanism in the mammalian kidney', *Amer. J. Physiol.* **200**, 1119–24 (1961).

308. SCHMIDT-NIELSEN, KNUT, and NEWSOME, A. E. 'Water balance in the mulgara (*Dasycercus cristicauda*), a carnivorous desert marsupial', *Austr. J. Biol. Sci.* **15**, 683–9 (1962).

309. —— Unpublished data.

310. SERGENT, EDMUND, and LHÉRITIER, A. 'Note sur la température rectale des dromadaires', *Compt. Rend. Soc. Biol.* **82**, 172–5 (22 Feb. 1919).

311. SHANTZ, H. L. 'History and problems of arid lands development', in *The future of arid lands* (G. F. White, ed.), Washington, D.C.: Amer. Assoc. Adv. Sci. Publ. No. 43 (1956), pp. 3–25.

312. SHAW, W. T. 'Duration of the aestivation and hibernation of the Columbian ground squirrel (*Citellus columbianus*) and sex relation to the same', *Ecology*, **6**, 75–81 (1925).

313. SHELLEY, WALTER B., and HEMINGWAY, A. 'The effects of thermal polypnea on the energy metabolism, respiratory quotient and water loss of dogs', *Amer. J. Physiol.* **129**, 623–30 (1940).

314. SHOCK, NATHAN W., and HASTINGS, A. B. 'Studies of the acid-base balance of the blood. IV. Characterization and interpretation of displacement of the acid-base balance', *J. Biol. Chem.* **112**, 239–62 (1935).

315. SIMPSON, GEORGE G. 'The principles of classification and a classification of mammals', *Bull. Amer. Mus. Nat. Hist.* **85** (1945), 350 pp.

316. SMITH, HOMER, and SILVETTE, H. 'Note on the nitrogen excretion of camels', *J. Biol. Chem.* **78**, 409–11 (1928).

317. —— *The kidney*, Oxford University Press: New York (1951), 1049 pp.

318. —— *From fish to philosopher*. Doubleday: Garden City, N.Y. (1961), 293 pp.

319. SPERBER, I. 'Studies on the mammalian kidney', *Zoologiska bidrag från Uppsala*, **22**, 249–431 (1944).

320. STARLING, E. H. (C. L. Evans, ed.), *Principles of human physiology*, Lea & Febiger: Philadelphia, 12th ed. (1956), 1233 pp.

321. STEBBINS, R. C. 'Adaptations in the nasal passages for sand burrowing in the saurian genus *Uma*', *Amer. Nat.* **77**, 38–52 (1943).

322. —— and EAKIN, R. M. 'The role of the "third eye" in reptilian behavior', *Amer. Mus. Novitates*, No. 1870, 1–40 (1958).

323. STEWART, R. E., PICKETT, E. E., and BRODY, S. 'Environmental physiology with special reference to domestic animals. XVI. Effect of increasing temperatures, 65° to 95° F., on the reflection of visible radiation from the hair of Brown Swiss and Brahman cows', *Univ. Mo., Agric. Exp. Sta., Res. Bull.* No. 484: 1–23 (1951).

324. STODDART, LAURENCE A., and SMITH, A. D. *Range management*, Amer. Forestry Series, McGraw-Hill: New York (1955), 433 pp.

325. STRELNIKOW, I. 'Importance of solar radiation in the ecology of high mountain reptiles', *Zoolog. zhur. SSSR*, **23**, 250–7 (1944) (Russ. with Eng. summary).

326. STROHL, J. 'Wasserhaushalt und Fettbestand bei Steppen- und Wüstentieren. Physiologische Gesichtspunkte zum Verständnis des Kamelhöckers', *Verhandlungen der Naturforschenden Gesellschaft in Basel*, **40**, 422–40 (1929).

327. SUTHERLAND, ALEXANDER. 'The temperature of reptiles, monotremes and marsupials', *Proc. Roy. Soc. Victoria*, **9**, 57–67 (1896).

328. —— 'The temperature of reptiles, monotremes and marsupials', ibid. 378–94 (1897).

329. TALBOTT, J. H., and MICHELSEN, J. 'Heat cramps. A clinical and chemical study', *J. Clin. Invest.* **12**, 533–49 (1933).

330. TECHNAU, G. 'Die Nasendrüse der Vögel', *J. Ornithol.* **84**, 511–617 (1936).

331. TEMPLETON, JAMES R. 'Respiration and water loss at the higher temperatures in the desert iguana, *Dipsosaurus dorsalis*', *Physiol. Zool.* **33**, 136–45 (1960).

332. TENNENT, D. M. 'A study of water losses through the skin in the rat', *Amer. J. Physiol.* **145**, 436–40 (1946).

333. THACKER, E. J., and BRANDT, C. S. 'Coprophagy in the rabbit', *J. Nutrition*, **55**, 375–85 (1955).

334. THOMPSON, J. J., WORSTELL, D. M., and BRODY, S. 'Environmental physiology with special reference to domestic animals. V. Influence of temperature, 50° to 105° F., on water consumption in dairy cattle', *Univ. Mo. Agric. Exp. Sta., Res. Bull.* No. 436, 1–18 (1949).
335. TOWBIN, E. J. 'Gastric distention as a factor in the satiation of thirst in esophagostomized dogs', *Amer. J. Physiol.* **159**, 533–41 (1949).
336. TROUGHTON, ELLIS. *Furred animals of Australia*, Angus & Robertson: London, 5th ed. (1954), 376 pp.
337. TUCKER, VANCE A. 'Diurnal torpidity in the California pocket mouse', *Science*, **136**, 380–1 (1962).
338. TURNAGE, W. V. 'Desert subsoil temperatures', *Soil Sci.* **47**, 195–9 (1939).
339. TURNER, H. G., and SCHLEGER, A. V. 'The significance of coat type in cattle', *Aust. J. Agric. Res.* **11**, 645–63 (1960).

340. USHAKOV, B. P., and DAREVSKII, I. S. 'Comparison of the heat tolerance of muscle fibers and behavior toward temperature in two sympatric species of semidesert lizards', *Akad. nauk SSSR, Doklady*, Biol. Sci. Sec. **128**, 770–3 (1959).

341. VAUQUELIN, LOUIS N. 'Examen des excrémens des serpens qui l'on fait voir en ce moment à Paris, rue Saint-Nicaise', *Ann. Chim. et Phisique*, 2me sér., **21**, 440 (1822).
342. VOIT, E. 'Die Zusammensetzung von Organen und dem Gesamtkörper bei Homoiothermen und Poikilothermen', *Zeitschr. f. Biol.* **89**, 114–38 (1929).
343. VORHIES, CHARLES T., and TAYLOR, W. P. 'Life history of the kangaroo rat, *Dipodomys spectabilis spectabilis* Merriam', *U.S. Dept. Agric. Bull.* No. 1091, 1–40 (1922).
344. —— 'Do southwestern quail require water?', *Amer. Nat.* **62**, 446–52 (1928).
345. —— and TAYLOR, W. P. 'The life histories and ecology of jack rabbits, *Lepus alleni* and *Lepus californicus* ssp. in relation to grazing in California', *Univ. Arizona, Agric. Exp. Sta., Tech. Bull.* No. 49: 471–587 (1933).
346. —— —— 'Life history and ecology of the white-throated wood rat *Neotoma albigula albigula* Hartley, in relation to grazing in Arizona', ibid. No. 86: 455–529 (1940).
347. —— 'Water requirements of desert animals in the Southwest', ibid. No. 107: 487–525 (1945).

348. WALD, G., and JACKSON, B. 'Activity and nutritional deprivation', *Proc. Nat. Acad. Sci.* **30**, 255–63 (1944).
349. WEINER, J. S., and VON HEYNINGEN, RUTH. 'Lactic acid and sweat gland function', *Nature*, **164**, 351–2 (1949).
350. —— and HELLMANN, K. 'The sweat glands', *Biol. Rev.* **35**, 141–86 (1960).
350a. WHITE, GILBERT F. (ed.). *The future of arid lands*, Washington, D.C.: Amer. Assoc. Adv. Sci. Publ. No. 43 (1956), 453 pp.
351. WHITEHOUSE, A. G. R., HANCOCK, W., and HALDANE, J. S. 'The osmotic passage of water and gases through the human skin', *Proc. Roy. Soc. Lond.* B, **111**, 412–29 (1932).
352. WIGGLESWORTH, V. B. *The principles of insect physiology*, Methuen: London (1950), 544 pp.

353. WILHOFT, DANIEL C., and ANDERSON, J. D. 'Effect of acclimation on the preferred body temperature of the lizard, *Sceloporus occidentalis*', *Science*, **131**, 610–11 (1960).

354. WOLF, A. V. *Thirst: Physiology of the urge to drink and problems of water lack*, C. C. Thomas: Springfield, Ill. (1958), 536 pp.

355. —— PRENTISS, P. G., DOUGLAS, L. G., and SWETT, R. J. 'Potability of sea water with special reference to the cat', *Amer. J. Physiol.* **196**, 633–41 (1959).

356. WOODBURY, A. M., and HARDY, ROSS. 'Studies of the desert tortoise *Gopherus agassizii*', *Ecol. Monogr.* **18**, 145–200 (1948).

357. WORSTELL, D. M., and BRODY, S. 'Environmental physiology and shelter engineering with special reference to domestic animals. XX. Comparative physiological reactions of European and Indian cattle to changing temperature', *Univ. Mo. Agric. Exp. Sta. Res. Bull.* No. 515: 1–42 (1953).

358. YAMANO, J., and ONO, Y. 'Rassenanatomische Untersuchungen der Hautstruktur von Büffel, Zebu, Formosarind und Friesisch-Holländer im Hinblick auf das Problem der Tropenanpassung', *Mem. Fac. of Sci. Agr., Taihoku Imp. Univ.* **19**, 57 (1936) (quoted from Dordick, *Acta Tropica*, **6** (1949)).

359. YEATES, N. T. M., LEE, D. H. K., and HINES, H. J. G. 'Reactions of domestic fowls in hot atmospheres', *Proc. Roy. Soc. Queensland*, **53**, 105–28 (1941).

360. —— 'Photoperiodicity in cattle. I. Seasonal changes in coat character and their importance in heat regulation', *Austr. J. Agric. Res.* **6**, 891–902 (1955).

INDEX